Radical Embodiment

Princeton Theological Monograph Series

K. C. Hanson, Charles M. Collier, and D. Christopher Spinks,
Series Editors

Recent volumes in the series:

Charles Bellinger
The Trinitarian Self: The Key to the Puzzle of Violence

Linda Hogan
Religion and the Politics of Peace and Conflict

Chris Budden
*Following Jesus in Invaded Space: Doing Theology
on Aboriginal Land*

Jeff B. Pool
*God's Wounds: Hermeneutic of the Christian Symbol
of Divine Suffering, Volume Two*

Lisa E. Dahill
*Reading from the Underside of Selfhood: Bonhoeffer
and Spiritual Formation*

Samuel A. Paul
*The Ubuntu God: Deconstructing a South African
Narrative of Oppression*

Jeanne M. Hoeft
*Agency, Culture, and Human Personhood: Pastoral Thelogy
and Intimate Partner Violence*

Ryan A. Neal
*Theology as Hope: On the Ground and Implications
of Jürgen Moltmann's Doctrine of Hope*

Scott A. Ellington
Risking Truth: Reshaping the World through Prayers of Lament

Radical Embodiment

David H. Nikkel

PICKWICK *Publications* · Eugene, Oregon

RADICAL EMBODIMENT

Princeton Theological Monograph Series 125

Pickwick Publications
An Imprint of Wipf and Stock Publishers
199 W. 8th Ave., Suite 3
Eugene, OR 97401

www.wipfandstock.com

isbn 13: 978-1-55635-578-3

Cataloging-in-Publication data

Nikkel, David H., 1952–

    Radical embodiment / David H. Nikkel.

    x + 192 p. ; 23 cm. —Includes bibliographical references and index(es).

    Princeton Theological Monograph Series 125

    isbn 13: 978-1-55635-578-3

    1. Mind and body—Religious aspects. 2. Postmodernism. 3. Religion and science. I. Title. II. Series.

BD438.5 .N49 2010

In Memory of William H. Poteat

Contents

Preface

MUCH OF THE MATERIAL FOR THIS BOOK ORIGINALLY COMES FROM several discrete articles. While relying upon these as a base, I have significantly modified and expanded this material over the years, as well as forging new content. It struck me that this cumulative process of creating and re-interpreting meaning—hopefully in more inclusive and complex ways, all the while relying upon a meaningful base, parallels the processes of my "habit body," to use Merleau-Ponty's phrase, and of the life of our traditions. While several themes reappear throughout the book, I have attempted to avoid mere repetition, essaying instead to progressively develop these themes in different contexts.

It is my conviction that our modern culture has lived under an insane picture of human nature, which has conspired to deprive us of a meaningful life and world. It is my hope that this project will accomplish some small work in advancing a picture of our meaningful, radical embodiment in our biosphere and in our social traditions, within a universe regarded as the body of God.

David H. Nikkel
Pembroke, North Carolina
September, 2008

1

Discerning the Spirits of Modernity
and Postmodernity

I COUNT MYSELF AMONG THOSE SCHOLARS OF RELIGION (AND OTHER disciplines) who believe that we live in the midst of a major shift in Western culture—that we are moving from the modern age into a post-modern age. "Postmodern" has gained supremacy over the alternative terms "postcritical" and "postliberal." Michael Polanyi's "postcritical" stands as probably the best single word for conveying the substance of the shift from modernity as I construe it in this chapter. The term, as I understand it, does not suggest the impossibility or undesirability of appropriate critical reflection, but rather modernity's failure to rec-ognize the limits of critical reasoning. "Postliberal" does connect with "postcritical" insofar as one of those limits is the impossibility of totally transcending tradition (and the wrong-headedness of attempting to do so). However, one cannot answer with generalities the question of how far one can or should transcend tradition in a particular cultural or religious context. It should not surprise us then that "postliberal" is the term of choice for those with a conservative orientation clinging tightly to their tradition.

In the opening sections of this chapter I will delineate some distin-guishing characteristics of the postmodern versus the modern spirit. I will proceed by describing respective *controlling assumptions* and con-comitants of first modernity, then postmodernity. One key postmodern assumption is precisely that every individual and culture holds basic assumptions, models, images, pictures that control the way one views the world. Such controlling assumptions function like eyeglasses—one *looks with* or *through* them, but does not normally *look at* them. (And indeed some assumptions are so basic or prereflective that, like one's own eye, one cannot look at them at all.)[1] Next I will discuss historical and logical relationships between the modern and postmodern spirits.

Postmodern sensibility would caution against any absolute postulating of the essence of an era, especially in contrast to another era. So I offer my understanding of the modern versus postmodern spirit not as an absolute or monolithic schema that disallows countervailing tendencies or alternative schemas, but as a general description of some contrasting tendencies involved in this cultural shift. Given, in addition to this general caveat, my characterization of the movement from modernity to postmodernity as long and gradual, astute readers should have no problem identifying some exceptions to my distinctions.

In the final sections of the chapter, I will consider the relationship of the postmodern spirit to theology, primarily through selected and hopefully representative movements and figures. In light of the judgment that the move to postmodernity has been a protracted one, I will look at some trends in theology, from Schleiermacher to the contemporary scene, in terms of their affinity with the postmodern spirit. Finally, I will examine three types of self-descriptively postmodern theology and assess them in relation to the spirit or logic of postmodernity as I have construed it. While I intend this construal to be acceptable to all three camps—the radical or deconstructionist/poststructuralist, the conservative or "postliberal," and the moderate, an important purpose of this project is to take a stand for moderate postmodernism. So I write in that section as a critical and constructive theologian of the moderate postmodern strand, contending that it alone among the types consistently draws out the implications of the postmodern spirit—while the other two end up being more modern than postmodern in crucial respects. This project thus counters the use of "postmodern" as a synonym for "deconstructionist" or "poststructuralist" by some scholars, both sympathetic and unsympathetic to radical postmodernism. My attempt to define "postmodern" is thus an enactment of the postmodern insight that reality is (in part) defined, enacted by us.

---

1. I am indebted to my mentor in postmodernity, William H. Poteat, for the concept of the controlling "picture," as well as for the idea, developed later in this chapter, that idealism and empiricism represent flip sides of the same dualistic coin. (Poteat in turn was influenced by French phenomenologist Maurice Merleau-Ponty on this latter point.)

The Modern Spirit

An original hallmark of modernity has been its stress on the individual and its great faith in individual critical reason. Let me note that in this book I will use the term "critical reason" in a general sense, meaning reason as it questions and/or attempts to establish or justify or make explicit meaning and value. Religiously speaking, Martin Luther's standing alone before the Diet of Worms dramatically signaled the coming of modernity. While the Protestant Reformation elevated the authority of Scripture, individual critical reason and conscience—hopefully guided by the Holy Spirit—received new freedom to interpret Scripture and sit in judgment. Correspondingly, this development greatly diminished the collective authority of institutions and tradition.

Certain Renaissance paintings represent the artistic beginnings of modernity as they reveal a controlling assumption or "picture" of modernity.[2] In contrast to actual vision, everything in these paintings, including all elements of the foreground and background, appears crystal clear. A basic assumption of modernity is that the individual can leave behind all limitations of one's body and perceptual equipment, temporality, language, and culture and reach an absolutely privileged position where one can "see" everything (including oneself) with complete clarity. Descartes, controlled by this picture, signaled the beginning of modern philosophy. Finding that all of his knowledge failed according to such a criterion of absolute—and explicitable—certainty, Descartes finally felt he reached the privileged position in his reflexive and self-conscious subjectivity—"I think, therefore I am." In comparison with the Reformation, the ensuing Enlightenment of course radicalized the role of critical reason with respect to Scripture and tradition.[3]

I will now consider some ramifications of this controlling picture of modernity, mostly confining my remarks to the realm of Western thought[4] (while mentioning that the alienation, absolutism, relativism,

2. Poteat, *Polanyian Meditations*, 59.

3. Martin Luther, taking a much more critical stance toward Scripture than subsequent Protestant scholastics, foreshadowed critical activities of the Enlightenment by denying the historical accuracy of parts of the Bible and by judging as theologically invalid certain biblical books (Harvey, *Handbook*).

4. Though certainly specific practical and social consequences, both positive and negative, have issued as well. For example, on the positive side: 1) many accomplishments of science, medicine, and technology, 2) the overthrowing of many superstitions,

and malaise stemming from this picture produce some effects not readily specifiable):

1) Probably the most significant consequence of modernity's picture
of the absolutely lucid and self-possessed subject was its dualisms between subject and object, mind and matter, including the body. If the
individual human subject or mind is the absolutely privileged starting
point, it becomes difficult or impossible to reach or have any meaningful connection with the object or the physical (especially by the
criterion of absolute certainty). The question becomes, how can mind
impose meaning on inherently meaningless matter? For the absolute
object constitutes the flip side of the absolute subject: critical, distancing reason tends to turn what is in its gaze into nothing but an object. If,
conversely, the simply material object and sense perception that supposedly mirrors the object serve as the absolutely privileged starting point,
then it becomes difficult or impossible to reach or find any meaningful
role for the human subject—which tends to be reduced to simply an
aggregate of matter and energy. As with Humpty Dumpty, no one could
put subject and object or mind and body back together again, given the
controlling assumption of modernity.

In either its idealist or physicalist manifestations, modernity's
controlling picture leads to loss of meaning and, in the extreme, to personal and cultural insanity: idealism by sundering us from our bodies,
emotions, and our embodiment in the world; physicalism by leaving no
place for the meaning, the sacredness of human and animal life. While
physicalism emphasizes the body as physical system, it is as discarnat-
ing as idealism, alienating us from our experiential, intentional bodies.
Idealism divorces purpose from the world; physicalism divorces the
world from any purpose.

---

and 3) a sense of universal human rights; on the negative side: 1) the exploitation of
nature and ecological crisis, 2) the common practice by physicians of treating patients
as just physical organisms (a practice that many medical schools now discourage in
something of a postmodern trend), and 3) striving in the workplace for absolute technological efficiency regardless of bodily consequences 4) the positing of an absolute
consummation which has been a factor in much (though certainly not all) modern
mass death, as in some religious violence and in the excesses of fascism and commu-
nism. Given my contention that postmodernity corrects excesses of modernity and is
impelled by a more truthful controlling assumption, a reader might get the impres-
sion that I regard modernity as "bad" and postmodernity as "good." As my preceding
remarks suggest, such simplism does not represent my overall position.

2) Having (assumedly) left behind the nitty-gritty of existence in time, modern thinkers have been wont to claim to see *the* essence of being, human nature, history, the Bible, or Christianity. Such claims have often involved the positing of absolute categories, often paralleling the fundamental subject-object and mind-matter dualisms, often hierarchical. Examples include the human world versus nature, inner versus outer, reason versus emotion or sense perception, an enlightened age versus past benighted ages.

3) In principle, everything could come under the gaze of the absolute subject; everything should be assimilable to the individual's critical knowledge. What critical reason's categories and logic could not assimilate tended to be ignored, dismissed, or destroyed. Diverse images that come to mind include Thomas Jefferson's version of the New Testament with all supernaturalistic passages deleted, the humanities attempting to establish their relevancy before the bar of science, and the unparalleled ideological violence (at least in scale) of the modern age.

4) The model of the absolutely privileged and neutral position assumes all objects of knowledge as already fully constituted apart from the individual's coming to know. Truth is simply correspondence to a reality already "out there" (for those on the object side of the dualism) or already "in here" (for those favoring the subject side).[5]

The Postmodern Spirit

A person standing in the world forms the contrasting controlling picture of postmodernity, with always at least "one foot in" one's body, temporality, society, culture, language, history, tradition, etc. While humans do indeed have reflexive, critical, transcending capabilities (far greater than those of any other animals on earth), such capabilities are not absolute as modernity tended to assume. One's ability to take off the eyeglasses through which one looks at reality and to look at those eyeglasses is limited. One cannot get out of one's own skin! One implication of the postmodern controlling assumption I would claim is that

5. While Kant came to deny that we can know any "thing in itself," as he grappled with the implications of modernity's subject-object split, what is noteworthy is his very assumption of a fully determinate object in itself, albeit unknowable, behind any perception.

a person always stands embodied, enmeshed, enculturated in meaning and value. Normally we do not need critical reason to establish or justify meaning a la Descartes and his successors. Rather, critical reason can come into play when questions arise in our practice or when meanings break down.

Following are ramifications of postmodernity's controlling assumption paralleling and contrasting with those of modernity:

1) Neither subject nor object constitutes the privileged starting point for postmodernity. In terms of individual epistemology—granting an inalienable social component—someone knowing or perceiving something is the only starting point. Any attempt to completely "get behind" the act of knowing, to reach the subject "in itself" (that is, in total distinction from any object known) and likewise to reach the object in itself (that is, in total distinctness from any subject knowing it), is rejected. The postmodern spirit disowns this attempt not just because of its practical impossibility, but as misguided in principle: no absolute or pure subject exists to abstract out of the world and society in which one is embodied. The postmodern spirit regards a person as a mindbodily continuum or whole. "Mind," as our awareness of and our attempt to make sense of things, and "body," as that with which we relate to a natural and social world, are radically interrelated, and both come into play at some level in all our acts.

2) In similar fashion, postmodernity views related distinctions or polarities—such as inner versus outer, reflective versus prereflective, the human versus the natural world, linguistic versus prelinguistic— as continuous, interrelated, and relative to context (never absolutely distinguishable). Besides eschewing dualisms, the postmodern spirit also runs counter to attempts to find *the* (necessary) essence of being, human nature, history, a religion, or a text. In general, it distrusts any rigid or absolutistic scheme of classification or categorization, on the grounds that such totalizing endeavors miss the richness, complexity, and contextuality of life, especially in its temporal and changing character and it its prereflective and tacit dimensions.

3) Compared to modernity's overemphasis on the individual, postmodernity elevates the value of what transcends the individual. Descriptively and prescriptively, the cruciality of the social dimensions

of life, including the authority of the group and tradition, are (or should be) recognized.

For the postmodern spirit, what appears different from or other than one's self, beliefs, or values should ultimately be neither assimilated or dismissed nor reduced to a mere object. Instead one should encounter—an encounter that partially defines oneself—or engage in dialogue with the other, dialogue that appreciates and respects real differences (without entailing that one must ultimately equally accredit all the differing beliefs and values). In postmodern logic no privileged or neutral position exists to which contrary views must summarily reconcile or else face elimination.

4) The postmodern spirit holds that our perceiving, knowing, and acting play a significant role in creating the world we experience. On a very prereflective level, the truth of this contention becomes evident by imagining how different a lake looks to a bird flying over it or to a fish swimming in it than to a human being. Each creature's perspective brings what is there into definition—there is no *fully* determinate lake in itself nor any perspectiveless perspective on the lake.[6] (A la Heisenberg's uncertainty principle, our "measuring" or perceiving always has some effect on what we know—our knowing always leaves some trace!) On a more reflective level, the vast array of languages, cultures, worldviews, and religions across the globe and through the ages suggests humanity's vital role in creating the worlds of meaning which we indwell.

Discerning the Spirits

Some have characterized modernity as an era (increasingly) aware of the historical and cultural conditionedness of everything human, an era that diminished or vanquished absolutisms.[7] Can we square that characterization with my claim that the picture of the absolutely privileged subject controlled modernity? While modernity's critical reason slew the authoritarianisms and absolutisms of the past, it tended to do

---

6. Note that my wording entails that, in knowing, something is there—something "stands against" us. Postmodernity's logic does not (or should not) permit the subjectivistic and solipsistic tendencies of modernity. We, individually or collectively, only partly create the world we know. The correspondence theory of truth is not entirely wrong.

7. E.g., Hopper, *Understanding Modern Theology II*; Wall, "Meaning, Mystery."

so with an assumption of its own absolutely privileged position! The ideas and values of a growing number of individuals and cultures were unhesitatingly exposed as historically relative, but modern thinkers tended less to sense the conditioned nature of their own critical reflection. Marx and Hegel saw the relativity of all past periods of history, but nonetheless constructed an absolute master plan and final period of history. Freud discovered the falsity of the model of total and explicit human consciousness and self-control, yet he used his general awareness of the subconscious realm to devise absolutistic explanations of such things as women's nature and the origin of religion.

Premodern absolutisms were uncritical and relatively prereflective. The absolute authority and rightness of a tradition or a way of life were (again relatively speaking) simply assumed. They represent a first-order naivete. Modern absolutisms were/are reflective. Supposedly neutral critical reason arrives at them. They represent a second-order naivete. The naivete of critical reason is like a child who learns a new skill, such as riding a bicycle, and feels so giddy with the newfound power and possibilities that the limitations of this capability, like all things human, escape notice.

Realizing or assuming the unavoidably incarnate, finite, temporally and culturally conditioned nature of *even one's own thinking and valuing* constitutes the crucial notion for admission into the postmodern age. To say that the postmodern spirit can be "realized" or "assumed" allows its appropriation to be either relatively reflective or relatively prereflective. Thus, the postmodern spirit overcomes or circumvents the second-order naivete of modernity.

Describing the relationships between the modern and postmodern spirits as I have above implies the inappropriateness of selecting one circumscribed period as *the* time Western culture left modernity and entered postmodernity. By the nineteenth century intellectuals arose who were "postmodern" in certain aspects of their thought, including Soren Kierkegaard and William James. As art had "announced" the beginnings of modernity, so also of postmodernity. Impressionist renderings of the same scene at different times of day pointed to the inescapability of temporality and of perspective. Cezanne's "out of focus" paintings suggested the necessary human component in bringing our world into definition.[8] We have been gradually entering the postmodern age and we continue to do so. The combination of the modern spirit slaying many authoritarianisms and a growing postmodern spirit has, I judge, influenced an overall (if quite uneven) trend of the lessening of absolutism and a growing tolerance for diverse viewpoints in Western culture.

Parenthetically, I will mention an ambiguity pertaining to the postmodern truth of the embodied and conditioned nature of everything human. On the one hand, this truth contains a summons to self-criticism—it has a *critical* side. It is sometimes both possible and appropriate to look at our individual and (sub)cultural eyeglasses and consider whether our lenses need a correction. In this enterprise, those wearing different spectacles can help us to see assumptions we ourselves miss. Also, the postmodern spirit calls us to guard against absolutizing our own perspective (or assuming we do not have one, which is tantamount to absolutism). On the other hand, the inescapability of our embodiment and enculturation has an acritical or *precritical* side: it is often inappropriate or impossible to look at our eyeglasses. Michael Polanyi noted the acritical nature of all tacit acts of knowing.[9] We can only devote a limited portion of time to the reflective enterprise of making explicit the normally tacit or prereflective—the rest of the time we must live. And any such reflective attempts can only partly succeed, for critical reflection entails some temporal and perspectival distancing and separation. Finally, as indicated earlier, some assumptions are so basic that one cannot get behind them—they are more like one's eye than like eyeglasses. Polanyi's term "postcritical," consonant with what I am calling "the postmodern spirit," takes in both the critical and the acritical or precritical. Polanyi assented to—critically—"the greatly increased powers of man," granting us a "capacity for self-transcendence of which we can never again divest ourselves."[10]

The Postmodern Spirit and Modern Theologies

If postmodern sensibilities already emerged in the nineteenth century, they manifested themselves more strongly in Protestant theology than

8. Poteat, *Polanyian Meditations*, 59.

9. Polanyi, *Personal Knowledge*, 264.

10. Ibid., 268.

in most other areas of Western thought. The modern spirit had unceremoniously dethroned theology as "queen of the sciences." Theology's past pronouncements on scientific and other "secular" matters were clearly recognized as historically limited. While theology's competence or worth was under challenge with respect to more narrowly "religious" spheres, the cultural conditionedness of its religious formulations had not been as clearly established. Friedrich Schleiermacher, anticipating the further reach of critical reason, made a rather remarkable and rather postmodern acknowledgment: *all* of our characterizations of "the Absolute" are linguistically, culturally, and historically conditioned. With some justification this "father of modern theology" might also be called the "father of postmodern theology."

However, Schleiermacher could not let go of one area of absolute privilege, one absolute human connection with the divine: the allegedly universal human "feeling of absolute dependence." (Note that the issue here is not the absoluteness of the divine, but the absoluteness of the claimed human connection.) Granted, attempts to express this feeling are always conditioned. Granted, too, this feeling manifests itself only in and through the particular contingencies of each moment of experience. Nevertheless, as a necessary component of every human experience rather that just a potentiality which some people realize some of the time, this feeling heralds its unconditioned and absolute character. Moreover, the particularities of this moment of experience versus that moment finally do not make any difference. We have the basic sense of our absolute dependence regardless, so in that sense this feeling remains unconditioned and pure in relation to any linguistic and historical particularities.

Most nineteenth and twentieth century theology followed Schleiermacher in clinging to one absolutely privileged divine connection. For Tillich, it was the "mystical a priori"; for Whiteheadian process theology, awareness of the "initial aim" for each occasion of experience; for neo-Thomism, implicit awareness and love for God; for existentialist theology, the courage to live authentically despite existential anxiety. Note the prereflective nature of all these connections. Modern theology had abandoned the attempt at an absolute reflective knowledge of God. But there remained the attempt to get underneath all cultural conditions through the prereflective.

Karl Barth, of course, denied any absolute or other connection coming from the human side. Instead, the absolute connection comes from God's intentional revelation in Jesus Christ. As with Schleiermacher, human attempts to express this connection are relative (and Barth would add prone to idolatry). But this human connection (albeit provided by God) receives absolute privilege.

I will now further consider some movements in twentieth century thought that, although in some aspects very much imbued with the modern spirit, evidence important postmodern elements and implications. Existentialist philosophy and theology in good postmodern fashion attacked modern and earlier attempts to abstract out and reify an atemporal human essence. Existentialism also found earlier categorizations of reality too abstract and out of touch with the temporal and historical character of existence. Much of existentialism, though, turned only outward in postmodern critique, not recognizing the historical limitedness and tendencies to absolutism of its own definitions of human nature and categorizations of reality. For example, human beings in many contexts do not feel "thrown" into the world, but rather feel quite at home in it. On a related note, our normal embodiment and enculturation in some meaning belies the notion that one could or should always *explicitly decide* to take on authentic meaning. (My faulting of this aspect of existentialism does not deny the fiduciary and interpretative elements of personal commitment in all knowing and valuing.) In different ways, therefore, existentialism tended to shortchange both the self-critical and the precritical aspects of the postmodern spirit. In one aspect most of existentialism remained under the sway of the modern spirit: its pronounced individualism.

In contrast to existentialism, process philosophy and theology is postmodern in its focus on, and consistently positive evaluation of, the social nature and inter-connectedness of reality. Its emphasis on the temporality of all existence (which it shares with existentialism) and its denial of anything concrete about the self that is unchanging through time also resonate with the postmodern. On the "down side," its Whiteheadian metaphysical system seems firmly entrenched in the rationalist or idealist branch of modernity, arising out of a desire to please the (absolute) thinking subject with its all-encompassing neatness. Idealism animates its theory that "occasions of experience" comprise all reality, with matter in effect only apparent, resulting from our abstract, partial inclusion or "prehension" of numerous low-grade (sub-atomic) experiences in our own experiences. Idealism likewise imbues its theory of causation, in which all causation is a matter of experience, prehension, or sympathetic feeling. To be fair, Whitehead does write of prehension in "the mode of causal efficacy"—we cannot help but to take account of what enters into our experience from the past. Yet the meta-phorical reliance on experience and on our taking in or grasping what affects us does not adequately account for materiality and exteriority, that is, causal efficacy that happens quite apart from any type of aware-ness or desire.[11]

Even as modern theologians subscribed to the notion that their work was relative to their era, they generally did not notice its relativ-ity to their identity as Western European and North American middle and upper class white males—they typically assumed they spoke for the whole of culture of their era. As suggested earlier, postmodernity's recognition of the difficulty of looking at our own embodied, histori-cal, and subcultural perspective on reality entails that those from an-other perspective can often look at our "eyeglasses" better than we can. Liberation theology has certainly performed this service for mainline theology, showing how it has traditionally ignored or subsumed the otherness of persons of color, women, gays, lesbians, or the underclass and ignored or complied with their oppression. Theology should value the other voices of homosexuals, women, blacks and the Third World to fulfill the postmodern spirit's call to mutually engage the other.

The Postmodern Spirit and Postmodern Theologies

Over the past generation theologies consciously or self-descriptively postmodern have tended to fall into radical, moderate, and conserva-tive camps. I now take up the (perhaps presumptuous) task of evalu-ating the contributions and prospects of those three types in light of the postmodern spirit as I have construed it—a postmodern scorecard, if you will.[12] The thinkers who inform this typology are mostly North Americans in the Christian tradition (though the radicals would gener-

---

11. It is no coincidence that David Ray Griffin typically identifies modernity and its negativities with its materialistic and sensationalistic side, while largely overlooking its idealist side (Griffin et al., *Varieties*).

12. For a related evaluation, see Klemm, "Toward a Rhetoric."

ally characterize themselves as influenced by, rather than part of, that tradition).

The Radicals

The postmodern theology that has caused the biggest splash, or the most waves, is the radical branch—deconstruction and other forms of poststructuralism.[13] As a tool, it performs a valuable postmodern function in critiquing or "deconstructing"—exposing the assumptions and contradictions attending—the absolute and self-contained subject, absolute text, or absolutely privileged place in or beyond time. As an a/ ontology, radical postmodernism is more problematic.

This type of theology has drawn the labels "severe," "negative,"[14] or "eliminative" postmodernism because it purportedly eliminates concepts of God, self, history, and truth.[15] The late Jacques Derrida constitutes the premiere philosophical influence behind this branch. Representatives of this type of theology in the Protestant tradition were Mark C. Taylor and the late Charles Winquist; D. G. Leahy and John Caputo offer versions in the Catholic tradition (though in Leahy's case more rooted in American pragmatism than in French poststructuralism). Though Taylor has since moved beyond his deconstructive phase, I judge that he most consistently developed the implications of Derrida's philosophy for theology (especially before Derrida himself began to write about religion). Therefore, I will be in conversation with him more than any other poststructuralist theologian.

Deconstructive postmodernism arises from a problem or "crisis of representation" growing out of modernity's controlling picture—which assumed that we could transcend to reality "in itself," a reality which our perceptions or words merely represent or to which they merely correspond, but in no way constitute. The postmodern spirit, of course, senses that interest, desire, perception, interpretation, commitment, personal and communal history influence every experience. Deconstruction reacts radically against modernity's picture of transcendence and interprets postmodern insight to entail the total immanence

---

13. Though radical pragmatism-historicism has affinities with continental post-structuralism, this American variety has not been as influential among theologians.

14. Beardslee in *Varieties*.

15. Griffin in *Varieties*.

of a person in one's experiences: We lie trapped in our perceptions, our words, our interpretations, our constructions of reality—and there is nothing else (except perhaps the "nothingness" of utterly unpresentable *differance*). Because of its reliance on linguistic metaphors, some have falsely accused deconstruction of denying non-linguistic elements of experience. (Though it may well be that deconstruction's reliance on reflective and linguistic metaphors for reality—such as, "writing," "text," "interpretation"—hinders it from acknowledging our [more] prereflective and bodily grounding in meaning.) What deconstructionists have maintained is the heavy influence of language on most human experience (a position that other postmodernists would accept). The key point here, though, is that no attainable reality exists beyond our constitution of experience through language, perception, etc.

As with the modern and general postmodern spirits, art heralded deconstructive postmodernism, through much so-called "modernist" visual art and literature. While William Beardslee may be correct in his generalization that aesthetic modernism, unlike deconstruction, did not abandon the quest for "a vision of the whole,"[16] I believe that the related observations of Stephen Moore and Karl Raschke are more to the point: Modernism did tend to downplay or abandon the attempt at representation or realism.[17]

To be totally immanent in one's representations is, in Derrida's words, to plunge into "the horizontality of a pure surface."[18] For deconstructionists everything is surface, appearance, horizontality. Not only do they deny absolute transcendence, but even relative height or depth. This conflicts with Polanyi's insight that knowing involves levels wherein tacit components contribute to wider, deeper, or higher focal contexts of meaning. Critical reason or reflective distance takes a penultimate role in deconstructing particular contexts of meaning, but from an ultimate perspective (although deconstruction's "a/theistic" premises disallow such a perspective) human beings lie trapped in the largest context of

---

16. Beardslee in *Varieties*, 64, 149.

17. Moore, "The 'Post-Age' Stamp," 544–49; Raschke, "Fire and Roses," 675–76.

18. Derrida, *Writing and Difference*, 298.

meaning,[19] a (predetermined?) humanly undecidable, flowing whole. Everything is as it ought to be, leaving no room for sin or guilt.[20]

In keeping with the postmodern spirit, deconstruction emphasizes the relativity of meaning to context, the connectedness of the elements within a context, and the openness of a context to further and future interconnections. This openness implies the inexhaustibility of reality. Ironically, though, by placing everything on the same level of "appearance," deconstruction instead offers a one-dimensional, flat, exhausted reality, lacking a genuine sense of mystery. Similarly, deconstruction undermines its valuing of otherness and difference by reducing all alterity to distances between points on the same plane (or to an unreachable beyond)—or as components of an enclosed, fragmented self. This is one of the ironies of radical postmodernism its advocates tend to overlook.

In the first place then, deconstruction holds that we are immanent and incarnated, totally inscribed in our bodies, culture, contexts of meaning. Forgoing explanation of how we can transcend our interpretations enough to come to such a second-order conclusion, deconstruction's next move is this: since practically speaking only interpretation or appearance exists, and given diverse, competing, and even apparently contradictory interpretations, one cannot seriously commit to any one interpretation. Indeed, the microcosm of the self and its meanings is so fragmented that it mirrors the inconsistencies and incoherencies of the macrocosm. Hence deconstruction's relativistic turn to irony or playfulness. Herein lies the supreme internal irony of radical postmodernism: the human being is regarded as totally embodied, immanent, committed, interested and at the same time called to be totally discarnate and disinterested. If, per impossible, one could fully take to heart deconstruction's anthropology, schizophrenia would result. Deconstruction's freedom from commitment to particular values or worldview can never work in practice; deconstructionists like all creatures are standing somewhere. (One commitment driving many radical postmodernists is opposition to totalizing ideologies that pretend to speak for the interests of all.)

In a radical appropriation of the postmodern rejection of modernity's search for absolute truth, Taylor offers wandering or "erring" as

---

19. By "meaning," I connote both sense and value.

20. M. Taylor, *Erring*, 121, 151–58, 166–69.

the primary metaphor for the human quest for meaning.[21] This accords with deconstruction's belief that we can only reach the "sign" but never the destination. Given the postmodern insight that we humans can never possess absolute presence or truth, deconstruction's claim that each moment of experience involves the interplay of the presence and absence of meaning is correct. From my personal and my Christian perspective, though, even granting these two equal billing in a polar relationship errs: the presence of meaning is more basic and stronger in normal human and animal experience.[22] However, deconstruction goes further and gives pride of place to the pole of absence. Its vocabulary and metaphors—such as erring, trace, shiftiness, undecidability, appearance(s) (and disappearance), marginality, darkness—suggest the insecure, unsettled, insubstantial, abysmal, and deconstructing nature of all meaning. Given the postmodern recognition of the impossibility of *absolute* self-presence, truth, and value, one might note that the cup of meaning is either relatively empty or relatively full. Why does deconstruction opt for (relative) emptiness? Perhaps pessimistic or skeptical personalities of its proponents play a part in deconstruction's temperament. Undoubtedly, deconstruction's emphasis on absence is partly rhetorical, an effort to counter-balance modernity's (and the Western Greek-rooted philosophical-theological tradition's) emphasis on absolute self-possession and truth. But the decisive factor, as I have implied, now claim, and later will argue, is the hidden yet controlling spirit of modernity and its haunting standard of absolute truth.

With its emphasis on the absence of meaning, deconstruction takes its standing nowhere in ironic relativism to at least the brink of nihilism. Having radically undermined all particular meanings, deconstruction can avoid the standing nowhere of nihilism only by trying to stand everywhere—by unqualifiedly affirming the interconnected totality of all that has or will transpire[23]—which is tantamount to standing nowhere relative to competing and contrasting possibilities, interpre-

---

21. Ibid., esp. 9, 149–58, 179.

22. I believe Sallie McFague granted deconstruction too much in *Models of God*, in writing that "absence is at least more prevalent than presence" (25). This conflicts, or at least stands in tension, with her assumption that Christian faith is "most basically a claim that the universe is neither indifferent nor malevolent but that there is a power (and a personal power at that) which is on the side of life and its fulfillment" (x).

23. M. Taylor, *Erring*, 151–58, 166–69, 182.

tations, and choices for individuals and societies. Practically speaking, such a universal attachment to every particular is no more possible than the ironic detachment that constitutes the flip side of the same coin.

Deconstruction's primary images for humanity and divinity do cohere: Even as the person is wholly immanent in one's body and experiences, so divinity is wholly immanent with respect to the world. Taylor writes of "the ever-never-changing-same [that] is the eternally recurring play of the divine milieu in which *all things* [emphasis his] arise and pass away."[24] Leahy also expresses the radical postmodernist vision: "As never before the divine flows absolutely. In this flow every notion of self is completely dissolved."[25] In this conception of divinity, more radical than most historical forms of pantheism, no place remains for transcendence, personality, or purposive agency ontologically prior to the world.[26] Deconstruction takes "the death of God"—meaning the denial of any divine transcendence or selfhood—to be concomitant with the absence of any absolute human meaning. Here deconstruction "errs" in a sense different than Taylor's, in assuming that the contextual relativity of all human existence and meaning contravenes the existence of an Absolute Reality.[27] The absence of any absolute human connection to the Absolute does follow from a consistent upholding of the contextuality of all human meaning; but the acknowledgement of human contextuality does not at all settle whether the Absolute exists and can be known—relatively, of course. Without denying deconstruction's claim that the traditional understanding of God reinforced modernity's picture of the absolute human subject, one can imagine God as having a perfect knowledge and self-possession impossible for human beings (without entailing impassibility or immutability).

The great historical irony of deconstruction, which often denigrates "seriousness," is that it has taken modernity's controlling picture far too seriously. Its extreme reaction against that picture of neutral and absolute truth—its affirmation of total immanence with its implications of relativism—forms the mirror image or the underside of the coin of modernity. Radical postmodernism's pessimism regarding meaning is

24. Ibid., 112–20, 183.

25. Leahy, "To Create the Absolute," 786.

26. M. Taylor, *Erring*, 118.

27. By "absolute," I do not mean to suggest that divinity is unrelated to or unaffected by creation.

quite appropriate relative to modernity's standard of *absolute* presence and meaning that must be critically established, but quite inappropriate in light of postmodernity's assumption of our inalienable embodiment and enculturation in some meaning. An absolutistic reflective move—the positing of total immanence in divergent meanings—permits the reversal of postmodern optimism about our embodiment in meaning. In spite of this pessimism, Peter Hodgson discerns an irony stemming from the obsession with absolute presence: deconstruction ends with a "total 'having' of divinity, and an undialectical immediacy," with God as "totally incarnate in worldly inscription."[28] On one level the radicals strenuously denounce modernity's quest for the place of absolute privilege. Yet on a deeper (or perhaps better, more shallow) level—in the human possession of the highest possible meaning of an experience, the "surface" meaning, which is also the possession of totally immanent divinity, and in the unqualified affirmation of the totality of experiences—the absolutistic spirit of modernity reigns.

To be fair to Derrida and his legacy, we must finally consider his later writings that explicitly deal with religion. In particular, some writings develop a concept of messianism—endorsed and expounded upon by John Caputo—but a messianism "without content and without identifiable messiah."[29] While Derrida grants that this messianic notion perforce comes from the particularities of tradition(s), it is intentionally a formal concept, a wholly other that challenges in the name of justice the privileged claims of any historical social structure or meaning. These later works reveal both the ethical intent of radical postmodernism to undermine absolutistic regimes and its insufficient ontological base on which to do so. Here Derrida comes to sense the absolutistic dangers of immanentism (as Taylor explicitly did[30]). But in doing so he posits a third companion on the transcendent side of the binary, to go with ironic detachment and unpresentable *différance*. Just as with the other two, we lack any direction in deciding on the justness of concrete structures and meanings.

---

28. Hodgson, *God in History*, 37. I think that Taylor in his latest work, *After God*, correctly diagnoses the undialectical total presence of divinity in the eschatology of Altizer's "Death of God" theology (the latter influenced Leahy) (202–4).

29. Derrida, *Specters of Marx*, 28.

30. M. Taylor, "Politics of Theo-ry."

Descartes in his exercise in radical doubt at the philosophic beginning of modernity failed to recognize his inevitable standing in the world and in meaning. Even as those controlled by the modern picture believe (falsely) that they stand nowhere in the world, so radical postmodernism, in its refusal to go beyond either a version of transcendental relativism or an unqualified affirmation of the whole, refuses to (claim a) stand in the world. Taylor wrote, "Though always enacted over a bottomless abyss, festive play is never grave."[31] If my preceding analysis is correct, rather than dancing over the abyss of meaning, radical postmodernism is mourning at the coffin of modernity.

The Conservatives

Both Protestant and Catholic postliberal theologians emphasize the importance of enculturation in a tradition or worldview. The Protestants regard secularists as ensconced in a competing tradition or worldview, while the Catholics tend to view them as tradition-less, homeless, and needing to return to (the authority of) the Church. Protestant postliberals include George Lindbeck, Stanley Hauerwas, and the late John Howard Yoder, with John Milbank and others adding a "Radical Orthodox" twist. The former Joseph Cardinal Ratzinger, now Pope Benedict XVI, former Lutheran Richard John Neuhaus, and George William Rutler advocate Catholic postliberalism. The Protestant postliberals engage in sophisticated postmodern discourse while the Catholics' postmodernism largely confines itself to critique of modernity for its individualism, materialism, and utilitarianism.

My following remarks on postliberal anthropology apply more directly to the Protestants, who have explicitly engaged in this postmodern argumentation. The conservative postmoderns join the radicals in emphasizing human immanence in our experiences and viewpoints (though implicitly or explicitly parting company on whether a reality exists beyond our interpretations, especially with regard to ultimate reality).

Noting both the deep rooting of persons in differing cultural-linguistic frameworks and the absence of a privileged position from which to adjudicate such differences, these thinkers have concluded that genuine understanding between basic perspectives is unlikely or

31. M. Taylor, *Erring*, 164.

impossible. Different worldviews must either contradict each other or—drawing (or misdrawing, I believe) on Wittgenstein's concept of different "language games" for different contexts—bypass each other. Even apparent similarities and commonalities between Christianity and other cultural-linguistic frameworks allegedly prove discordant when viewed within their differing contexts. In terms of the basic assumption or picture of postmodernity, such thinkers do not see human beings as getting even one foot out of one's society, culture, history, or tradition. The critical side of the postmodern spirit is downplayed or absent. Such a conclusion also violates the postmodern spirit's respect for otherness: The other poses either a threat or an irrelevancy.[32]

Such tribalistic thinking allows postliberal theologians to believe that the Bible or Christianity comprises its own world (view) in need of no authentication or corroboration by critical reason or any non-Christian perspective. The posture of this conservative wing of postmodernity is defensive; it hopes to save Christianity from further critical attacks by modernity. Postmodern logic implies that Christianity or any worldview carries (and to some extent creates) its own self-authenticating context of meaning. However, it does *not* imply denying or downplaying the importance of corroboration and questioning by critical reason and by alternative perspectives. As Adam and Eve could not return to the garden of innocence, so as we leave modernity's second-order naivete about critical reason, we cannot return to the uncritical first order naivete of premodern orthodoxy. We will be the poorer in added misunderstanding and conflict and foregone cooperation if each worldview and religion naively assumes its absoluteness—absolute here in the sense of an entity unto itself, unrelated to others. In addition, this notion of a more or less unbridgeable gap between differing worldviews has very negative implications for a traditional Christian concern—evangelism.

Postliberals do offer a positive contribution to contemporary theology by challenging Christians to be genuinely immanent in their tradition, to recognize and claim what is meaningful in Christianity, and by increasing awareness of how Christians allow other viewpoints to define us. (An irony appears here. The postliberal belief in the incommensurability of worldviews arises in tandem with a fear of

32. Charles W. Allen describes tribalism's threat-irrelevancy polarity in "Primacy of *Phronesis*."

Christianity's corruption by secularism; yet postliberals fail to recognize the implausibility or impossibility of such contamination to the extent of the truth of incommensurability.) Though in considerable tension with belief in incommensurability, postliberalism does provide hope for the evangelistic efficacy of a community whose authority lies in the attractiveness of its praxis. (By contrast evangelistic hope for Catholic postliberals rests on the prospect that people in want of a moral and religious authority will return to the Church.)

Having provided Christianity intellectual sanction through the postmodern notion of culture or worldview as self-authenticating context of meaning, conservative postmodern theology then refuses to play by the logic of that notion, by the rules of the postmodern game. Christianity escapes the application of the relativity and contextuality at the heart of this postmodern idea. On what basis? On an absolutistic assumption in the modern or pre-modern spirit: that religious truth entails that God intentionally and infallibly (though acting through cultural-linguistic realities) constitutes a religion as *the* religion. At most one religion correctly claims to know an extra-cultural-linguistic and ultimate reality. Publicly speaking, in the short term we cannot adjudicate these competing claims of religious traditions, in keeping with the postliberal immanentist assumption. In the long term, the one true religion established by God will survive, while other worldviews may not. Postliberals recognize that Christianity appears as relative as any other religion to outsiders. But privately speaking, the Christian can know this God-given absolute connection. Clearly this theology will not settle for Christianity as one context of meaning among many—it must reign as the absolute religion, the one grand exception. Though this theology acknowledges the relativity of everything human on one level, in the tradition of Barth (whether or not Barth is cited), ultimately God overrides human epistemological finitude.

Given the strong Polanyian influence on this project, I will address the thought of Esther Meek, who has authored an excellent book on Polanyi's epistemology.[33] Postliberals and the Radical Orthodox do not assume the violation or superseding of natural processes in the unique authority of the Bible. By contrast, in step with evangelical tradition, Meek does hold to supernatural interventionism to guarantee the

33. Meek, *Longing to Know.*

historicity of the biblical witness. On several interconnected fronts I find Meek's stance on revelation and biblical authority problematic from a Polanyian perspective. Historical biblical criticism constitutes a well-established tradition supported by general evidence that pre-modern people judge truthfulness by mytho-poetic, theological, and existential rather than modern historical standards, as well as by particular evidence that many biblical narratives are in fact not historical. In the face of such direct challenge one cannot retreat to an uncritical haven. The cruciality of science for Polanyi compounds the difficulties inherent in Meek's position, and not only through the breaking or supersession of scientific laws that grounds her view of religious authority. While an intuitive, unspecifiable, and tacit dimension underlies all science, scientific knowledge often defies common sense or naïve realism. Likewise we need to recognize an unscientific naivete of ancient "common sense" concerning the "historical."[34] In the tradition of liberal Protestantism (and Judaism) we need to distinguish between theological/ethical and historical truth, as Polanyi himself suggested by endorsing "modern theology('s)" acceptance of historical biblical criticism "as its guide for reinterpreting and consolidating the Christian faith in a truer form."[35] Only then can we do justice to the "universal intent" of faithful scientific and historical investigation.

While radical postmodernism images humanity and divinity consistently—total immanence prevails, conservative postmodernism downplays human transcendence and freedom, even as it stresses them with respect to God. God chooses to reveal God's self within one particular tradition. Personal particularity wins out over a wider, more consistently immanent revelation—a revelation consonant with both human and divine universal intent and with indeterminate future manifestations.[36]

34. See Polanyi, *Personal Knowledge*, 267.

35. Ibid., 282–83.

36. See Cannon, "Longing to Know"; Rutledge, "Knowing as Unlocking"; and Meek, "*Longing to* Know," for additional discussion of Meek's theology relative to Polanyi's post-critical philosophy.

The Moderates

Not being aware of a representative movement or figure that has spelled out the relevant characteristics of moderate postmodernism, I now presume to write constructively from that perspective. The moderate wing takes to heart postmodern freedom from the modern burden of explicating and justifying all basic assumptions and all meanings. It enjoys the postmodern assurance that Christianity has meaning for those incarnated and enculturated in it. This assurance frees it to use critical reason appropriately to address problems and opportunities as they arise. It alone among the three postmodern camps can be genuinely hopeful. Part of its relative optimism stems from it alone fully disowning absolutism. It avoids the deconstructive emphasis on the extreme tenuousness or absence of meaning relative to a hidden standard of absolute truth. It also averts postliberalism's impossible burden of maintaining or proving to the Christian community its religion's absoluteness.

I have delineated how both the radicals and the conservatives bounce back and forth between immanentist relativism and respective absolutisms. Moderate postmodernism attempts to chart a course between relativism and absolutism. For it, the absence of an absolute beginning and end does not entail deconstruction's "erring" or "aimlessness." Rather, in their bodily becoming in the world humans and animals normally find purpose and direction in a multiplicity of goals and meanings, some more immediate or short-term, some long-term or overarching, some more definite or particular, some more provisional or general. Despite foreclosure from any absolute perspective, creatures normally come to perceptual, kinesthetic, and cognitive closure, contrary to deconstructive "undecidability."

To the extent poststructuralists would acknowledge the above description of normal experience, they might still contend that upon radical reflection (in the modern spirit, I would add) ironic skepticism is a more appropriate attitude. But moderates realize that lack of meaning and skepticism are parasitical upon meaning, upon standing somewhere. In normal experience we realize we are in touch with some truth and value, even though upon reflection or further experience we discover that we erred in some (perhaps crucial) respect or missed the greatest possible value (and, indeed, perhaps even caused great evil in the process).

Crucially moderates realize and claim that we know reality, a reality partly but not wholly constituted by us. There is always a givenness not constructed by any individual or cultural group. Except in the case of other experients (and unless one accepts a panpsychic viewpoint without remainder, which I earlier rejected as an expression of modern idealism), the given element is not itself already fully constituted or definite, not a "world" apart from our participation, but open to our fuller definition. From a postmodern perspective, it is neither necessary nor plausible to postulate either a concrete, fully constituted physical realm or a reified moral order completely independent of a world evolving and under construction. Yet neither is the given simply indefinite or amorphous. Certainly no one can directly or concretely describe the given fully, for any description involves our constituting activity. Here we can helpfully contrast the moderate postmodern vision with other options. While radical postmodernism denies any world beyond our constituting activity and Kantian modernism postulates a fully constituted world independent of, but partially accessible through, our constituting activity, moderate postmodernism sees given elements and our constituting activity as together forming the world.

Because of the uncompromising commitment that we live embodied *in reality*, contra both radicals and postliberals, moderates reject any strong doctrine of incommensurability and credit others with some grasp of truth. Even radically divergent perspectives may apprehend at some level the same given element of reality. Moderate postmodernism holds that error is corrigible—not by some absolutely privileged, infallible, inherently different method, but by our normal ways of coming to know in the world; that there are better and worse; that in moving from one perspective to another, we not only achieve something aesthetically novel (as in Lyotard's "paralogy"[37]), but can stretch to fuller truth. In short, moderate postmodernism places us in the muck and mire of real existence with all its ambiguity, where none of us has any absolute possession of the truth but none of us is totally blind either, where we may be "often perplexed, but not defeated," where we can and should reach for fuller truth and greater value.

With the radicals, moderates recognize that part of Christianity's largest context of meaning involves its interconnections with differ-

37. Lyotard, *Postmodern Condition*.

ing worldviews. While maintaining Christianity's relative identity, it eschews the notion of Christianity's absolute difference from other religions and worldviews. It willingly and hopefully enters into dialogue with the other. While acknowledging that a Western Christian cannot know Buddhism, for example, precisely as someone enculturated in Buddhism from birth, it believes that mutual translation and understanding are possible. It shares its viewpoints and commitments in the faith that they (and those of the partner in dialogue) can have relevance to more than an isolated context, can have more universal meaning. Change and even conversion are possible outcomes of dialogue. Such faith involves the basic assumption that continuous with our rootedness in a particular culture and tradition lies our rootedness in the being/becoming of the world.

The moderate branch recognizes our immanence in contexts of meaning in a way that modernity did not and disavows its assumption or standard of absolute transcendence. But unlike the other two branches, it does allow a significant place for freedom and transcendence, as the preceding analysis suggests. Humans have the potential and sometimes the obligation to critique smaller and larger contexts of meaning and to embrace or reject them, the potential to change our judgments regarding truth and our moral commitments. The middle branch alone consistently gives the critical side of the postmodern spirit its due.

As does radical postmodernism, the moderates image humanity and divinity harmoniously. As some balance of transcendence and immanence pertains to humans, so too to God. A stronger sense of divine immanence prevails than in classical theology, even as greater immanence characterizes its portrait of humanity. To the extent they directly address concepts or metaphors for God, postmodern moderates may favor panentheism, as do Protestants Sally McFague and Peter Hodgson and Catholic David Tracy. Chapter 6 will have more to say about this.

Epilogue

A sense of rootlessness and of the arbitrariness of ways of life has grown in Western civilization over the past century or more. This rootlessness and disembodiment derives in part from the controlling picture of modernity, a picture that denies our roots.

Modernity initially hoped that critical reason would banish the arbitrariness of individual and institutional beliefs and practices. As reason failed to establish absolute truth, hope for overcoming arbitrariness increasingly banked on the prereflective; however, this hope was dashed as well. The past century also saw an increasing awareness of alternative cultures and worldviews.

While preliminarily acknowledging bodily and social rootedness, radical postmodernists, like some existentialist forerunners, applaud rootlessness and arbitrariness-relativism. The desire to feel "at home" in the world, for things to "hang together," is finally inappropriate and unhealthy. Postliberals by contrast attempt to purchase at-home-ness by positing an absolute grounding in a tradition. Given an increasing sense of uprootedness in modern and postmodern worlds, it should not surprise us that both radical celebration and postliberal exorcism of rootlessness and arbitrariness have appeal.

Refusing either extreme, moderate postmodernism acknowledges both our rootedness in meaning—through our bodies and traditions I would claim—and the element of arbitrariness in all ours ways of viewing and doing. Nothing is absolute or necessary in a logical sense, yet this does not preclude meaning and coherence. Our rootedness in our bodies and world is not one of stasis, but of openness both to new constitutions of the world and to fuller apprehensions of the world's givenness. Ensuing chapters will elaborate upon these three postmodernisms with respect to rootlessness and rootedness. The postmodern insight that everyone must stand somewhere can be startling. Radical and conservative postmodernism see everyone as standing irreconcilably far apart. The radicals, though, attempt to overcome such incommensurability by the standing everywhere-nowhere of endorsing every position equally. Moderate postmodernism recognizes our differences, but affirms that through our embodiment in the world we do not stand irreducibly far apart.

The abandonment of the modern assumption of and search for the privileged position of absolute self-possession, absolute transcendence with respect to time, and absolute clarity and certainty in knowledge, will sadden some. But perhaps renouncing any absolute human perspective should not unsettle us. Those who disbelieve in God or divinity presumably have no reason to expect any absolute perspective. Those who believe might well confess that there is only one absolute perspective, and that it belongs to the divine.

2

Postmodernism(s) and Tradition

Introduction

"WITHOUT TRADITION OUR LIVES WOULD BE AS SHAKY AS ... AS A FID-
dler on the roof." So intones Tevye in a (bodily) metaphor from *Fiddler
on the Roof.*[1] As the play suggests, the role of tradition came under
increasing threat in the modern period. Indeed, the dominant modern picture of human rationality, and by extension of human life, has
been deracinate and discarnate—without roots in tradition or in the
human body. I will argue that tradition and the body are—and should
be acknowledged as—thoroughly interconnected. And I will attempt to
reclaim the cruciality of tradition and the body for human rationality
and life.

Modern epistemological assumptions discounted, indeed dismissed, the role and value of tradition. As William Poteat has argued and
as indicated in Chapter 1, Renaissance paintings, where all appears crystal clear in foreground and background, reveal a "controlling picture" of
modernity: the reasoning subject can reach a place of absolute privilege
beyond mediating structures such as the human body, language, and
tradition.[2] Observations on the negative attitude of the Enlightenment

---

1. Bock, *Fiddler.*

2. Poteat, *Meditations,* 59. 1) Crucial aspects of the Protestant Reformation evidence
the influence of this picture. Apart from its actual relationship to tradition, the rhetoric of the Reformation entailed bypassing centuries of corrupt tradition to recover a
pure origin. Likewise tradition was dethroned from an authoritative role in interpreting Scripture, in favor of individual reason and conscience under the guidance of the
Holy Spirit (again in rhetoric if not always in reality). 2) Given Radical Orthodoxy's
claim (Milbank et al., *Radical Orthodoxy*) and earlier Tillich's (*Theology of Culture,*
16, 19), that late medieval nominalism formed the juncture where Western theology

toward tradition are commonplace. Alasdair MacIntyre has gone so far as to claim that *the* essential project of enlightenment liberalism has been to remove all vestiges of traditional communal authority.[3] I will note the essentializing and hyperbole of that claim. And I will grant countervailing tendencies in the Enlightenment, a very complex phenomenon indeed. Certainly Enlightenment thinkers manifested great interest in historical, social, and political contexts—though still the dominant mode was to emphasize discontinuity over continuity with the past. As Karsten Harries and Susan E. Schreiner have shown, anxiety about the deceptiveness of putative privileged perspectives pervaded the late Renaissance and the early Enlightenment.[4] Yet the very breadth and depth of this anxiety and doubt reflects the pull of the ideal of absolute knowledge. This present project cannot encompass arguing such issues further. So I will claim the following as a scholarly consensus in the humanities and social sciences: on the whole the Enlightenment did indeed enthrone the ideal of a universal reason not dependent upon particular traditions. Descartes, signaling the philosophical beginnings of modernity, assumed a radical—albeit anxious—skepticism of all tradition and convention in the search for absolute certainly based on reason. This was a *critical reason*, in the senses that 1) claims based on tradition or convention demanded critical evaluation, and 2) any truth claim required explicit justification or proof.

Such enlightenment rationality exhibited initial confidence in establishing a universal religion and morality. However, given the standard of absolute proof, this project was doomed to failure. The assumptions of modernity—that knowledge required explicit justification from neutral premises—ineluctably led to the polarized opposites of absolutism and relativism, flip sides of the same epistemological coin. In the wake of Humean skepticism, Kant attempted to negotiate the limits of

---

and philosophy went tragically astray, I will share a word on nominalism's relationships to modernity. With Tillich (*Theology of Culture*, 16–18) I judge that Aquinas did posit an autonomy (and even an aspect of superiority) of reason vis-à-vis faith. This was not yet modernity's absolutization of reason. But this elevation of reason drew a Scotistic-Occamist reaction which paralleled at the same time both deconstructive and postliberal reactions to modernity: skepticism regarding reason's ability to establish any truth about God *and* the reassertion of tradition in the form of church authority guaranteeing absolute divine truth.

3. MacIntyre, *Whose Justice?* 228.

4. Harries, *Infinity*; Schreiner, "Appearances and Reality."

human reason, yet still relying on critical doubt to find the supposedly indubitable, to "gain for ourselves a possession which never again can be contested."[5] Alas, it was not to be. The relativistic failure of universal reason left only historically conditioned particularisms, constructed by communities and individuals, with no means for adjudication. Here critical reason concluded that religious, ethical, and other value claims were unjustifiable. Standing in or preferring one tradition to another was wholly arbitrary. This helped set the stage for modern uprootedness.

If the anti-tradition "tradition" of modernity is clear, the anti-body dimension is no less real, if more complex.[6] Modern epistemology, either implicitly or explicitly, has attempted to locate a place of absolute privilege and certainty on one side or the other of Cartesian mind-body dualism. Rationalists obviously have had little use for the body. Yet even empiricists such as Locke and Hume offered strangely disembodied understandings of perception, focusing on immediate mental contents. Many of their contemporary realist, empiricist successors champion a reductionistic physicalist version of the body, where the body becomes merely an object, an object with little or no connection to anyone's lived or experiential body. Such objectification of the body when placed under the gaze of scientific critical reason should come as no surprise. Even idealist Romantics glorying in the prereflective and emotive often split these from any rational bodily connection with the actual world. While one can point to particular pernicious effects of modernity's anti-tradition and anti-body assumptions,[7] these symptoms point to a deeper malaise: these assumptions call into doubt—radical doubt—the fundamental meaningfulness of life. Indeed, if we alienate ourselves from our traditions and our bodies, what remains but the most abstract forms of meaning? Furthermore this doubt is invincible given modernity's absolutistic/relativistic epistemological assumptions. Paul Tillich famously observed that the dominant existential anxiety and threat of the modern era was meaninglessness.[8] If as I believe we have been entering a postmodern age, the premiere existential issue remains that of meaning(lessness), at least for affluent Westerners. Compounding

5. Kant, *Critique of Pure Reason*, B805–6; quoted in Polanyi, *Personal Knowledge*, 270.

6. For a corroborating perspective, see Midgley, "Soul's Successors," 54ff.

7. See footnote 4, Chapter 1, for such a list.

8. Tillich, *Courage to Be*, 60–62, 113ff.

the atmosphere of uprootedness bequeathed by modernity's denials of tradition and the body are various interrelated twentieth-century developments: increased mobility, exponential technological change, the knowledge explosion, and sea changes in social roles and status.

Embodied organisms instinctually orient themselves to their environment. Human beings, because of our reflective abilities to stand back from our immediate environment, have the capability to orient ourselves to ever larger natural and cultural environments. The perspective I will develop regards religion, at least in one of its functions, as the human attempt to orient ourselves to the largest environment we can imagine, to the universe, to the whole of things insofar as we might know that, and often to an ultimate/divine source or overall purpose of the universe. Thus, religion's roots lie in a basic aspect of biological embodiment, even as it expands upon that basic impulse. Some forms of religions, in the face of life's evils, have of course promoted alienation from the body and the world. But I would judge that the healthier forms of religion have provided people with a sense of at-home-ness in the world. Implicitly or explicitly this has involved acknowledging and celebrating our embodiment in the world and our embeddedness in tradition(s). Thus growing modern and postmodern rootlessness threatens a primary meaning constituting/confirming function of religion.

Before proceeding to consider various postmodernisms with respect to tradition, I will offer a general word on postmodernism and epistemology, recapitulating and expanding upon my considerations in Chapter 1. While "postmodernism" is a multivalent term used in diverse contexts, insofar as a reaction against epistemological assumptions of modernity constitutes postmodernity's raison d'etre, widespread and perhaps surprising agreement exists among numerous lists of postmodern epistemological assumptions and claims:

1) Knowledge always comes mediated, always constructed (at least in part), involving the engagement of the knower. There is no absolute, privileged epistemological space and no fully determinate objective reality, which our language simply represents, to which our perceptions or ideas simply correspond.[9]

---

9. Aichele, "Literary Fantasy," 325; Evans, "African-American Christianity," 214; Kort, "Religion and Literature," 576; Raschke, "Fire and Roses," 672–73.

2) The subject is not transparent to itself, never strictly autonomous, totally present to itself, or fully in possession of itself.[10] Gone then is the "transcendental subject" capable of absolute knowledge of world or self.

3) As a corollary to the first two, totalizing schemas are suspected or rejected. Essentializing misses the complexity of life in its temporal and contextual dimensions.

4) Modern dualistic schemas especially draw postmodern ire, both for absolutizing and hierarchicalizing difference. The binarisms challenged include mind-body, subject-object, reflective-prereflective, culture-nature, and high-low culture.[11]

5) If not polarized and absolutized though, difference and otherness are highly valued. In the absence of an Archimedian standpoint, particular standpoints and mediating structures deserve a presumptive respect.[12]

6) The interconnected, interdependent nature of reality finds affirmation.[13] This is construed so as to recognize complexity, porosity, and otherness, while rejecting essentialism and dualism.

Radical Postmodernism

In the face of this situation some radical postmodernists like some existential forerunners ultimately follow modernity in its anti-tradition and anti-body attitudes—at best exhibiting ambivalence about the body, despite not infrequent invocations of it. If modernity assumed we could bypass the mediation of tradition and body, some poststructuralists regard tradition and the body as arbitrary constructs in principle always subject to deconstruction or replacement—thus likewise negating the

10. Dean, "Challenge of New Historicism," 266; Evans, "African-American Christianity," 216; Scharlemann, *Theology*, 2; Winquist, *Epiphanies of Darkness*.

11. Lowe, *Theology and Difference*; Merleau-Ponty, *Phenomenology of Perception*; Poteat, *Recovering the Ground*, 28–30; M. Taylor, *Erring*, 8–10, 108–9.

12. Evans, "African-American Christianity," 216; Jameson, "Postmodernism," 75; Klemm, "Toward a Rhetoric," 456–57; Lawson, *Reflexivity*, 78, 123; Lowe, "Deconstructionist Manifesto," 329–30.

13. Evans, "African-American Christianity," 215; Griffin et al., *Sacred Interconnections*; Kort, "Religion and Literature," 576; Raschke, "Fire and Roses," 676.

necessary mediation by tradition and body. Commendably this brand of constructivism uplifts contextuality and intertextuality. And I would follow it as far as the following point: because of the temporal flow and intertextuality of reality, contexts and attendant givenness constantly change, and such change should be acknowledged rather than stifled— thus no abstract or absolute rule can decide for us. However, it also posits an arbitrary givenness to our experience, even to the point that we become ciphers of apparently deterministic social, political, and cultural forces. We appear to be wholly immanent in representations and constructions, language, perceptions. One response to this contextuality and intertextuality appears in Mark C. Taylor's deconstructive phase: the Nietzschean "Dionysian" affirming of the whole of life and all its constitutive parts, the endorsement of all constructions (or at least all those that do not negate other constructions).[14] On the other hand, this deconstructionist approach suggests two notions, not unrelated, which appear to challenge total immanentism regarding constructions. Derrida denied outright that we are stuck in our constructions, given his overarching goal of valorizing otherness.[15] Ambivalence, however, pervades this goal, as we can never reach the unpresentable— *differance*—which remains beyond our constructions. Our bodies and language (and traditions) then cannot mediate difference—through them we can only recognize the existence of an unbridgeable gap. An ironic corollary follows: despite the intertextuality that assumes our constructions always interconnect with those of others, out of respect for the principle of "otherness" we can never actually reach the other.[16] Secondly, Taylor and other radical postmodernists urge us (somehow) to resist any *dominant* constructions, including influential traditions, again valorizing the marginal and the trace, the "not," the imperceptible always escaping our grasp. Therefore, even stopping short of the ironic detachment—and implied disembodiment—which often accompanies radical postmodernism, we have only the criteria-less criterion of the

14. M. Taylor, "*Erring*", e.g., 167. Mark C. Taylor probably represented the premiere proponent of deconstructive and poststructuralist thought relative to religion. In more recent work Taylor has reacted against and moved beyond deconstruction's immanentist and nihilistic tendencies.

15. Derrida, "Deconstruction," 123; *Limited, Inc.*, 136–37, 146–47; see also, Creech et al., "Deconstruction in America," and Caputo, "Good News."

16. M. Taylor, *Erring*, 30–31; *Alterity*; *Nots*, 89–91.

unpresentable or "not" that ever eludes us. This leaves us no means to decide among contested, "living, forced, momentous" options, to use William James' language,[17] no means to choose whether to resist or accept a given construction or interpretation in our actual contexts—except perhaps to try to resist any dominant one. In short, this leaves us with relativism.

In contrast to deconstruction, the very notion of embodiment entails both correlation/consonance and differentiation of the body with respect to its environment. This in turn entails the following: the givenness of an individual body of a particular species necessitates some non-arbitrary constructivism which sets parameters for how we engage our environment—much common to the species, some unique to the individual. At the same time, the givenness of our natural and social environments means we do make contact through our own bodies—though of course never "absolute" contact—with the other, with other bodies and physical realities. The body then (like tradition) is not just a passive medium constructed by various forces and possibly by a (non) author resisting said forces, not just a text to inscribe; no, the body—which includes an active, non-arbitrary biological givenness, both physiological and experiential—also constructs, also inscribes. If modernity imagined the transparency and incidental nature of our language and bodies (in the case of our perceptions claiming we can get beyond the mediation entailed in "secondary" qualities and discern "primary" qualities), radical postmodernism clings to this incidental nature. The key difference, of course, lies in modernity's hope that one reaches the truth beyond incidental mediators, while for deconstruction one only has incidental mediators with no beyond—except for unreachable alterity. As radical postmodernism resists any closure in favor of eternal deferral, the desire to feel at home in the world, for things to hang together, becomes an unhealthy illusion we best abandon.

Not coincidentally, pictures and metaphors of surface and of texts inscribed on a surface pervade radical postmodernism's understanding of meaning, with a concomitant eschewal of metaphors of depth. If the danger of depth metaphors is hierarchy and dualism, the danger of surface metaphors is relativism—all values lie on precisely the same plane. Literary texts consist of two dimensions while bodies and embodied life

17. James, "Will to Believe."

inhabit three; literary texts typically do bear multifarious contextual interpretations over extended periods of time. Radical postmodernism's picture in effect crunches these interpretations into an abstract instant on a flat, "utopian"—"no place"—space. Difference constitutes the unreachable third dimension. Interestingly, this tendency to abstraction comes out as Derrida (echoing Sartre and consonant with Levinas) writes of our equal ethical obligation—an absolute duty—to each of various others.[18] Yes, of course we must decide, but here any decision appears arbitrary. By contrast the givenness of the concrete depth of particular situations at a place in time more readily elicits valid judgments of better and worse: as we must always stand somewhere, this givenness calls us to take a principled stand as traditioned bodies.

Radical postmodernism shares with postmodernism in general the rejection of modernity's premise and promise of absolute truth through reason. But, to elaborate upon tradition, French poststructuralism and deconstruction regard reason's totalizing pretentions evident in modernity—"logocentrism," as not only present but dominant in Western philosophy and theology from the beginning. Thus a proclivity exists to reject much of Western tradition—especially dominant traditions. At the same time, as suggested above, more marginalized traditions, texts, subtexts, and fragments that work against the dominant discourse come highly prized. Yet this does not represent a gain for tradition(s) overall. For (a) tradition to possess authority, a certain degree of continuity and integration is requisite. But poststructuralism tends to deny precisely this, doubting any decidability on the meaning of a tradition, instead championing fragmentation and discontinuity. Add to this the Foucaultian suspicion that suppressive power interests invariably corrupt tradition's construal, and postructuralism refuses tradition any of its traditional value—as an authority. In this postructuralism echoes modernity's basic attitude toward tradition.

Taylor's deconstructive phase engaged the question of the (in) commensurability of interpretive traditions. Note that I will use "incommensurable" in the following sense in this book: two traditions are incommensurable when, in the face of difference, 1) they cannot credit the other as a valid alternative and 2) no adequate means exist to reconcile outright disagreements. I mentioned earlier the strong "Dionysian"

18. Derrida, *Gift of Death.*

element, which plays off of the Saussurean-Derridian understanding of language and culture as differential system of signifiers, where apparently opposite positions require and define each other.[19] The Dionysian side of Taylor's thought entails a "post-critical" moment, a refusal of the modern charge to critical reason to justify all values, and with it an immanentism, as mentioned above. However, in one sense this immanence cannot be complete. For when difference, the trace, the "not", the unspoken, the imperceptible get turned in on the self rather than applied to the other "outside," inalterable alterity within the self reigns: we can never totally identify with our own words and perceptions. Taylor finds positive value in this incompleteness, insofar as it discourages immanence as return to undifferentiated primitive origin, as disastrously exemplified in fascism.[20]

Deconstruction does then affirm porosity and interconnectedness in the sense that something of the other beyond the self also lies within the self. Yet, ironically, because of the impossibility of actually reaching the other as above, for the deconstructive Taylor an ultimate incommensurability among options, an unalterable alterity among individual viewpoints and among traditions, reigns.[21] Finally no effectual commonality and no basis for adjudication or decidability exists.[22] Because one can neither reach the other nor stand fully committed to one's own perspective because of the alterity within the self, the radical postmodernist is not rooted, not affirmatively present, in any of these traditions. This accounts for the attitude of ironic detachment that one finds at some points in Taylor, Derrida, and other deconstructionists. Taylor's thought issues in an either/or, oscillating between a Dionysian, non-critical embracing of the whole with its interconnected traditions or a

19. M. Taylor, *Erring*, 107–12. One can interpret Saussure as claiming that the meaning of signs is constituted *only* negatively, in relation to the other signs that a given sign is not (e.g., Murphy, *Anglo-American Postmodernity*, 135). Taylor is unclear as to whether he endorses that interpretation. I would insist that some degree of positive intrinsic content or identity of the referent of a sign also constitutes meaning; but this identity or content is never separate but always involves interrelationships.

20. M. Taylor, "Politics of Theo-ry," 32–33.

21. M. Taylor, *Erring*, 172; *Alterity*; *Nots*, 155.

22. Brian McHale has claimed that if you push epistemological uncertainty hard enough, you get ontological pluralism (*Postmodernist Fiction*, 11). Philosopher Nelson Goodman has argued that human beings and cultures create multiple, incommensurable worlds (*Ways of Worldmaking*, 1–6, 110).

critical, detached refusal to commit to any of separate(d) traditions. In common both contain a haunting, hidden standard of absolute proof and certainty, which forces a relativistic undecidability or an absolute endorsement of all decisions

Before moving to the postliberals, I will note another strand of postmodernism's "left wing"—the new historicism's more radical contingent. This group includes philosophers Nelson Goodman and Richard Rorty and religionists William Dean and possibly Jeffrey Stout. What distinguishes this new historicism, at least in its radical versions, from the old is its acceptance of "sheer historical contingency," in the words of Dean.[23] Neither a transcendent efficient or final cause nor an underlying logic or immanent *telos* guides history.[24] Given no constraints on historical contingency, these thinkers envisage robust freedom of interpretation; yet past decisions do constrain present ones. Regarding the threat of relativism, Dean and Stout condemn such egregious evils as Nazism or torture on a gut-feeling level.[25] However, they offer no epistemological or ontological basis for this intuition, no basis for transcending the "henotheism" that Dean concedes the new historicism permits.[26] Though strongly influenced by continental poststructuralism, these thinkers—rooted in American pragmatism—take historical community as their starting point. Tradition, as the past interpretations of a community, possesses some authority and provides a basis for decidability. Theoretically, rootedness in *one* tradition is no problem for radical new historicism. Relativistic problems arise though on how to decide among competing traditions. Here incommensurability applies. Without deconstruction and poststructuralism's positing of some interpenetration of traditions for the sake of (internal) alterity, a picture of self-enclosed traditions informs radical historicism.[27]

---

23. Dean, "Challenge of New Historicism," 262.

24. Ibid., 262, 266, 272.

25. Ibid., 280; Stout, *Ethics after Babel*, 245.

26. Dean, "Challenge of New Historicism," 281.

27. Rorty, *Mirror of Nature*, 315–94. Jean-Francois Lyotard, influenced by a certain reading of Wittgenstein's language games, also operated under such a picture: each language game is heterogenous, with its own unique rules, the purity of which should be protected (*Postmodern Condition*, 66; *Just Gaming*, 96). In a subsequent work, Lyotard embraced the quest for rules to link language games (*Differend*).

Postliberals

On the opposite side of the spectrum postliberals attempt to purchase at-home-ness by positing an absolute rootedness in a tradition. It regards Christianity as a particular form of life and practice deriving from a canonical text and its interpretation, with its own internal logic and coherence. The premiere theoretician of this camp, George Lindbeck, influenced by Wittgenstein, has expounded Christianity as a cultural-linguistic semiotic system. Doctrine for Lindbeck performs a regulative function for Christian language games and the Christian form of life.

The overarching concern of Lindbeck and other postliberals, such as Protestants Stanley Hauerwas, the late John Howard Yoder, and Ronald Thiemann and Catholics Richard John Neuhaus and George William Rutler, as well as of Radical Orthodoxy, is to define Christian identity over against the larger culture. One danger of such a project consists in over-determining identity, in failing to acknowledge sufficiently the plurality within Christianity. It would be quite unfair to characterize the postliberals as blithely unaware of the contested and changing nature of Christianity historically, relative to formation of the canon, interpretation of Scripture, and communal practice. For example, Lindbeck cites the significant adaptations that resulted from the encounter of pacifistic early Christianity with militaristic Germanic culture,[28] and he generalizes that a religious tradition *may* need to change in changing historical contexts.[29] Yet despite the ability to recognize a certain plurality on the level of historical facticity, I judge that the following overarching picture unites the postliberals: the essential, defining features and logical structure of Christianity were present in the earliest canonical Scriptures as interpreted by the first Christian community (Protestant postliberals) or earliest ecclesiastical practice (Catholic postliberals). This essence is readily decidable, at least for the discerning with eyes to see and ears to hear. And despite variations, adaptations, explicitations, unfaithfulness, or outright heresy, this essence itself has remained intact, unchanging, at least for the Protestants.[30] The Catholics are more open to development

---

28. Lindbeck, *Nature of Doctrine*, 33–34.

29. Ibid., 39.

30. Lindbeck clearly affirms a "self-identical story" of Christ and a constancy of basic Christian grammar or rules (ibid., 83–84). In speaking of a Christian essence for postliberals, I am not suggesting an abstract, philosophical essence. Many Protestant postliberals contend that the (essential?) form of the Christian message is narrative. Yet this narrative consists of unchanging essential features, the "self-identical story."

and maturation of the original essence.[31] Of course, postliberals disagree as to the nature of this essence. In particular, Yoder and Hauerwas believe that the mainstream Constantinian church, in refusing pacifism, abandoned an essential feature of Christianity.

Lindbeck's admission of the plausibility of a correspondence theory of truth, or realism,[32] points to a final crucial aspect of postliberalism. Undoubtedly part of Lindbeck's concern is to defuse any suggestion that the partially constructed nature of a religious cultural-linguistic system precludes a reality transcending the system, in this case, God. And this point has legitimacy. However, I also sense a more dubious move, smacking of epistemological absolutism. As indicated earlier, postmodern epistemology recognizes the inevitable interest and participation of the knower, over against pre-modern or modern models of an already determinate truth and reality. The rest of Lindbeck's project relies upon precisely such postmodern logic in the exposition of Christianity as one constructed, mediating cultural-linguistic system, among others.[33] Lindbeck senses the unenforceability of claims to Christianity's unique absoluteness on postmodern logic; so he relies on eschatological verification of Christianity's unique and final truth (that is, we will know in the afterlife).[34] Therefore, while Christianity may appear to be humanly constructed and mediated on the same ontological plane as all other traditions, for the postliberal it is not: only Christianity comes divinely constructed, possessing an absolute givenness. A revelation from the Wholly Other overcomes the finitude and partiality entailed in our embodiment as "Adam—earth beings"—and supersedes our normal

31. Fiorenza, "Tradition."

32. Lindbeck, *Nature of Doctrine*, 63–64, 68–69.

33. Nancey Murphy has observed that "postliberal theologians appear as fideists to liberals but as relativists to conservatives" (*Beyond Liberalism*, ix, 155). It is Lindbeck's reliance upon this postmodern logic that raises the ire of conservatives. Problems arise for liberals when Lindbeck's postmodern epistemology runs into a Barthian kind of revelatory positivism. While Terrence Reynolds is correct that Lindbeck "does not explicitly adopt a Barthian stance on revelation" ("Walking Apart," 63), his strong valuation of the authority of the biblical narrative combined with an unwillingness to "demythologize" its revelatory claims implies such a stance. In addition, Lindbeck depends upon the Barth-influenced Hans Frei. Also relevant is Scott Cowdell's observation that Lindbeck allows ontological (or metaphysical) claims of Christ's unsurpassability without enforcing them (*Recent Christology*, 272). Indeed, Lindbeck not only allows but makes such claims.

34. Lindbeck, *Nature of Doctrine*, 56ff.

epistemological limitations or (Barthian) impotency in divine matters. While this revelation comes hidden within fallible human construction and divine fulness remains concealed, still an absolute connection from the divine side guarantees to this "mediation" a correspondence to reality unique to Christianity. Radical Orthodoxy finds more nuance with its Patristic affirmation that the whole world reveals God, but the upshot is the same: only revelation in Jesus Christ provides absolute truth.

As with the radical new historicism, a picture of self-enclosed traditions, of separate(d) cultural-linguistic systems,[35] stands behind post-liberalism's endorsement of incommensurability, though its motive in adopting the picture differs diametrically. While the radical wing would protect the otherness of all traditions, the conservative wing would protect the identity of the Christian tradition. Indeed, defensiveness constitutes postliberalism's raison d'etre: to preserve Christian identity over against other religious and secular traditions. It is thoroughly post-critical, rejecting any need to justify Christian claims contested by other traditions. This does not deny countervailing tendencies: 1) William A. Werpehowski and others see Lindbeck's thought as amenable to an "ad hoc apologetics," which would assume commensurability with non-Christian worldviews at some key points.[36] 2) An irony attends the postliberal position, as suggested in Chapter 1. If Christianity were as self-identical and self-contained as postliberalism pictures it, no need would arise to defend it against an encroaching secular culture. Postliberalism thus overestimates the degree of identity and ease of decidability within Christianity even as it overestimates the degree of difference and strength of boundaries among traditions.

Moderate Postmodernism

A moderate postmodernism stands in the best position to avoid extremes of relativism or absolutism. It consistently refuses the Cartesian assumption of a fundamental subject-object, idealist-realist split. In all our acts of knowing, doing, and valuing, subjectivity and objectivity, self and world, stand in inescapable correlation. Moderate postmodern philosophy and theology fall into certain camps: neo-pragmatist historicists, not as radical as the previously considered strand; hermeneutical

---

35. See ibid., 48–49.

36. Werpehowski, "Ad Hoc Apologetics," 287–98.

thinkers; neo-romantic expressivists; and finally "bodily "philosophers who inform the perspective of radical embodiment. The neo-pragmatists include philosophers Hilary Putnam and Richard Bernstein and theologian Cornell West; the hermeneuticists, philosophers Hans-Georg Gadamer and Paul Ricoeur and theologians David Klemm and David Tracy; neo-romantics, philosophers Stanley Cavell and Charles Taylor. Moderate postmodernists position themselves to give due in a correlative "both/and" fashion to (partial) givenness and (partial) constructivism in knowledge in general and to continuity/creativity, the a-critical/ critical, and the prereflective/reflective with respect to tradition. Among such moderates, Gadamer, Ricoeur, Tracy, Charles Taylor, Polanyi, and Poteat directly consider tradition.[37] Moderate postmodernism, as much as and probably more consistently than poststructuralism (given its tendency to ironic detachment) or postliberalism (given its objectivist tendencies with respect to revelation), emphasizes that knowledge is an activity, a practice, that involves our desire, participation, interpretation, commitment. Examples include Ricoeur's figuration, Gadamer's mimesis as performance, Bernstein's and the just-mentioned thinkers' appropriation of Aristotle's *phronesis*,[38] Cavell and Taylor's knowledge as expression, including Taylorean "strong evaluation" and Cavellian conviction "to mean what we say,"[39] Polanyi's "personal knowledge," and Merleau-Ponty's active perception.[40] For these moderate postmodern thinkers the act of knowing always involves judgment. Judgment is not limited to aesthetics, as in Kant, but applies to scientific, ethical, religious knowing, etc. As Bernstein has observed, Gadamer's *Truth and Method* argues that finally no method exists for determining truth[41]; one must instead rely upon judgment. For Polanyi human knowing relies upon a tacit dimension in principle unamenable to total specifiability.[42] For

---

37. Polanyi, *Personal Knowledge*, esp. 53–55, 374ff.; Poteat, *Philosophical Daybook*, 146–47.

38. Ricouer, *Time and Narrative*; Gadamer, *Truth and Method*, 102; Bernstein, *Beyond Objectivism*.

39. C. Taylor, *Sources of Self*; Cavell, *Must We Mean?*

40. Polanyi, *Personal Knowledge*, e.g., 157–62; Merleau-Ponty, *Phenomenology of Perception*, 28ff.

41. Bernstein, *Beyond Objectivity*, 115.

42. Polanyi, *Personal Knowledge*, 55–65; *Tacit Dimension*, 3–25; *Knowing and Being*, 138–57.

Wittgenstein rules run out: every act includes a moment where one must judge how to apply the rules of a language game or form of life.[43] (This usually more or less prereflective judgment is sometimes distinguished from a reflective "interpretation."[44]) And Merleau-Ponty describes judgment as "the hidden art of the imagination" in all human knowledge and consciousness.[45] For these thinkers then there is no decidability by rules, yet a non-arbitrary decidability obtains.

Tradition in particular involves a givenness from the past in correlation with present judgment, interpretation, and partial construction (as in Gadamer's fusion of horizons). Of course, the tradition(s) we inherit have been formed by this correlative process of givenness from the past meeting present construal. This correlation means that tradition is never absolutely continuous or discontinuous. A fortiori, sociologist Paul Connerton notes that even revolutionary change relies centrally upon social memory of the tradition it attempts to displace.[46]

The appropriation of tradition can be relatively self-conscious, reflective, and critical, as when one defends a discrete facet of a tradition or selects certain classic texts for interpretation.

Or its appropriation can be more subconscious, prereflective, and acritical—and more pervasive, as in a tradition's consensual authorization of a canonical religious text or in the background one brings to the interpretation of any text or idea. Here tradition is not what we think about but what we think with. It is Gadamer's "prejudices" or prejudgments, Ricoeur's "prefigurations," the communal aspect of Charles Taylor's "situatedness" and the preconscious dimensions of language,[47] a part of Polanyi's "tacit dimension,"[48] and Wittgenstein's "customs"[49] or "forms of life."[50] I will refer to this aspect of tradition as its prereflective or tacit givenness. Because "we know much we cannot tell," "the transmission of knowledge from one generation to the other must be

43. Wittgenstein, *Philosophical Investigations*, nos. 28, 84–86, 186, 198; 227.

44. Ibid., no. 201.

45. Merleau-Ponty, *Phenomenology of Perception*, xvii; see also, 32ff.

46. Connerton, *How Societies Remember*, 13.

47. C. Taylor, *Sources of Self*, 232.

48. Polanyi, *Personal Knowledge*, 53–55; *Tacit Dimension*.

49. Wittgenstein, *Philosophical Investigations*, no. 337.

50. Ibid., no. 241, 226.

predominantly tacit," according to Polanyi.[51] At the same time, what Polanyi writes about scientific tradition extends to all tradition: though traditions themselves always involve interpretations beyond mere facts or experiences, our appropriations involve further interpretations that modify the tradition in light of present concerns[52]—again the inevitable element of discontinuity or dissent. Furthermore, Tillich rightly noted that all ethical traditions—and we can add religious, political, and others (which often overlap)—contain both genuine wisdom from the past as well as the desire of those with power to maintain their privileges.[53] The concern to unmask the latter probably constitutes the most valuable contribution of radical postmodernism.

The dominant model for the appropriation of tradition in the hermeneuticists and neo-romantic expressivists involves the above-mentioned selection of classical texts. Some have criticized this approach for providing no criteria of selection and for neglecting the element of social power in designating texts as classics. David Tracy, an advocate of the classics model following Gadamer and Ricoeur, has felt chastened by such concerns, without rejecting the model. He has admitted the instability of criteria for selection and the moral ambiguity of classic texts. While Tracy's self-criticism is admirable, especially with regard to morality and power, I would not take it as far he does, for such blanket criticism of a lack of explicit selection criteria is itself problematic. Given the importance of judgment for moderate postmodernists, trusting the judgment of past others as to the value of a text may constitute a legitimate reliance on authority, a valid acritical knowing. That much of tradition is inevitably and legitimately prereflective, as indicated above and as I will elaborate in chapter 4, makes the case for such trust even stronger. Only when the value of a particular "classic" text becomes problematic or contested does an obligation arise in the realm of critical reason. Then arises the occasion to make explicit and to justify criteria for one's own and one's authorities' judgments. As implied above, critical reason also has a role in challenging morally objectionable elements within a text one otherwise deems valuable. I will note that the contestation of an authoritative text within a (sub)tradition is made from within

51. Polanyi, *Tacit Dimension*, 61.

52. Polanyi, *Personal Knowledge*, 160.

53. Tillich, *Theology of Culture*, 139.

some other (sub)tradition(s), such as the Judeo-Christian prophetic heritage, the Western enlightenment project of individual rights, social scientific hermeneutics of suspicion, or feminism.[54] Even as one gains critical, reflective distance on a problematic (aspect of a) text, one stands somewhere—never at an Archimedian point of world-transcending absolute privilege, but within one or more linguistic, cultural, ethical, or religious traditions, embodied in the world. The enlightenment picture of critical reason insofar as discarnate and deracinate is simply false.

While its premises avoid most of the either-or's of radical postmodernism and postliberalism, still many of the exemplars of moderate postmodernism—hermeneuticists, neo-romantic expressivists, and moderate neo-pragmaticists/historicists—join the above movements in their emphasis on the linguistic dimensions of tradition, to the neglect of the natural and the bodily. William Dean has indicted not only his fellow neo-pragmatists/historicists, but also deconstructionists and postliberal narrative theologians for regarding meaning as "literally and entirely constituted by the language of narrative conversation, or chains of signs," thus "neglect(ing) the natural world as it is experienced in cognitive, noncognitive, sensory, and affective ways."[55] Dean attempts to correct such neglect through his proposal of the "convention," defined as a social construct that takes on an objective historical reality. The convention involves both cultural and natural experience.[56] However, both the normal connotations of a "convention" and Dean's definition of it as social construct seem to favor the cultural over the natural, even as does "history" as primary category. In the absence of the development of an ontology or epistemology of the body or nature, Dean alerts us to a problem with the new historicism but fails to overcome it. This is not to say that all of the above postmodern thinkers deny non-linguistic aspects of human experience; however, they do subsume the natural to the cultural-linguistic. Linguistic-cultural construction so dominates, that experiences of nature and body become linguistic through and through. Causal influence travels one way. Here enlightenment culture-nature binarism still rules, albeit not separation but hierarchical reductionism. The cultural-linguistic may indeed so pervasively affect our

54. Various thinkers have recognized that, in spite of its anti-tradition pedigree, the Enlightenment has perforce spawned its own traditions and subtraditions.

55. Dean, "American Religious Thought," 749–50.

56. Ibid., 750–51.

lives that no "pure" bodily experience of the natural world "untainted" by language and culture exists. Overlooked however is the profound, prior, foundational, inalienable effect of the body and nature upon language and culture, especially in the realm of prereflective givenness. Language radically depends upon the human body. Only a perspective of radical embodiment can adequately develop the implications of moderate postmodernism for tradition(s).

3

The Body in Tradition

BEFORE DIRECTLY EXPOUNDING THE SUBSTANCE OF THE BODY IN TRA-
dition, I will begin with a more formal consideration of the "radicalness"
of radical embodiment. Etymologically, *radical* literally means getting to
the roots of something. Our bodies as they orient us in an environment,
a world, are the very roots which make possible all our living, knowing,
and valuing. As such they limit and define us at the same time they grant
us all our potentialities. Constructivist-essentialist debates are parasitic
upon (and typically tacitly assume) the range of possibilities our bodies provide. We are normally *aware* of our ubiquitous rootage in and
reliance upon our physiological and experiential bodies in only a tacit
manner. Neurobiologist Antonio Damasio has characterized this "hid-
ing of the body" as an "adaptive distraction," meaning that we become
"distracted" from directly attending to our bodies so we can attend to
our environment.[1] But when this tacit dimension is assumed but not acknowledged in philosophical and religious discourse—and the cultural
attitudes allied with such discourse—the results can be disastrous.

Radical embodiment then regards the body as an irreplaceable
mediator in all our doing and knowing. Does this mediating status
mean that the values we realize lie beyond the mediation, extrinsic to it,
that the body is mere means but not end? Absolutely not. The body constitutes the very correlation of subjectivity and objectivity. Embodied
values are not those of a pure subject(ive body) in itself nor of objects
in themselves but always of a lived body engaging its world: moving,
dancing, seeing colors, viewing spatial relationships and configurations,
hearing sounds, pitch, and rhythm, smelling, tasting, touching, feeling
warmth and divers skin sensations, sexual desiring and pleasuring, as

1. Damasio, *Feeling*, 29.

45

well as less immediate ideas and images—not directly perceptions of our primary senses, but nevertheless relying upon bodily orientation and movement in order to mean anything.

The radicality of radical embodiment is not that of biological determinism. The perspective of radical embodiment does not deny the tremendous creativity and the diversity of human culture; it simply recognizes that all culture relies substantively upon bodily meanings. Radical embodiment does not minimize our human capability to forgo pressing bodily needs; it only affirms that such sacrifice draws substantively on other bodily meanings. Radical embodiment does not gainsay the element of contingency in human existence, the element of chance and even arbitrariness. Yet the presence of contingency—the lack of absolute logical necessity to any aspect of our existence—does not contradict the overall coherence and meaningfulness of that existence. As some thinkers have noted, embodied rationality is not that of necessary and sufficient conditions.[2] Nagatomo Shigenori declares that "the living body *is* already *placed*, or to use Heidegger's terminology, 'thrown' into a meaningful ambience or environment."[3] While the usual connotations of existentialist "thrownness" conflict with Nagatomo's position, he is exactly right on the larger substantive issue: we are rooted in a meaningful world through our human bodies—and the bodies of our traditions.

Before leaving the more formal implications of radical embodiment for the substantive development of the body in tradition, I want to address a possible concern of feminists and gender theorists: that my focus on the bodily basis of meaning could end up supporting the privileged status of certain bodies. Poststructuralists and probably most feminist and gender theorists urge the socially constructed nature of the body, gender, and sexuality. Conversely, a minority of feminists and certain scientists hold to some form of gendered bodily essentialism or biological determinism. Where does radical embodiment stand in this debate? I believe it offers a viable tertium quid between the relativistic tendencies of constructivism and the absolutistic ones of essentialism. For her part premiere gender theorist Judith Butler attempts to overcome modern binaries with her concept of the indissolubility of bodily

2. Johnson and Lakoff, *Philosophy in the Flesh*; Varela et al., *Embodied Mind*.
3. Nagatomo, *Attunement*, 30.

materiality and linguistic signification.[4] (However, I do see the earlier-mentioned tendency to prioritize the linguistic over the bodily in her rhetorical affirmation that language is "the very condition under which materiality may be said to appear."[5]) As a moderate postmodernist, I agree with Butler that every instance of our knowing and being is a constitutive action. So in a genuine sense gender and everything human is "performative." However, the perceptual modalities and the structure and shape of our motile bodies that we bring to every constitutive action constrain our possibilities within human ranges. Human perception and sexuality differ from, say, hippopotamus perception and sexuality. A biological givenness then pertains—though our concrete reality never becomes fully determinate until we act. This does not deny within the applicable ranges innumerable, even inexhaustible, possibilities. For example, to use myself as an individual example, I could run a 100-yard dash in many possible ways, but there is no possibility I could set a world record—or even come close. What about alleged human gender differences? Short of a sex-change operation (which is not the kind of de/construction constructivists usually have in mind), male/female anatomical genital-sexual differences entail some differences in the opening up/constraining of sexual expression. Furthermore, evidence exists that a combination of genetic, physiological developmental, and early psychological factors constrains a particular individual's sexual preferences. For example, a study of self-identified homosexual, bisexual, and heterosexual men found that the bisexual men generally exhibited strong genital arousal to sexual images of either males or females, but not to both.[6] This still leaves ample room for heterosexual, homosexual, bisexual (given some sexual attraction to the less "preferred" gender), and transgender possibilities.

More broadly, a cascade of studies that support gender variations in learning, playing, working, perceiving, thinking, and communication styles continue to capture the popular imagination. For example, the headline, "Hear, hear: Genders listen differently," announces a study concluding that men listen to language using only the left of the brain's

4. Butler, *Bodies That Matter*, 29–31.

5. Ibid., 31.

6. Rieger et al., "Sexual Arousal Patterns."

hemispheres, while women use both.[7] Another study finds that most children born without a penis but otherwise normal males, castrated at birth and raised as girls, come to identify themselves as boys.[8] A *Reader's Digest* article cites higher testosterone levels in males than females and suggests its likely influence on early mental differences between genders: two to three times as many boys as girls are hyperactive; relatively speaking, girls perform better in verbal tasks, boys in spatial tasks[9]; and so on. What is the upshot of research in this area? While the accuracy and significance of particular studies await definitive confirmation, I judge the overall trend to be clear: 1) there are some statistically significant differences among gender groups inexplicable by social conditioning alone 2) the performance ranges of men and women largely overlap, with differences falling at the edges of these ranges. This is to say that male and female bodies have much more in common (in terms of perceptual, intellectual, and locomotive abilities) than in contrast. This is further to say that no biological justification exists for gender segregation in the overwhelming majority of social roles in contemporary society—given that the major gender differences relate to genital anatomy, female birthing and lactation capabilities, and musculature. While mothers can have some initial advantage in bonding with children through pregnancy and breastfeeding, men can, should, and, more frequently than in the past, do become first-rate parents. Separate teams or venues for men and women in certain sports make sense. And one should expect to see many more men than women in the few jobs that feature heavy lifting. However, as a committed feminist, I happily vouchsafe that radical embodiment offers no succor for the privileging of certain bodies, no comfort for gender stereotyping.

Radically Embodied Language

To begin my argumentation for the body in tradition, it is obvious yet worth noting that human language arises only from human bodies. Not merely for its instrumental physical expression but for its substantive meaning, human rationality and language build upon the base of— radically and tacitly rely upon—our bodily being in the world, upon our

7. "Hear, Hear," *Los Angeles Times.*
8. "Sex Reassignment Fails," *Associated Press.*
9. Sullivan, "Why Do Men?"

seeing, hearing, smelling, tactile, motile, sexual bodies. The very nature, structure, and logic of human conceptual systems are rooted in our embodiment. As Poteat put it, "language is structured *upon* and therefore structured *like* our sentiently oriented and motile mindbodies."[10] All language is "body-shaped." This has been recognized by Polanyi in his claim of tacit reliance upon the body for all practical or intellectual knowledge, by Merleau-Ponty in his argument that the *meaning* of language is understood with our bodies, and by Wittgenstein on the biological underpinnings of our language games and forms of life.[11] As Polanyi expounded, human intellectual superiority vis-a-vis animals is due almost entirely to language, yet language does not arise from language but rather from human prelinguistic abilities—abilities that are only slightly better at problem solving than those of animals. Therefore, we must account for human "acquisition of language by acknowledging . . . the same kind of inarticulate powers as we observe already in animals."[12] Suggestively, primate observations and studies have debunked the discarnate theory that, since pointing allegedly depends upon language, only humans do so: chimpanzees spontaneously point with their hands and their whole bodies, while some monkeys point through head jerks or with their whole bodies.[13] And as Poteat cogently argued, only because a child has an understanding of "form, wholeness, and meaning" prior to language acquisition, as "the very modalities" of one's bodily being in the world, can the child become "a speaking animal" who can understand and generate meaningful words and concepts.[14] None of this denies that human evolution may have favored a larger neo-cortex able to utilize language more precisely; but some type

10. Poteat, *Polanyian Meditations*, 187–88

11. Polanyi, "Preface," *Personal Knowledge*, x, *Personal Knowledge*, 398–99, *Tacit Dimension*, 15–16, *Knowing and Being*, 147–48; Merleau-Ponty, *Phenomenology of Perception*, 174–99, 400–409; Wittgenstein, *Philosophical Interrogations*, nos. 25, 244, 281, 283, 415; 178, 188–89, 230.

12. Polanyi, *Personal Knowledge*, 69–70.

13. De Waal, "Pointing Primates." An interesting thesis comes from primatologist Carole Jahme as to why her field is the sole area of science where women outnumber men: women are generally better at nonverbal communication than men and thus have greater desire and abilities to read the nonverbal communication of nonhuman primates (*Beauty and the Beasts*).

14. Poteat, *Polanyian Meditations*, 20ff., 189.

of symbolic communicative ability must already have existed to make possible the selection of enhancing variations of it.

More recently philosopher Mark Johnson (with linguist George Lakoff) has argued persuasively for the cruciality of (non-proposition-al) embodied schemas for the very intelligibility of language. These schemas arise from our perceptual interactions with the world, bodily movements, and manipulation of objects.[15] Many types of schemas orient us spatially. These include the container schema (in-out), the source-path-goal schema (from-to),[16] and bodily projection schemas such as front-back, near-far, left-right, up-down, straight-curved.[17] Force-dynamic schemas rely upon bodily movements and interactions: "pushing, pulling, propelling, supporting, and balance"[18]; compulsion, blockage, counterforce, diversion, removal of restraint, enablement, and attraction.[19] The roots of other less easily categorized schemas also lie in bodily interactions with the world, including part-whole, full-empty, mass-count, cycle, iteration, link, contact, and adjacency.[20]

Head's classic studies of traumatized patients in 1920 uphold the plausibility of such schemas: memory of real-world events depends upon building a body schema in terms of motor and sensorimotor interactions.[21] A series of experiments by cognitive scientist Eleanor Rosch further buttresses the case for embodied schemas by identify-ing a "basic level of categorization" for all concrete objects. This level is the most inclusive, wherein category members share similar motor actions and imagible perceived shapes, possess "humanly meaning-ful attributes," and are identifiable by young children.[22] The research of Elizabeth Spelke and associates shows that prelinguistic infants construct images or concepts of cohesion, boundaries, substance, and spatiotemporal continuity.[23] Drawing upon such experimental data on

15. Johnson, *Body in the Mind*, 29.

16. Ibid., 30ff.; Johnson and Lakoff, *Philosophy in the Flesh*, 31ff.

17. Johnson, *Body in the Mind*, 30ff.; Johnson and Lakoff, *Philosophy in the Flesh*, 34–35.

18. Johnson and Lakoff, *Philosophy in the Flesh*, 36.

19. Johnson, *Body in the Mind*, 44ff.

20. Ibid., 121–26; Johnson and Lakoff, *Philosophy in the Flesh*, 35.

21. Edelman, *Remembered Present*, 141.

22. Varela et al., *Embodied Mind*, 177.

23. Spelke, "Origins," 168–84; cited by Edelman, *Remembered Present*, 144. See also Edelman, *Bright Air*, 244–45.

infant cognition, Jean Matter Mandler illustrates how infants use perceptual information to think preverbally, theorizing that infants utilize the image schemas introduced by Johnson and Lakoff, as well as that of animacy-inanimacy, in inferential thought and language learning.[24] Johnson's work finds support also in psychology from Harry T. Hunt's contention that consciousness and knowledge stand upon the structure of perception of all motile organisms. Such perception fuses two dimensions[25]: 1) "direct perception," that is, orienting oneself to and navigating one's ambience or "streaming array" 2) recognition of particulars.[26] Hunt connects this dialectical fusion to William James' recognition of human consciousness both as a continuous stream and as pulse-like, the latter relating to drive or need reduction behaviors.[27] (In our computer age we might note the analogy of general orientational perception to an analog mode and perception of particulars to a digital one.) In particular, Hunt draws connections between orientation to the flow of our environment and transitive language. The logic and grammar of "and," "but," and "if-then" are rooted in feelings of relation, tendency, or direction of our bodily orientation to our ambience.[28] Hunt's views in turn coincide with an outlook of radical embodiment from the East. Nagatomo, formed by Asian tradition and informed by Ichikawa's view of the body and Yuasa's body-scheme, concludes: "Directionality is the primary function of the living body with respect to its environment or ambience."[29]

While much of the preceding discussion has centered on spatial orientation and movement, perception of colors instantiates an additional realm in support of the embodied nature of language. While the tremendous variety in color terminology across cultures could seemingly serve as a poster child for purported linguistic constructivism in perception, research by Rosch points in the opposite direction. Building upon the groundbreaking work of Berlin and Kay which identified eleven basic color categories as "pan-human perceptual universals," Rosch

---

24. Mandler, *Foundations of Mind*.

25. Hunt, *Nature of Consciousness*, 90; Gibson, *Senses*.

26. Hunt, *Nature of Consciousness*, 68ff; Neisser, "Direct Perception."

27. James, *Principles of Psychology*; Hunt, *Nature of Consciousness*, 246–48, 250–52.

28. Hunt, *Nature of Consciousness*, 90, 121–22.

29. Nagatomo, *Attunement*, 29.

studied a tribe (the Dani of New Guinea) virtually devoid of color ter-minology. She found the central members of these basic color catego-ries to be "perceptually more salient," readily learnable, and more easily remembered, with very similar structures of color memory for both the tribespeople and English speakers.[30] Recently researchers have cor-roborated these findings with speakers of 110 non-literate languages.[31]

Perhaps at this point many will concede that basic human lan-guage stands rooted in our embodiment in the world. Yet must the most abstract language remain rooted in our bodies in order to be meaning-ful? The pervasiveness of metaphor in language and conceptualization suggests that it does. Johnson contends that more abstract language and propositional reasoning stem from metaphorical and metonymical ex-tensions of bodily schemas. A supporting illustration comes from work on modal verbs and gestalts of force by Eve Sweetser, who concludes that "must" relies upon the root meaning of compulsion, "may" upon removal of restraint, and "can" upon enablement.[32] In addition, Sweetser has highlighted an extensive subsystem of metaphors that conceptual-izes the mind itself as a body. This subsystem has four branches: think-ing is moving, perceiving, object manipulation, and eating.[33]

More widely, Johnson claims that conceptual tools for subjective judgments and experiences come mostly from sensorimotor domains. He theorizes that young children conflate subjective experiences and judgments with sensorimotor experiences. An infant, for example, as-sociates the experience of affection with that of warmth, the warmth of being held. Later, children are able to differentiate the domains, yet the cross-domain associations abide with understanding dependent on the meaning of the source domains.[34] Hunt for his part cites a few of the many instances in which subjective or abstract language is strik-

30. Varela et al., *Embodied Mind*, 168–69.

31. Regier et al., *Proceedings*. A recent experiment concludes that Russians, who do not have a word equivalent to the English "blue," but rather two distinct words for "dark blue" and "light blue," more quickly distinguish between shades of blue than do English speakers (Boroditsky, "How Does Our Language?"). While this shows that language can influence perception of finer distinctions, it does not appear to challenge the findings about more basic color perception.

32. Sweetser, *From Etymology*, 48ff.

33. Johnson and Lakoff, *Philosophy in the Flesh*, 235ff.

34. Ibid., 45ff.

ingly rooted in bodily perception of the physical world: "hard" decisions, "deep" or "shallow" ideas, "colorful" or "rigid" persons, thoughts and feelings we "carry," hopes that are "kindled," and insights that come in "flashes."[35]

Mathematics constitutes a form of human language that can reach the heights of abstraction. Yet Lakoff and compatriots have devoted a whole book to the contention that all of mathematics rests upon bodily bases.[36] An interesting primate mathematical experiment at Duke University concerns "semantic congruity," namely that people in numerical comparisons, say of two small things, more quickly pick out the smaller rather than the larger of the two. Scientists had assumed that this phenomenon hinged entirely upon language. However, the experiment demonstrated semantic congruity in macaque monkeys choosing between two randomized groups of dots.[37]

Neuroscientist Gerald Edelman corroborates the metaphorical, embodied nature of all language with his theory that the neural correlates of general concepts in mammals and humans constitute higher-order cortical mappings abstracting from mappings in other areas of the brain associated with more immediate perceptual, memory, or feeling content.[38] Interestingly, Shaun Gallagher notes that the language-focused Broca's area of the human brain "is homologous with areas of the premotor cortex in the primate."[39] Linguistic syntax permits far-flung extension and manipulation of body schema concepts or perceptual images. Edelman regards the human ability to place concepts in an ordered relation as operative not only in syntax but in a "pre-syntax" of some animals and prelinguistic infants.[40] Hunt cites psychological experiments supporting the theory that gesture is a key stage of the organization of sentences, externalizing their otherwise implicit spatial design.[41] Gallagher elaborates how congenitally blind persons use certain gestures when speaking.[42] All of this is to say that syntax itself

35. Hunt, *Nature of Consciousness*, 124.

36. Lakoff et al., *Where Mathematics Comes From*.

37. *Duke Magazine*, "Monkeys Don't Monkey with Math," 19.

38. E.g., Edelman, *Wider Than the Sky*, 50, 104ff.

39. Gallagher, *How the Body Shapes*, 127.

40. Edelman, *Remembered Present*, 147.

41. Hunt, *Nature of Consciousness*, 154–56.

42. Gallagher, *How the Body Shapes*, 121–22.

emerges from bodily semantics. Lakoff has categorized examples of this dependency: hierarchical structure stems from part-whole schemas, head and modifier structures from link schemas, and categories from container (in-out) schemas.[43]

The fact that persons make sense of certain language without having had the relevant full bodily experience constitutes an argument against my claim of bodily roots for all language, according to some. For example, Joanna Bryson in an interesting piece bounces off Dawkins and Dennett's concept of "memes," of conceptual units able to replicate themselves and evolve in human culture. She specifically argues for a "disembodied semantics," claiming that, whatever role embodiment may have played in the origins of semantic meaning, "it is no longer the only source for accessing a great deal of it" and, moreover, that "some words (including their meanings) may well have evolved more or less *independently* of grounded" or embodied experience (emphasis hers). Or to put it another way, "semantics is another form of automated perceptual learning"[44] and "can be acquired through purely statistical methods."[45] Bryson claims proof for the reality of disembodied semantics from experiments involving "semantic space," a model based on "the observation that whatever the reason that two words are similar in meaning, that similarity shows up in the distributional profiles of the words, that is . . . the sorts of words they co-occur with."[46] This claim, though, appears to beg the fundamental question of whether patterns of similar usage ultimately depend upon embodied or disembodied semantics.

Granted a young child may use the word "justice" in a linguistically appropriate manner. However, I see syntax here but not necessarily semantic understanding. Moreover, I have just argued that correct use of syntax itself relies on bodily schemas. Also, as an implication of upcoming comments about the possible evolution of language, the child may grasp some poetic meaning of language which may fall short of its referential meaning. To cut to the chase, I contend that for the child to have significant, relevant understanding of "justice" in human society

---

43. Lakoff, *Women, Fire*, 289ff.

44. Bryson, "Embodiment *vs.* Memetics," 3.

45. Ibid., 6.

46. Ibid., 5.

does indeed entail embodied grounding. Granted, too, that congenitally blind persons use color terminology in meaningful and usually correct ways. However, the meaningful use of such language by the congenitally blind is parasitic upon the embodied experiences and meanings of vision by the sighted. Furthermore, making sense of color terminology by blind persons relies upon some analogy with their own embodied perceptions. Lastly, I grant that a disembodied artificial intelligence, a "*perfect* meme machine" as a conversation partner a la Searle's Chinese Language Room,[47] might conceivably "generate new cultural content."[48] However, only a human could assess the absurdity or meaningfulness for embodied human beings of a permutation produced by the meme machine.

To conclude this subsection specifically on language, I quote Poteat, who has succinctly and forcefully expressed the bodily basis of language: "language—our first formal system—has the sinews of our bodies which had them first; the grammar, syntax, meaning, semantic, and metaphorical intentionality of our language are preformed in that of our prelingual mindbodily being in the world which is their condition."[49]

Non-Linguistic Meaning

Growing evidence of non-linguistic dimensions of meaning, knowledge, and symbolism directly contribute to my overarching and underlying claim that all human meaning is radically embodied, as well as implying bodily bases for linguistic meaning. Perhaps this should come as no surprise to scholars of religion, given the importance for religion of ritual, music, and art, visual and kinesthetic symbolism.

Hunt discriminates three basic perceptual modes: audition-vocalization, vision, and touch-movement (though cross-modal syntheses often occur). Audition-vocalization constitutes the mode that includes the linguistic or propositional. One specific piece of evidence Hunt cites

47. Searle's thought experiment invites you to imagine yourself in a room with the task of translating Chinese pictograms into English in accordance with an instructional book. Even with no knowledge of Chinese, you could get the job done if the book were extensive and accurate enough. Searle likens computers to this imagined process, unable to understand or produce meaning ("Minds").

48. Bryson, "Embodiment *vs.* Memetics," 13.

49. Poteat, *Polanyian Meditations*, 9.

concerns the modes of vision and touch-movement: whatever the style of painting, psychological experiments indicate that a fundamental dynamic shape looms out as its basic physiognomic or expressive structure. In particular, horizontal lines suggest stability and calm, vertical lines more excitement and upward striving, and diagonal lines greater degrees of tension.[50]

Neuroscientist Damasio holds that *all* knowledge is embodied in "dispositional representations."[51] "Dispositional" means that neural networks are patterned in such a way that representations can become active "images," whether visual, auditory, kinesthetic, body-state, or other. Damasio concludes that thought consists largely of such images. While acknowledging the obvious, that thought includes words and non-image, abstract, arbitrary symbols, he urges that focusing on this truth causes many to miss a converse fact: "both words and arbitrary symbols are based on topographically organized representations and can become images." Indeed, Damasio continues, if our words "did not become images, however fleetingly, they would not be anything we could know."[52] The import of Damasio's words here can hardly be exaggerated: Any and all human signs and symbols must involve some connection with bodily sensorimotor and feeling imagery to be comprehensible, indeed to exist in the first place. It is a truism among neurobiologists, primatologists, and other zoologists that at least the "higher" non-human animals use mental representations or images to negotiate their worlds, images patently non-linguistically based.

I will expand upon Damasio's above contention that words and signs only have cognitive meaning in connection with images. Radical embodiment entails that not just non-verbal but linguistic symbols as well are never totally arbitrary. Cartesianism by contrast assumes that symbols function as arbitrary tools which correspond to subjective reality (which is to say that language is incidental to thought) or to objective reality. Johnson notes that first-generation cognitive science fell under the sway of such a Cartesian picture: the mind could "be studied fully independently of any knowledge of the body and brain, simply by

50. Hunt, *Nature of Consciousness*, 171.

51. Neither Damasio nor Edelman regard mental "representations" as mirrors of a world determinate without our enactment (e.g., Damasio, *Feeling*, 322; Edelman, *Wider Than the Sky*, 104ff.).

52. Damasio, *Descartes' Error*, 106.

looking at functional relations among concepts represented symboli-
cally." Such functionalism held that meaning is "only an abstract relation among symbols" (in the subjective view) or "between symbols and
states of affairs in the world" (in the objective view).[53] On the contrary,
there exists no "computational person, whose mind is like computer
software" and "somehow derives meaning from taking meaningless
symbols as input, manipulating them by rules, and giving meaningless
symbols as output," nor any "Chomskyan person for whom language is
pure syntax, pure form insulated from and independent of all meaning,
context, perception, emotion, memory, action, and the dynamic nature
of communication."[54] Supporting Damasio's position that all cognition
involves images and in keeping with an intuition I have long held concerning our embodied attempts to orient ourselves to and negotiate our
world, Johnson in his latest book argues that an aesthetic element lies at
the heart of all meaning.[55] This claim also relates to Damasio's theory of
background feelings, to be discussed later in this chapter.

I will note that radical postmodernism, in spite of its endorsement
of the mediatory materiality of language, appears to be under a Cartesian
picture as well: symbols are arbitrary signs which derive whatever un-
stable meaning they have only in relationship to other signs. Given the
tremendous variety of words in different languages for similar objects,
much arbitrariness in human language is more than obvious. But this is
not tantamount to absolute arbitrariness. Hunt finds a synthetic resonance, though largely suppressed or unconscious in ordinary language,
between the nature of sounds and meaning, a resonance highlighted
in poetry and music.[56] In this connection, he cites an intriguing hypothesis by Mary Foster, who maintains that primordial language was
based on metaphorical similarities between movements of the mouth
and aspects of the environment. For example, the *pl* or *fl* sound suggests
that which is extended or broad.[57] I will note the similarities among
languages in basic words, such as childhood names for parents (*ma*,

53. Johnson and Lakoff, *Philosophy in the Flesh*, 78. See also Damasio, *Descartes'
Error*, 25.

54. Johnson and Lakoff, *Philosophy in the Flesh*, 6.

55. Johnson, *Meaning*.

56. Hunt, *Nature of Consciousness*, 152. This connects to Johnson's recent focus on
aesthetics.

57. Foster, *Growth of Symbolism*; Hunt, *Nature of Consciousness*, 154.

pa, etc.). Poteat provided evidence for this perspective: infants move their bodies in meaningful resonance, indeed in precise synchrony, with the speech patterns of their parents, long before they understand the propositional meaning of that language.[58]

An interesting angle on non-verbal insight concerns innovative scientists and other creative people who come to know through visual and kinesthetic images and emotions, through play-acting and empathy, rather than through linguistic or mathematical symbols. Polanyi noticed this phenomenon, as have Hunt and Damasio.[59] Indeed, Robert S. and Michele Root-Bernstein have now devoted a whole book to this phenomenon, *Sparks of Genius: The Thirteen Thinking Tools of the World's Most Creative People.* The most celebrated exemplar of this kind of creativity was Albert Einstein, who wrote:

> The words or the language, as they are written or spoken, do not seem to play any role in my mechanism of thought. The psychical entities which seem to serve as elements in thought are certain signs and more or less clear images.... [T]he desire to arrive finally at logically connected concepts is the emotional basis of this rather vague play with the above mentioned elements.
>
> [These] elements are, in my case, of a visual and ... muscular type. Conventional words or other signs have to be sought for laboriously only in a secondary stage, when the mentioned associative play is sufficiently established and can be reproduced at will.[60]

Also supporting the reality of non-linguistic dimensions of knowledge and meaning is the tremendous span of unconscious mental processes that forms the substrate of our linguistic awareness. Polanyi, with his concept of tacit knowing, was extremely cognizant of this. Johnson for his part notes "that most of our thought is unconscious, not in the Freudian sense of being repressed, but in the sense that it operates beneath the level of cognitive awareness, inaccessible to consciousness and operating too quickly to be focused on."[61] Referring to this as the "cognitive unconscious," Johnson goes on to list a dozen processes occurring

58. Poteat, *Philosophical Daybook*, 34–35.

59. Polanyi, *Personal Knowledge*; Hunt, *Nature of Consciousness*, 161, 172; Damasio, *Descartes' Error*, 107.

60. Damaiso, *Descartes' Error*, 107.

61. Johnson and Lakoff, *Philosophy in the Flesh*, 10.

"below the level of conscious awareness" in everyday conversation—while this tally represents just a fraction of all that transpires at this level.[62] Damasio and Edelman perforce regularly refer to neural processes unavailable to our conscious awareness. In particular, Damasio offers an analysis of intuition as a process whereby we subconsciously avoid entertaining negative options while bringing more positive ones into consciousness.[63] Polanyi had noted how scientific innovation relies on tacitly knowing which data to ignore and which to focus on.[64]

A suggestive aspect of unconscious neural activity indirectly supports the bodily, physical, spatial nature of knowledge. While it would be naive to presume that the whole complex of cognitive brain activity for spatial patterns and locations simply corresponds to perceived spatial relations in the world, Damasio advances the following theory: in seeing or recalling a face, if we were able "to inspect the patterns of activity occurring in . . . early visual cortices," we would probably find that those patterns "had some relation to the geography of" that face.[65] Experiments already support this theory, including the finding that "when a monkey sees certain shapes, such as a cross or square, the activity of neurons in early visual cortices will be topographically organized in a pattern that conforms to the shape the monkey is viewing."[66]

Emotions powerfully argue the reality of non-linguistic dimensions of meaning and knowledge. Emotion has been an explicit and implicit factor in the preceding discussion of this section. But given the dualistic tendency to split feeling from reason, it is instructive to focus on emotion. A non-dualistic, common sense view, classically developed in psychology by William James, recognizes the bodily nature of emotions. As James penned:

> If we fancy some strong emotion and then try to abstract from our consciousness of it all the feelings of its bodily symptoms, we find we have nothing left behind, no "mind-stuff" out of which the emotion can be constituted, and that a cold and neutral state of intellectual perception is all that remains. . . . What kind of an emotion of fear would be left if the feeling neither

62. Ibid., 110–11.

63. Damasio, *Descartes' Error*, 187–89.

64. Polanyi, *Personal Knowledge*, 134ff.

65. Damasio, *Descartes' Error*, 103–4.

66. Ibid., 103.

of quickened heart beats nor of shallow breathing, neither of trembling lips nor of weakened limbs, neither of gooseflesh nor of visceral stirrings, were present, it is quite impossible for me to think.[67]

Damasio indicates that what makes feelings different from other cognitive components is that

> they are first and foremost about the body, that they offer us *the cognition of our visceral and musculoskeletal state* as it becomes affected by preorganized mechanisms and by cognitive structures we have developed under their influence. Feelings let us *mind the body* attentively, as during an emotional state, or faintly, as during a background state.[68]

Clearly Damasio rejects Cartesian reason/emotion dualism. While not cognitive in the precise way sense perception is, emotions are cognitive in their own fashion. Moreover, embodied reason is highly dependent upon emotion. "Emotion is in the loop of high reason," as Damasio put it during an interview.[69] Damasio's insights come especially from observing "Elliott," a man who suffered ventromedial prefrontal brain damage. Elliott scored well above average in various cognitive tests, including those of moral judgment. But Elliott was quite dysfunctional in personal and social planning and decision-making; an inability to decide constituted one major component of this dysfunction. Elliott was also emotionally flat.[70] Damasio determined that the neural systems damaged in Elliott's brain play a role in planning and deciding, processing emotions, and holding in mind over time the image of a relevant though not present object.[71] Thus, emotions are inextricably linked to assigning values to options. Emotionless reason could never value or decide. Damasio disputes a Cartesian dualistic assumption of traditional neuroscience—that emotions are processed only in subcortical parts of the brain, while the cortex and neo-cortex deal solely with reason and higher reason, respectively: "Nature appears to have built the apparatus of rationality not just on top of biological regulation, but

67. James, *Principles of Psychology* (quoted in Damasio, *Descartes' Error*, 129).

68. Damasio, *Descartes' Error*, 159.

69. Wheeler, "Neurologist Steps Back."

70. Damasio, *Descartes' Error*, 46–47.

71. Ibid., 78–79.

also *from* it and *with* it." Rationality results from the "concerted activity" of both "the older brain core" and the neo-cortex.[72] Jesse Prinz has recently published a book consonant with Damasio's outlook: though emotions are most immediately perceptions of changes in the body, they provide "embodied appraisals" of our world, as his title, *Gut Reactions*, suggests.

The preceding section has been premised on various non-linguistic dimensions of meaning and knowledge. Now I will highlight a few facets of non-verbal *communication* of knowledge. It is a given in communication theory that much or most of the meaning of human speech is non-verbal. Certainly the emotional and value-laden aspects of a tradition involve a heavy dose of the non-linguistic dimensions of meaning. In a work consonant with Polanyi's intuition that many of the tacit elements of tradition are learned from observing practitioners, Paul Connerton (focusing on commemorative rituals as prime example) has argued that bodily ritual, techniques, and properties in their own right constitute traditions as much as does linguistic inscription.[73] Primatologists are well aware of "culture" among monkeys and apes. From both observations in the wild and experiment, it is clear that distinctive behaviors learned by individuals and particular groups get passed on to future generations.[74]

I believe that my integrative work makes a strong case for the radical dependence of all human knowledge and meaning upon the body. If my argument has succeeded, the vast repertoire of knowledge and meaning transmitted through cultural traditions (that is, not garnered through individual discovery or simple instinct) is radically rooted in the body, whatever the respective roles of the linguistic and the non-verbal in this transmission. But I do want to elaborate on specific implications of this bodily basis of meaning for religious and ethical traditions.

Religious Meaning

Radical embodiment offers a non-reductionist biological theory of religion. Polanyi describes the confluence of animal perception with the epistemological commitments of the highest forms of human culture,

72. Damasio, *Descartes' Error*, 128.

73. Connerton, *How Societies Remember*.

74. De Waal, "Culture and Nature."

including religion.[75] Thus, religious attempts to orient ourselves and to make sense of our world are biological, though a biological feat which apparently only human bodies can achieve. Earlier, William James also regarded religion as a biological and psychological attempt to find—and partially make—a meaningful world to which we belong and which makes life worth living.[76] To expand upon a function of religion described above, religion involves the embodied attempt to discover and partially create a larger or holistic meaning for humans to indwell, traditionally in light of power(s) regarded as divine or sacred. (Theologians or religious thinkers within a particular religion traditionally have believed in the existence of such power(s). Scholars of religion of course may or may not believe in the existence of any such powers.)

Religions commonly understand these powers as more or greater than the world as scientifically known; thus religions often regard them as transcending the world in some sense, or at least to possess a transcendent dimension. Terry Godlove, building upon Davidson's understanding of language, declares that the meaning of religious transcendentals depends on their everyday perceptual counterparts.[77] I would add that the meaning of transcendence relies upon our bodily perceptual grasp of such orientational schemas as "in-out" and "near-far." These are not merely optional metaphors for something we could know more directly; without them concepts of transcendence are literally inconceivable. That all metaphors of transcendence rely upon our embodiment provides bases for critiquing these metaphors and adjudicating among conflicting ones. Consider discarnate models purporting human transcendence with respect to the body and nature. Such models bank upon certain bodily metaphors, particularly those involving vision. These models capture/are captured by vision's objectifying qualities, its ability to perceive from a distance a vast expanse in its totality "in an instant," its relative atemporality compared to audition, touch, and motion. (By way of contrast, when we tacitly indwell the particulars of something we enable ourselves to perhaps find a holistic meaning.) As suggested at the beginning of this chapter, we can discern this type of model in Renaissance paintings where all is in focus. Actual vision

75. Polanyi, *Personal Knowledge*, 374ff.

76. James, *Varieties*, 51–52, 504ff.; *Will and Other Essays*, 39, 51ff., 116ff., 134.

77. Godlove, *Religion, Interpretation*, 149–50.

by contrast depends upon a series of muscular movements over time, but because we are normally only tacitly aware of these while focusing on our ambience or on particular objects, we become vulnerable to discarnate metaphors of transcendence. Such metaphors result in false anthropologies, but may also lead to models of divinity where physical reality and the bodies of creatures hold little or no value for the divine, where embodied life is not in any sense sacred.

Supposed human transcendence of the body and nature has influenced many religions' beliefs about life after death. Given the absolute cruciality of our embodiment for our very life, consciousness, rationality, meaning, and value on earth, radical embodiment could plausibly lead to skepticism about any subjective immortality. The final word for "Adam"—the "earth being"—might be "dust to dust." Certainly radical embodiment should reject disembodied versions of an afterlife present in some forms of religion. Interestingly, when many believers imagine life as an allegedly immaterial soul in a heaven or even have near-death or other "out of body" experiences, they tacitly bring along their bodies and (imagine they) see and hear.

If religions have commonly viewed the divine or sacred as possessing a transcendent dimension, they have also commonly regarded it as also in some sense immanent. As with transcendence, the meaning of immanence relies upon our bodily comprehension of the "in-out" and "near-far" orientational schemas. What of radical embodiment's claim that religion functions to orient humans to a purported larger whole? To understand claims that we are part of God (panentheism), the *Tao*, *sunyata*, creation, or the universe requires understanding bodily perceptual schemas such as "in-out" (container), "part-whole," and "empty-full." Again these do not function as optional metaphors for what we could know in a non-bodily way. (In a cross-cultural simplification, we might say that Western religion emphasizes transcendence more, in the sense of our distinction from others and the divine, while Eastern religion emphasizes wholeness more, but that both dimensions are present in either.) Similarly making sense of concepts or metaphors of divine action or holy power stands necessarily upon the meaning of embodied forceful interactions in the world.

While radical postmodernism tends to emphasize immanence with respect to any notion of divinity and postliberalism transcendence,[78] moderate postmodernisms, in accord with their correlative "both-and" orientation, want to do justice to both divine immanence and transcendence, tending towards panentheistic models. Radical embodiment fleshes this out by embracing the metaphor of the world as the body of the divine. While this metaphor obviously emphasizes immanence, neither the panentheistic model nor the body metaphor requires the reduction of divinity to the physical universe. Divine embodiment bears some analogy to human embodiment, in that the human personality is not simply reducible to the component physical processes of its body—granted though that such human transcendence is relative while only divine transcendence has an absolute dimension. Eastern religions, though generally stressing immanence relative to Western, do not entertain such total immanence as does radical postmodernism. Indeed, I judge that some Eastern models can be classified as panentheistic, and not only *bhakti* Hinduism, but those found in Taoism and Mahayana Buddhism. The world moves within the *Tao* or *sunyata*; the world "bodies forth"[79] from the *Tao* or *sunyata*. Here the transcendent dimension beyond its manifestations in/as the world is modeled as transpersonal or formless rather than as personal with attributes.

The above function of finding our place in the whole is where religion might most enable us to feel at home as radically embodied in this world. Damasio discusses background feelings of our body states. Normally tacit rather than attended to with full consciousness, they are always actual. Damasio learns something from anosognosiacs (literally, "no knowledge of disease"), victims of left-side paralysis but with no immediate, internal, or functional knowledge of said paralysis.

---

78. In line with its immanentist tendencies, radical postmodernism first of all tends towards a total immanence with a Dionysian affirmation of all worldly inscription as divine, concomitant with "the death of (the transcendent) God." The later Derrida and John Caputo, reflecting radical postmodern oscillation between the constructed and what lies beyond all construction, arguably lift up as divine what does not fall under the constructed world—the transcendent unpresentable, wholly other, or messianic ideal (Derrida, *Gift of Death*; Caputo, *Prayers*). Postliberalism ultimately emphasizes divine transcendence as the divine becomes immanent in a very particular personalistic manner, only in the revelation in Jesus Christ.

79. Sally McFague has famously urged the metaphor of the world as the body of God, sometimes using the phrase "bodies forth" (e.g., *Models*, p. 92).

Anosognosiacs claim to feel fine; any knowledge of their paralysis is external and fleeting; they are emotionally flat and unconcerned about their future.[80] Damasio hypothesizes that, incapable of normal body-state background feelings, they remember and report a now quite out-dated image of their bodies.[81] Damasio goes on to hypothesize that such background feelings, such "primordial representations of the body," play an important role in consciousness, "provide a core for the neural representation of self."[82] By definition background feelings are not intense; rather they provide a backdrop for everything we experience, including more particular and more intense pleasant or unpleasant emotions. In his most recent work Damasio stipulates that emotions, here categorized as background, "primary," and "social," are never simply neutral.[83] In keeping with Damasio's understanding, I would stipulate that background feelings are normally positive (excepting certain diseased states like anosognosia associated with an impaired sense of self, systemic physical illness, or severe emotional disorders involving chronic negative emotions)—providing a positive feeling of integral bodily presence.[84] Joy, the primary emotion associated with preserving and enhancing the self,[85] might be viewed as an intensification of this normal background state. If this is so, it would support the affirmation of most religions of a basic and primordial goodness and beauty to life. As radically embodied we can feel a fundamental at-home-ness in the universe. A faith in the meaningfulness of life is then not contrary to reason but rather serves as its very basis. In this connection I will suggest another thesis whose development lies beyond the scope of this article: Even ancient religions and philosophies that subordinated or devalued the body (in favor of the mind or soul) typically used palpably bodily metaphors to make sense of our being in the world (for example,

80. Damasio, *Descartes' Error*, 62ff., 153.

81. Ibid., 154.

82. Ibid., 235ff.; see also *Feeling*, 110, 285–87. Looking psychologically rather than neurologically, feminist Nancy J. Chodorow devotes a book to the role of feelings in our sense of selfhood, a selfhood she finds more integrated than the poststructuralist fragmented self (*Power of Feelings*).

83. Damasio, *Looking for Spinoza*, 43ff., 93.

84. Of course intense short-term negative emotions or intense pain, short-term or chronic, may overwhelm these background feelings, so that one's overall affective state is negative.

85. E.g., ibid., 13–14.

Plato's charioteer on the relationship between the mind and passions). Cartesian enlightenment philosophy, on the other hand, has tended to expurgate such bodily metaphors in explicating mind and perception, resulting in a more extreme—and impoverished—dualism.

While usually affirming a primordial goodness to life, most religions have also offered mythological, philosophical, and/or theological explanations for the reality of alienation, of evil. Radical embodiment can offer interpretations of the self-centered sin or ignorance that many classical world religions posit. The most obvious such lies in the fact that one indwells one's own body most immediately and therefore usually appreciates the interests of one's own body more readily than those of other bodies. Of course most religions promote "pro-social" emotions through teaching that the interests of others are just as valid as one's own (and sometimes, as an over-reaction to selfishness and/or because of an anti-body ethic, through the implication of the greater validity of others' interests with the enjoinment to deny oneself). Another important angle on sin or ignorance involves 1) human finitude and fallibility as embodied creatures in an environment and 2) human reflective ability and our social nature, which lead us to form a self-image of our value to ourselves, society, and/or divine powers. We normally want to feel good about ourselves, to possess self-esteem. However, life's vicissitudes cause us to doubt ourselves. A powerful defense mechanism for individuals and social groups to sustain self-esteem is to posit the superiority of oneself or one's own group vis-à-vis others' inferiority. This of course has served as a prime way for traditions to attempt to preserve the power of the haves. In relation to self-denial, woman and other "inferior" groups especially have been targets of such enjoinment, either because they have more to deny as supposedly more "bodily" or in order to receive a deferred reward for greater service—perhaps in the afterlife. Clearly religions have provided significant resources for demeaning others as inferior—and when that inferiority has gotten translated as opposition to the divine or alliance with evil powers, adherents have perpetrated terrible wickedness in religion's name. The work of philosopher Martha Nussbaum and psychologist Paul Bloom on the emotion of disgust also provides perspectives on demeaning and dehumanizing others.[86] Facets and functions of the human body related to substances that evoke dis-

---

86. Nussbaum, "Danger"; Bloom, *Descartes' Baby*, 175–78.

gust become associated with or get projected onto particular individuals or groups. To the extent an anti-body ethos exists, the victims are then dehumanized as more bodily. Or to the extent some bodies receive superior regard, as with the Nazis and Aryan German, heterosexual bodies, disgust serves to differentiate evil from good bodies. In either case, presumed divine disgust or disfavor may buttress the dehumanization of those associated with evil embodiment. However, most religions do have powerful resources available to combat the positing of the inferiority and even dehumanization of others, precisely in their traditions of the self-centered sin or ignorance endemic to our human condition. Indeed, they typically call for self-examination to ferret out one's own sin or ignorance, often admonishing followers to refrain from judging others. William James certainly stresses the role of religion in helping us to recognize and overcome the wrongness in ourselves,[87] as well as in the world.[88]

If religion entails the biological attempt to orient our bodies with respect to larger meanings, what implications does radical embodiment have for religious epistemology, in terms of both limitations and opportunities? Even as postmodernism in general tends to doubt unmediated experiences of the divine, radical embodiment doubts claims that the transcendent dimension of the divine becomes immediately immanent, bypassing our bodies. This would certainly pertain to the type of mystical experience that claims to transcend any distinction between subject and object. But more theistic mystical experiences of communion as well as visionary, numinous, and more subtle religious experiences all engender suspicion *if* interpreted as immaterial contacts from the divine side that do not impinge in some tangible, indeed mundane, sense upon our bodies or embodied minds. (While applauding William James' pioneering of the biological basis of religion, I do find his model of rather direct or minimally mediated experiences of divine powers to lose any discernible sense of our bodily connection to the universe.[89]) Some of the experiences of religious geniuses may instead be radically embodied, involving the visual and kinesthetic imagery found in creative artists and scientists mentioned earlier. Though Mark

---

87. James, *Varieties*, 507–9.

88. Ibid., 49–50.

89. Nikkel, "Negotiating Mystical Experience," 35–36.

Johnson does not delve much into religion, he avers that "imaginative, empathetic projection is a major part of spiritual experience." Relative to the following quote, I would add that such projection provides one basis for the ecological ethic universal in primal religions and evokes a sense of the goodness and at-home-ness in the universe of non-human bodies:

> Part of the awe we feel observing animals in the wild—the trotting coyote, the soaring eagle, the playful porpoise, the aggressive jay, the magnificent diving whale . . . is that we too feel some of the sense of trotting and soaring, playing and diving. Shamans in aboriginal cultures . . . observe animals closely by empathetically "becoming" the animals, and ritual practices in a wide range of aboriginal religions employ the movements of animals to achieve an ecstatic experience, an experience of being in the body of a very different kind of being.[90]

In addition, the case can be made for even mystical experiences as mediated events comprising a distinctive bodily harmony, without reducing them to a type of erotic experience.[91] While acknowledging the tremendous differences between the human and the divine, radical embodiment maintains some analogy between our knowing of finite and of any divine realities: even as we know finite realities through their embodiment so we know the divine through its embodiment in the world. The transcendent divine does not bypass its body, namely, the world, in communicating with humankind.

This last point impinges on the fact that some religious thinkers and traditions have asserted the definitive nature of the revelation or foundational experience of the divine at the heart of their faith as unequivocally superior to those claimed by other religions. Traditionally religions have purported the supernatural origin for such events. For our purposes, however, the crux of the matter is whether the divine reality intends or means for this event to be the definitive and supreme manifestation of itself. For example, Barth, the postliberals, and Radical Orthodoxy have not insisted on supernaturalism, but rather have allowed that almost all of God's unique revelation in Jesus Christ has transpired without violating the laws of nature (the resurrection of Jesus perhaps the exception). Radical embodiment finds such claims

90. Johnson, *Body in the Mind*, 566.
91. Nikkel, "Negotiating Mystical Experience," 37–38.

of divinely authored uniqueness quite implausible. If the world is the body of God or divinity, one point where the analogy breaks down is this: animal and human bodies have evolved to enable us to relate to an external environment. However, the world religions do not generally consider God or the divine to have an external environment requiring a spatially circumscribed body in order to interact. From the perspective of radical embodiment (as well as panentheistic and pantheistic models of divinity), the "environment" for the divine is internal to it. This suggests an analogy of animal bodies considered internally to the body of divinity: as our bodies involve homeostatic processes allowing for growth and change, so the divine interacts with the world in terms of general processes of nature that achieve balance and relative stability while allowing for growth and change. As humans consider the various aspects and events of the body of the divine in order to make holistic sense of the universe, certain events do stand out as particularly helpful, paradigmatic clues to the possible meaning of the whole. But on an internal, "homeostatic," model of divinity, we should not expect one aspect or event to stand out as *the* exclusive "bodily" or "incarnational" event which by design definitively reveals divine intention and meaning.

Inspired by a recent class discussion, I will hearken back to Johnson's comment on shamanistic visions. In particular, his reference to the soaring eagle may call into mind primal art depicting the land they inhabit from a bird's eye view. How does this compare to the Renaissance paintings I have highlighted that cover significant expanses of space, with everything crystal clear? I would suggest that the primal art represents an embodied perspective, whether through the imagining of moving in the body of a bird and/or through a shamanistic spiritual journey. This latter should not be understood as a discarnate, completely "out of body" experience. Rather the shaman uses a form of his or her body appropriate to the spirit world. This is key: these visions do not escape nature nor express any desire to escape; the viewer and the viewed, the physical and spiritual, all live and move within the natural world in the broadest sense. By contrast, those Renaissance paintings represent precisely the desire to transcend nature—to know immediately in a discarnate manner. Of course, the classical world religions generally posited some transcendence of nature by humans vis-à-vis other animals through a (greater) kinship with the divine—as created in God's image or as closer to enlightenment about one's divine nature. The Western religions received strong influence from Greek philosophical strands regarding the body as inferior. Platonism of course viewed matter and the body negatively, as disorderly and chaotic in their own nature. It did have a place for the world as the body of the divine in some sense, through its notion of the World Soul; however, the very existence of the material world represented a fall. Artistotelianism regarded the body more positively, though clearly as inferior to mind or soul. In keeping with this hierarchy, Aristotle's God is completely disembodied. Yet despite these downplayings of the body, nature continued to have a fairly significant role and some positive evaluation in Western culture. The radicalism of modernity lay in its attempt completely to transcend nature, in its controlling picture of the individual human being as not at all grounded in nature. It is no coincidence that the early Enlightenment characterized nature as disorderly in its fallenness, in need of taming by human reason and technological instruments, indeed sometimes referring to subduing nature in terms of rape. Of course, if radical embodiment is on target, humans cannot escape bodily metaphors, as in such malignant Enlightenment language. More fundamentally, the inescapability of our bodiliness, as the human fell under the external stare of discarnate reason, led to the view of the human being as nothing but an object, as in reductionisitc physicalism. Radical postmodernism in its way also regards the human being as an object, albeit one trying—more or less futilely—to resist objectification.

Given the claim of radical embodiment that religion involves the biological attempt to orient ourselves to wider meanings, I should address scientists' conclusion that evolution has programmed our bodies and embodied minds to overestimate when an animate or intentional cause exists—and certain interpretations thereof. On the concrete level of making sure the rustling in the bush is not a tiger, one could hardly disagree. Some theorists of religion such as Pascal Boyer though go much further, claiming that evolution has programmed us counter-intuitively towards animism or, with more refinement, to imagine ultimate causes of the universe.[92] Evidence does exist that around the age of five, children tend to regard natural objects as having a purpose,[93] though not

---

92. Boyer, *Naturalness of Religious Ideas*, esp. 125ff.

93. Keleman, "Are Children 'Intuitive Theists'?"

unambiguous evidence.[94] A key question concerns the origins in children's thinking of supernatural agency as cause of natural phenomena. Zoology has not found evidence that other animals entertain animistic explanations or engage in magical thinking. Some recent research indicates that neither do young children—whatever causes beyond the natural they entertain to explain phenomena come from adults.[95] Such evidence suggests that supernatural or religious explanations depend on reflective abilities only humans of a certain age typically possess, thus standing at least one remove from our more immediate, pre-reflective attempts to assign causality. Clearly much traditional and current popular religious reflection assumes that karmic or divine forces orchestrate the details of life; however, much modern scholarly religious reflection and tradition deny such micro-managing as they account for freedom, spontaneity, and chance in a purposeful larger framework of natural processes. While hardly denying a biological basis for the human search for causal explanations, the evidence thus far does not support any "hard-wiring" for supernatural explanations nor for imagining an ultimate cause of the universe. To recognize our radical embodiment at least seems to leave open the question of whether that embodiment has some ultimate cause or larger purpose.[96] I will leave arguments that it does to the final two chapters.

While most or all religions have an ethical dimension (and I have already weighed in on religion and moral evil), I have promised a spe-

94. Keil, "Origins of Autonomous Biology."

95. Orem, "Magical Mind."

96. In his revision of his 1989 Gifford Lectures (*Creation of the Sacred*), classicist Walter Burkert argues for the biological basis of specific forms of religious expression, including sacrifice of the part for the whole (34–55), quest narrative (based on the search for food, though extended into human culture, including shamanistic quests) (58–69), and the presence of hierarchy (80–101). (One can recognize various bodily schemas involved in these forms.) While his project does not appear to explain adequately the genesis of a religious impulse or dimension itself, Burkert does demonstrate that comprehending certain common or even universal forms of religious expression entails acknowledgment of their biological, bodily substratum. For example, the dominant-submissive patterns of behavior common to apes do not explain why humans extend hierarchies beyond a dominant human, but they do illuminate the bodily ways, such as lowering oneself, that humans show deference to a "higher" power. While Burkert does not commit himself to reductionistic conclusions, one could take his type of program in that direction. Neurobiologist and psychologist Jay D. Glass, for example, purports that dominance-submission biological hardwiring fully explains human belief in a supreme being (*Animal within*).

cific word about the bodily bases of meaning for ethical traditions. Pragmatist social philosopher George Herbert Mead argued for the importance of taking the role of the other for symbolic communication and social ethics.[97] From the perspective of radical embodiment, our bodily bonding with, while at the same time differentiating from, other bodies is requisite for us to take this role. I would note that this empathetic capability is crucial for ethical judgment and agency. Contrary to Mead's premise that taking the attitude of the other requires language, recent observations of primates indicate that this bodily capability and its ethical implications are not unique to humans—rather our linguistic and generally superior ability to symbolize enhance a more ancient capacity. DeWaal interprets the following incident recounted in neuroscientist Robert M. Sapolsky's memoir to demonstrate that, while baboons may not be capable of full empathy, they have gone far beyond the apparently automatic responses to another's distress found in "lower" mammals and human infants (as when one baby's crying triggers another's)[98]: One first-time mother baboon

> couldn't seem to learn to position [her youngster] to ride on her back, so that he sprawled sideways, clutching the base of her tail. One day, as she leapt from one branch to another with the kid in that precarious condition, he lost his grip and dropped ten feet to the ground. We various primates observing proved our close kinship, proved how we probably utilized the exact same number of synapses in our brains in watching and responding to the event, by doing exactly the same thing in unison. Five female baboons in the tree and this one human all gasped as one and then fell silent, eyes trained on the kid. A moment passed, he righted himself, looked up in the tree at his mother, and then scampered off after some friends and as a chorus, we all started clucking to each other in relief.[99]

This next incident comes from news wire service reports: an adult male bonobo (close relative of the chimpanzee) named Kakowet noticed that water was about to flood a nearby moat where infant bonobos were playing at the Yerkes Regional Primate Center. Kakowet empathetically took the role of the other in realizing they could not yet swim and suc-

97. Mead, *Mind, Self, and Society.*
98. De Waal, "Do Humans Alone?"
99. Sapolsky, *Primate's Memoir,* 491.

cessfully warned zookeepers of the impending danger, thus saving their lives.[100] Finally, De Waal relates an episode of a bonobo showing concern, indeed compassion, for a non-primate, a non-mammal:

> Kuni noticed a starling strike a glass wall and plunge to the ground, first unsuccessfully attempted to help it fly, then guarded it for hours until it could fly on its own.[101]

Growing knowledge about "mirror neurons" provides evidence of a basis for animal empathy that goes beyond an automatic response devoid of meaning and at the same time differs from human reflective empathetic thought and decision, a tertium quid between empiricist materialistic and rationalist idealistic models. In general these neurons, located in the premotor cortex, become active when an individual either initiates a particular motor action or observes another perform the action. Gallagher rightly criticizes interpretations of the role of mirror neurons that involve subject-object dualism. Such interpretations assume a simulation, where a more or less conscious mental operation, translates the observation of the other into one's own frame of reference.[102] The "growing consensus that mirror neurons . . . play an important role in neonate imitation and the infant's ability to perceive intentions"[103] suggests a more holistic model of radical embodiment. Namely, that embodied beings recognize meaning, expressiveness, emotion, value in their perceptions of similarly embodied beings, starting with a neonate's observation and imitation of a parent's facial expression. Radical embodiment entails an inter-subjectivity at the very roots of human and animal existence.

100. Neergaard, "Scientists Rethink Origins."

101. De Waal, *Our Inner Ape*, 2.

102. Gallagher, *How the Body Shapes*, 9, 77, 220ff.

103. Ibid., 223.

4

Tradition as Body

HAVING ARGUED FOR THE BODY WITHIN TRADITION, I NOW ARGUE FOR
tradition as body. The metaphorical phrase, "the body of a tradition," is
well-known. Indeed, as such a conventional and familiar a metaphor,
its metaphorical power has long been lost in ordinary usage. I suspect
though that the original inventor(s) of the phrase intuited some vital
truth about the nature of tradition. In any case, I desire to make this
metaphor fresh again by arguing that the prereflective givenness of tradition strongly parallels the prereflective givenness of the human body.
Our traditions, like our bodies, constitute our life and identity—what
we live in and through, what we are—and function as that on which
we tacitly rely in order to meaningfully orient ourselves and to reflect,
in order to know, to value. Note that givenness here does not primarily
function as object of our knowledge—though we do have subsidiary or
tacit awareness involving content, but more as part of the subjectivity
of our experiential body—or tradition as body—that mediates our contact with the world. The very possibility of critical thinking presumes
the mediation of tradition(s) upon which we pre-critically and radically rely. Polanyi has written, "when we make a thing function as the
proximal term of tacit knowing [that which we are "attending from"],
we incorporate it in our body—or extend our body to include it—so
that we come to dwell in it."[1] Polanyi's remark generalizes from the use
of a tool and can profitably be applied to tradition: We dwell in traditions, extending our bodies through them, incorporating them within
our bodies; tradition then functions as a body through which we engage
the world and becomes part of our bodies. As Delwin Brown and Sheila
Greeve Davaney have stated, traditions are not just conceptual, but ma-

1. Polanyi, *Tacit Dimension*, 16. See also x.

terial, embedded in communities. And human beings are embedded, embodied, in communities and traditions.[2]

I would add that from the perspective of radical embodiment the prereflectivity and tacitness of much of tradition applies both to the material—ritual, architecture, moral behavior, and institutional practices to which Connerton attests[3]—and to the conceptual. While much of the linguistic, conceptual dimension of many traditions has received some explicitization, for any tradition a portion of it has not. Moreover, from a Polanyian perspective, every use of even a single word or concept involves a tacit coefficient as the speaker relates it to the particular context, including tacit knowledge of its application in many other contexts. Therefore, especially considering the complexity of religion, when a thinker in a tradition articulates any religious belief, only a small portion—the tip of the iceberg—of the full meaning of said belief can find explicit expression in that articulation. Of course, some of that meaning can find expression in other or further articulations. Yet a significant tacit operation always pertains when religious beliefs or doctrines stated explicitly in one context find application in new contexts. My sense is that, even in the realm of the linguistic, more of the meaning of any tradition remains unspecified and tacit than becomes explicit. In any case, as various elements of any tradition—again including the linguistic let alone all the non-linguistic—enter into wider applications and meanings in a contemporary context, the tacit dimension must always figure heavily. As Polanyi has put it, all knowledge is either tacit or explicit, and explicit knowledge relies on tacit knowledge for understanding and application; "a *wholly* explicit knowledge is unthinkable."[4]

Certain revisionist theologians have joined radical postmodernism in alleging the thoroughly contestable nature of all tradition. Comments from four out of five presenters at a session of the 1996 American Academy of Religion Annual Meeting, entitled "The Nature of Tradition and the Theological Task," included the following: Francis S. Fiorenza characterized identity within a tradition as a present contemporary constructive task rather than a historical inheritance.[5]

2. Brown and Davaney, "Theology and Tradition."

3. Connerton, *How Societies Remember.*

4. Polanyi, *Knowing and Being*, 144.

5. Fiorenza, "Tradition."

Kathryn Tanner rejected the legitimacy of any appeal to the authority of tradition, claiming that theology must establish continuity and "prove everything."[6] Finally, despite the above-cited remark on the material embeddedness of tradition in communities, Brown and Davaney argued that truth can be judged only by "contemporary canons of discourse," not by the authority of a tradition; traditions are negotiable throughout, they concluded.[7]

Brown in particular has written at length about tradition in his book, *Boundaries of Our Habitations: Tradition and Theological Construction*. Here Brown regards humans' relationship to tradition primarily as one of self-consciously "reconstructing . . . the house of history which they have inherited."[8] He does refer to ritual and feelings[9] and in a response to journal articles addressing his book explicitly identifies "a principle of materiality."[10] In this latter piece he commendably mentions the body's "reach into the cognitive life" and notes that the interaction of feeling, thought, and practice "far exceeds the force of language and conscious reflection."[11] However, he specifically writes only about bodily enactments of thoughts and feelings in ritual and in social institutions. What Brown does not significantly develop is a bodily or prereflective givenness that radically forms and informs traditions, a theory that recognizes the depth of the mediating function of traditions. Frankly, we do not have the house of history, with all its rooms fully accessible to us, to reconstruct.

The above comments reflect a strongly reflective model of tradition that ignores inherited and possibly authoritative prereflective or tacit givenness. As such, they are terribly redolent of enlightenment standards of critical reason: the explicitization and justification of everything. Despite post-enlightenment chastening, the enlightenment picture of absolute lucidity and accompanying standards still exerts

---

6. Tanner, "Tradition and Theological Judgment." Tanner came out of the Yale school of postliberalism but more recently has been significantly influenced by poststructuralism.

7. Brown and Davaney, "Theology and Tradition."

8. Brown, *Boundaries*, 118.

9. Ibid., 92ff., 145ff.

10. Brown, "Beyond *Boundaries*," 169–70.

11. Ibid., 170.

powerful influence as asymptotic ideal. As Poteat noted, this picture assumes that tradition and critical thought lie on the same logical plane:

> All the elements of their relationships . . . are taken to be logically homogeneous, suggesting that tradition and criticism have the same logical standing and, more important, that they have the same kind of weight; that tradition exerts its force in the way that an explicitly reflected premise does when construed in light of the above rationalistic model, whereas the force of all the unreflected premises, metaphors, analogies, images, pictures which determine the range and limits—and power—of critical thought is hardly felt at all.[12]

It is worth noting that radical postmodernism's embrace of surface metaphors and its reliance on a visual picture of language accord with this enlightenment picture: all the diverse elements of experience can in principle be brought to the surface and equally exposed (even as they equally harbor an unpresentable remainder).

The implications of my model are now perhaps clear: tradition—as a body with which we think, upon which we tacitly and radically rely— is not at every point contestable or negotiable. As medium, tradition then is not transparent nor fully penetrable. Limits exist on exposing the prereflective or tacit givenness of the flesh of tradition. A general limitation is that the relationship of the explicit to the previously implicit is never one of exact equivalency. Polanyi has pointed out one potential danger associated with this limitation: "an unbridled lucidity can destroy our understanding of complex matters. Scrutinize closely the [normally tacit] particulars of a comprehensive entity and their meaning is effaced, our conception of the entity is destroyed."[13] When we look at, rather than from or through, particulars we become alienated from their integrated meaning. Everyday examples include repeating a word while concentrating on its individual phonemes, a pianist looking at or thinking about finger movements, or focusing on small details of a face or other visual pattern.[14] Applying this phenomenon to tradition, analytically dissecting particular components of a tradition risks alienating one from its wider integrated meaning. The economy of grace or "the gift" might provide one such example. One might conclude that any

12. Poteat, *Philosophical Daybook*, 146.

13. Polanyi, *Tacit Dimension*, 18.

14. Ibid., 18; see also *Personal Knowledge*, 56; *Knowing and Being*, 146.

expectations of the recipient by the giver must vitiate the graciousness of a gift. Yet in lived experience the following occurs: someone gives a gift in *hopes* of some kind of appreciation or reciprocity, but without any condition that the gift should be returned if this does not eventuate. Some religious traditions of course believe that this occurs with regard to the divine's relation to human beings. Moreover, much human giving involves some mix of self-concern and concern for others. While the Protestant Reformers' doctrine of total depravity taught that any self-interest vitiated a loving deed, embodied religion is not bound to such absolutistic, all or nothing thinking. Fundamentalism offers an example from the other side. The authority of a scriptural passage becomes so tied to the historicity of a single detail that the deeper religious meaning becomes lost.

In brief, three categories pertain to contestability and explicitization: 1) That which is actively contested. Undoubtedly, our liberal thinkers want to avoid the appeal to authority as a trump-card discussion ender, as do I. In this case, discussants have already raised elements of tradition to a reflective level and critical reason becomes requisite. However, I disagree that any reference to an acritical dimension of trust in a traditional authority is necessarily an illegitimate move in every controversy. 2) That which is potentially subject to contestation/negotiation. Here a rule of thumb applies: to invoke critical reason, including prophetic reason, only as problems arise in practice. 3) The non-contestable and non-negotiable: a) Given temporal, practical constraints, only selected potential issues can in fact be contested. b) In principle, some aspects of tradition may be so deeply tacit and embedded as to defy adequate explicitization. These aspects would be assumed in any explicit affirmations or refutations—and would, I claim, include the meaningfulness of our bodily orientation of ourselves to our world.

Given my contention just above and in chapter 1 that some aspects of knowledge in principle defy specification, I will address contrary views even among Polanyians, notably by Zhenhua Yu, who maintains that "tacit knowledge cannot be fully articulated by verbal means, but can be articulated in action."[15] It seems to me, though, that if this were true, then the bodily actions of someone riding a bike, of a master craftsperson shaping a violin, or of a wordsmith using a term in a new

15. Zhenhua, "Tacit Knowledge: Wittgensteinian Approach," 11.

context would be more readily transferable upon observation than they in fact are. (Regarding the example of using a word, Polanyi holds that knowing how to use language always involves tacit elements themselves not verbally expressible.) Zhenhua grants that "the transference of tacit knowledge relies more on first-hand experience, examples and guided instructions of the master" and rightly observes that "in order to criticize tacit knowledge, we must appeal to action or practice."[16] Yet the process of non-verbal "articulation" or transference appears so different from the verbal process as to make the prospect of full articulation or explicitization most improbable. While the degree of understanding of a verbal explicitization of course varies from person to person, providing a certain minimum background knowledge, we can ensure that a hearer achieves a basic comprehension. That hardly is the case for many non-verbal attempts at transference of knowledge. Even assuming repeated practice according to the instructions of an expert, no guarantees exist that the pupil will ever get it, know it, do it like the master. Zhenhua's references to first-hand experience are indicative. Understanding verbal explicitation does not usually require contextual first-hand experience, while non-verbal knowing typically does. For the latter it takes internalization, indwelling of the tacit subsidiary elements to understand fully, to have the same knowledge as the original knower/doer. In the case of learning to ride a bike, transference finally does not best describe the process. Rather, a gap exists in the communication from teacher to learner that can only be bridged—if it ever gets bridged—by first-hand dwelling in the relevant tacit subsidiaries by the embodied learner. One can study the practice of and receive advice from an acclaimed public speaker, practicing devoutly, but the budding Demosthenes rarely matches the eloquence of the original due to that speaker's tacit, intuitive ability to use language. Since no formulas exist to actually cause the transfer of the tacit knowledge of the originator, I conclude that full non-verbal articulation is impossible regarding motion, art, and language use. This seems to me the intent of Polanyi himself:

> Things of which we are focally aware can be explicitly identified;
> but no knowledge can be made *wholly explicit* (emphasis his).
> For one thing, the meaning of language, when in use lies in its

16. Ibid., 12.

tacit component; for another, to use language involves actions of
our body of which we have only a subsidiary awareness.[17]

In an earlier piece, Zhenhua appears to attempt to carve out a
domain of human knowledge open to full verbal articulation. He distinguishes two types of tacit knowledge in Polanyi's corpus: 1) the inarticulate knowledge we share with other animals 2) the from-to nature of
knowing whereby we tacitly use subsidiaries while focusing on a larger
meaning. He claims that the former can become known only through
action, while the latter is amenable in principle to verbal articulation.
Zhenhua recognizes that for Polanyi the very understanding of the basic symbolic processes of language relies on inarticulate knowledge.[18]
Moreover, Zhenhua quotes Polanyian passages to the effect that moving
from an old articulate framework to a new one also relies upon such
inarticulate knowing.[19]

However, for Polanyi using a word in a new context or discovering
a whole new framework in a field of knowledge does indeed involve
tacit awareness of subsidiary clues while focusing on the relevant situation holistically. Therefore, I do not think Zhenhua's distinction, of tacit
knowledge subject to verbal articulation versus knowledge amenable
only to articulation through action, can stand, on Polanyian terms. For
Polanyi moving to a new framework involves a logical or heuristic gap:
if one could specify the movement in terms of the old framework, one
would have already reached it within that framework. The implication
of Zhenhua's analysis is that, while the heuristic leap defies verbal specification, it can undergo specification through action. Polanyi, however,
only writes about the unspecifiable nature of reorganizing and achiev-
ing new knowledge. What actions could specify how one moves from
an old to a new paradigm? Zhenhua might reply that the action itself of
the epistemological breakthrough by the knower provides the specification. But those still in the old paradigm fail to see any articulation of the
leap to the allegedly new.

My above analysis has implications for tradition: If *relatively*
simple actions of using a word, navigating a space, or crafting an object
resist total explicitation, the more complex linguistic, ritual, and social

17. Polanyi, *Personal Knowledge* with Preface, x.
18. Zhenhua, "Tacit Knowledge: Knowing," 15–19.
19. Ibid., 15; Polanyi, *Study of Man*, 18, 24–25.

organizational elements of a religious or other major tradition a fortiori resist the same (even more so to the extent they forge new knowledge over time).

The body in tradition and tradition as body bring resources for overcoming epistemological dualisms and aporias, for overcoming relativism and incommensurability. To develop the tradition as body metaphor, I will focus on the dynamic of integration. A common sense view assumes the highly integrated nature of a biological body (whereas the integrity of a tradition is not as obvious).

However, radical postmodernism would press discontinuity and fragmentation in body, self, tradition, etc. On the one hand it deplores the either-or of modern binaries like subject/object, sense/reason, emotion/reason, presence/absence. On the other hand, in the name of and for the sake of difference and alterity, it cannot bridge these binaries. Rather than any "both-and," the earlier Taylor opts for "neither-nor."[20] The object always remains at a frustrating remove from the subject; the self can never truly connect with the other[21]; reflection never catches up enough to perception or emotion to make sense of them; words slip and their meaning is ever ambiguous and ultimately undecidable; Goedel's mathematical theorem, demonstrating that not all the presuppositions of a system can be proven within the system, means that every system is "irreducibly incomplete"—further interpreted to mean every system is "inwardly torn" and "essentially opaque"[22]; the body's "analog" processes

<hr/>

20. M. Taylor, *Erring*, 11; *Disfiguring*, 316. In his latest work, Taylor's emphasis on self-organizing complex systems has much in common with my correlative model of reality. Interestingly, though, he still describes as "neither-nor" the "locus of the real" in such complex systems. Without explaining why, he characterizes monistic models as "both-and." Instead I would regard monistic systems as affirming only one side of relevant polarities—absolute presence and immanence and as Taylor himself puts it, "identity without difference" (*After God*, 37–41). Conversely, in complex, dynamic correlative systems of identity-in-difference and difference-in-identity, the ultimately "real" would seem to be both present and absent, both transcendent and immanent. In general Taylor characterizes the structuring/stabilizing and de-structuring/destabilizing elements of complex systems as complementary and coequal. However, I sense an overemphasis on the side of destabilization, when Taylor writes of the "virtual" and "elusive" real as "the source of the endless disruption that keeps complex systems open," where "(n)othing remains stable" (41). Perhaps a preference for the disfiguring pole keeps Taylor from endorsing presence, even in a "both-and" relationship with absence.

21. M. Taylor, *Alterity*.

22. M. Taylor, *Nots*, 238.

clash irreconcilably with its "digital" processes.[23] Indeed, the body itself "betrays."[24] Taylor, as a matter of general principle, rejects modern notions of the absoluteness of origin and primordiality. Tellingly, though, the deconstructive Taylor finds great import in the fact that the fetus' immune system must learn not to attack the body's own cells. Taylor interprets this as a primordial division of the body against itself.[25] In the gap between the binaries lies the trace, the unutterable, difference—neither present nor absent, neither being nor nonbeing. I have of course advocated the reality of the tacit and cognitive unconscious, of so much unavailable to language or to the full light of consciousness. For radical embodiment this "unpresentable" is as diverse as the scope of human experience. I would add here that radical embodiment definitely does not reify the "prereflective" as some unchanging entity. What functions as prereflective or tacit changes over time with experience, elements being added or subtracted—as long as we understand that some aspects of the physiological structures of our motility and perception ever abide as acritical ordainers/ constrainers of our potentialities. Neither does radical postmodernism intend to reify the unpresentable; in contrast to radical embodiment, though, it is largely incapable of explicating the unpresentable in any positive fashion. In all of radical postmodernism's emphasis on radical discontinuity, I detect the haunting standard of modernity, its standard of absolute lucidity and presence. Only judged by this standard does subject fail so abysmally to reach its object. Only with this standard as backdrop does radical postmodernism come to its nihilistic tendencies.

Moderate postmodernism advocates a both-and solution to overcome modernity's dualisms. Conceptually these binaries stand in correlation. In proper reflection, they mutually entail each other—their separation is unthinkable. As indicated in chapter 1, someone knowing something constitutes the epistemological surd. No pure object exists in itself nor pure subject in itself. Pure cognition without affect is absurd (or at least diseased, as in the case of Elliot; and even he does not lack minimal affect). In practice human bodies bridge the purported gap between subject and object all the time. Each body enjoys tremen-

---

23. Ibid., 236ff.
24. Ibid., 239ff.
25. Ibid., 246.

dous diversity whether considered at the cellular level or at the level of our various senses and mobile parts. Yet normally the body achieves adequate integration. The proper standard for embodied beings is adequacy (literally, "equal" [to the task]), not absolute oneness, presence, and lucidity—whatever that would mean. The body usually realizes physical health, successful coordination among our senses,[26] adequate integration of the habits and projects of our phenomenal body—or, failing that, an instinctive striving towards adequate integration, making adequate sense of words in the context of their utterance,[27] indeed making adequate sense of systems and traditions even when all their premises cannot be proven within said system (here Goedel's theorem only entails the impossibility of explicit proof of all premises—surds are inalienable not absurd, incompleteness means openness not opaqueness). The body stands as a diverse yet integrated complex system.

So with tradition. Postmodern epistemology assumes substantial diversity within any religious tradition, diversity incompatible with postliberal essentialism. Though a tradition defies reduction to an essence, if recognizable as that upon which some community effectively relies, it presumptively has found adequate integration. It is a diverse yet integrated system. Some of the diversity within a tradition involves contestation. Alasdair McIntyre has cogently argued that traditions themselves contain arguments—traditions are hardly unaware of questions, tensions, and multiple perspectives.[28] Contestation within a tradition in itself does not deny integration; rather it represents a striving for adequate integration.[29] And such integration within a tradition does not assume that important concepts—and their underlying primary

26. Merleau-Ponty, *Phenomenology*, 139–42, 148–53, 224–25. Recent research suggests that crosstalk among senses influences how the brain initially experiences perceptual input; integration among the senses begins early in the process (Guterman, "Do You Smell What I Hear?").

27. The observation that radical postmodernism relies upon a visual, literate "picture" of language rather than an aural, oral model pertains here (see Jardine, "Sight, Sound"). Written texts are subject to unending, sometimes incompatible, interpretation over time, while a spoken word normally elicits adequate comprehension in its context. Also, that a written text can be scanned in an instant promotes a picture of absolute knowledge—either as a goal, as for much of modernity, or as an unachievable standard that engenders epistemological pessimism.

28. MacIntyre, *Whose Justice?*

29. Of course, failure to adequately integrate can result in division into multiple traditions.

metaphors—are always propositionally consistent. All the same they may complement and cohere at a more tacit, prereflective level of embodiment. This relates to my above comments on the danger of losing holistic meaning when focusing on particulars. Noteworthily, philosopher of myth Ernst Cassirer and Polanyi independently have commented on how myth typically involves antimonies incompatible when considered separately, yet point to an import which encompasses their joint meaning—a sympathetic coherence, involving a "unity of feeling," in Cassirer's language.[30] Such polarities may include the one and the many (unity/multiplicity), creation/destruction, primordial goodness/evil, and order/chaos. As suggested earlier, moderate postmodernisms in general stand in the best position to correlate binarisms, while radical embodiment points to how the body regularly succeeds in bridging them, as above.

I move from consideration of diversity within a single tradition, to the diversity of the traditions within which any individual stands. I propose that these diverse traditions, each of which is individually analogous to a body, also collectively form a body of tradition(s). As the phenomenal body draws upon diverse senses and habits for integration, so the embodied individual draws upon diverse religious, ethical, or other traditions (in striving) for an adequately integrated worldview. As the person does not normally regard their body's members as separate bodies, so the person does not normally regard diverse traditions, insofar as useful for an integrated worldview, as simply separate but as members of a body of human tradition. This experience of diverse traditions as a body is normally a tacit or prereflective one. However, without the presumption of a certain level of fruitful interrelatedness and adequacy of integration among the traditions one relies upon, one would not use them. Of course, elements of some of these various traditions that a person tacitly integrates may harbor inconsistencies if separately made explicit. But the tacit, holistic way the person uses them may not itself involve contradiction. Of course, at times we reflectively struggle to integrate personally meaningful traditions that do clash. Yet this body of tradition(s) anyone relies upon *usually* is experienced as a diverse yet adequately integrated system.

---

30. Cassirer, *Essay on Man*, 81ff; Polanyi and Prosch, *Meaning*, 152ff.

The final move is significantly more problematic. It is to the diverse traditions among diverse individuals and communities. Postmodern epistemology opposes rigid boundaries within and between traditions, favoring instead porosity and interconnectedness. Only the moderate postmodernists, however, consistently uphold this vision. I have judged that radical postmodernists in the interests of difference and postliberals in the interests of identity both accept the ultimate incommensurability of systems. A given word for Wittgenstein, rather than subsumable under one essence or definition, consists of a series of differing yet overlapping usages, characterized by "family resemblances."[31] Though Wittgenstein's language games and forms of life have often been appropriated on behalf of a picture of self-enclosed traditions, these are better interpreted as likewise overlapping and porous. Indeed, Wittgenstein broaches the notion of a "family of language games"[32] and does refer to language as a "family of structures."[33] If we consistently grant porosity and interconnectedness, then the presumption must be against inexorable incommensurability.

But can I be so bold as to broach the metaphoric possibility of one body of tradition for the human species? I recognize that such a body is an abstraction in the sense that any human being can indwell only a portion of all of human tradition in any significant way. Yet may a person legitimately regard the traditions one encounters as part of a larger body? Any tradition will have certain interconnections and commonalities with any other tradition. But what of the clear differences among religious traditions? Of course in practice few individuals will deeply indwell more than one religious tradition, in part because of all the prereflective or tacit elements of tradition. Yet because of the bodily basis of all our indwellings, one may imaginatively enter into enough of another religious tradition to recognize some of its differences from one's own as a valid alternative embodiment, as an alternative indwelling of truth. In just writing of people normally indwelling simply "one" religious tradition, I was thinking primarily of Westerners. Of course many East Asians historically have indwelt two or more traditions, depending on how one counts. At the same time, the pertinent tradi-

31. Wittgenstein, *Philosophical Investigations*, ns. 66–67, 164.
32. Ibid., n. 179.
33. Ibid., n. 108.

tions in this regard clearly have mutually engaged, influenced, indeed, interpenetrated each other. The traditional religious life of China and Japan then can serve as an exemplar of what does or could happen in less obvious ways with religion elsewhere. Still, what of the blatant disagreements, the outright contradictions? I propose the following: for those willing to generously engage other traditions, it remains possible to imagine a body of tradition of the human race awaiting fuller integration, if in the face of contestation between traditions, implicit bodily bases for dialogue and adjudication exist, as I believe they do. Now we have cycled back to the body in tradition.

At this point a skeptic might ask, why should we trust embodied rationality in the first place, let alone the religious traditions that function as extensions of our bodies? Especially given that I have appealed to the integrative ability of our bodies with respect to elements at some level in tension or even in contradiction. After all, we have become aware of how "predictably irrational" human economic behavior can be,[34] how our strong evolutionary preferences for sugar, salt, and fat can debilitate and kill us, how we register disgust at the thought of eating out of a completely sterile bedpan,[35] and how our visual perception can create optical illusions as to relative length, etc. Radical embodiment would note how these behaviors, definitely irrational in certain contexts, nevertheless manifest a deeper rationality in terms of many or most embodied contexts, going back to animal and human evolutionary history. Certainly, the embodied perceptual functioning behind so-called "optical illusions" normally yields relevant truth in terms of judgments about animals and objects in motion (even though the judgments may be false in terms of abstract mathematical contexts). In a related vein, the phenomenon of semantic congruity cited in the preceding chapter—for example, of more readily picking out the larger of two large objects than of two small ones—manifests quite rational contextual, embodied logic rather than the logic of neutral computation. Disgust at certain types of substances that may sicken us betokens an evolutionary logic of "better safe than sorry," even if we naturally and "irrationality" feel disgust when confronted with (often contrived)

---

34. Ariely, *Predictably Irrational*.
35. Bloom, *Descartes' Baby*, 159.

situations that could not harm us.[36] Some economic and dietary choices confronting us clearly call for the employment of critical reason. But none of this denies the fundamental rationality of our embodiment in the world. Of course our religious traditions, though rooted in our basic embodiment, also reach beyond it. Yet when our critical reason stays in touch with our embodiment, we can place some trust in the rationality of human religious seeking.

As Terry Godlove following Davidson claims, human language use presupposes that the vast majority of our beliefs are held in common.[37] The body in tradition provides an account of the commonalities in human symbolic meaning, including the commonalities in language upon which Davidson builds. It is a truism that no one-to-one equivalence obtains among languages. This fact has influenced the dominance of the picture of finally self-enclosed incommensurability I see in various postmodernisms. But that languages all radically rely upon our embodiment enables adequate translation from one language/tradition to another. We can go further than a claim of diverse interconnections between a given tradition and any other. Such a claim entails that tradition A shares certain commonalities with B, and B with C, yet does not preclude the disjunctive possibility that A, B, and C have nothing jointly in common. Radical embodiment entails that all traditions hold in common something(s) very basic, not fully determinate but neither simply indeterminate, in terms of our human embodiment on the earth.

The previously noted integrative ability of the body offers one model for adjudication among contested traditions, namely, greater inclusiveness, which is a function of greater complexity. A tradition that is able to include and integrate within its body important features and dimensions of another tradition gains an epistemological advantage over that tradition, if the other tradition is not similarly able to include and integrate. An example might be a tradition that incorporates modern science versus a primal tradition unaffected by same—*if* that tradition at the same time maintains a deep sense of sacredness and divinity. A religious tradition that can integrate scientific truths about the natural world with mythological truths about the nature of reality and human nature possesses greater inclusivity than a primal tradition alone; it

36. Ibid., 159–61.

37. Godlove, *Religion, Interpretation.*

can integrate more traditions and more truth within its body. Recently Mark C. Taylor has written helpfully about the destabilizing effect of the growing interaction and competition among religious and other traditions in modern and postmodern times.[38] In such a situation, which we can label as "far from equilibrium," reside both special danger and special opportunity. The opportunity is to forge "new" or "revised" traditions of greater complexity (which term to favor depends on context). I would remark that even such major change does rely radically upon the traditions it engages (consistent with Connerton's observation in Chapter 2 concerning revolutionary change). Even in its rejection of the old, it incorporates elements without which the new would be impossible.

Above I referred to the indeterminacy associated with our embodiment in the world. One can even speak of an inexhaustibility to our radical embodiment. As our bodies encounter the world, we never exhaust all the possibilities, the dimensions, the angles for perceiving, moving, creating. Our bodies set ranges within which all our possibilities lie, but within that range for our embodiment inexhaustibility reigns. For the believer of divine purposiveness, the range of possibilities of divinity is vastly greater, indeed infinite. Thus our inexhaustibility does not rival that of the divine, yet we are created in the divine image with respect to inexhaustibility. Herein consists radical embodiment's principal disagreement with Radical Orthodoxy. Radical Orthodoxy identifies the dimension of inexhaustibility in creation, of "density," "depth," "surplus," exclusively with the divine.[39] And if it were not for that transcendent inexhaustibility, all rationality and meaning would indeed die from exhaustion; the nihilistic tendencies of radical postmodernism would be right on the mark.[40] For radical embodiment, such a move concedes game, set, and match. It underestimates the goodness of creation by positing an added, extrinsic, transcendent, dimension of inexhaustibility. Instead, inexhaustibility bubbles up immanent in creation, immanent with our radical embodiment in the world. The radical embodiment proponent who believes in divine purpose would add that the goodness

38. Taylor, *After God*, 23–28.

39. Milbank et al., *Radical Orthodoxy*, 1ff., 26–27, 220ff.

40. Ibid., 1–3, 24–27, 105; Milbank, Respondent, "Pickstock's *After Writing*."

and inexhaustibility of the world are sustained in each moment by the creative power of the divine.

I hope that the revisionist theological tradition (liberal Protestantism chastened by neo-orthodoxy and leavened by post-Vatican II Catholic, liberationist, and postmodern influences), which lies exhausted at this juncture, might find rejuvenation through radical embodiment. It would be apropos for theology of a faith claiming the descriptor, the religion of the Incarnation, to be thus revived. More generally for religious traditions, if the body in tradition and tradition as body get taken seriously, perhaps the Jamesian hope of our rootedness in a meaningful universe will flourish. For a long time meaning has been threatened by an absurd picture, discarnate and denigrating of tradition, vacillating between objectivism and absolutism on the one hand and subjectivism and relativism on the other. As Polanyi expressed it, humanity's striving for an enduring purpose "should become more feasible once religious faith is freed from pressure by an absurd vision of the universe, so there will open up instead a meaningful world which could resound to religion."[41] Or as Poteat expressed it through the words of an ancient psalmist, it may become possible again for Westerners to declare without embarrassment our natural intuition at our embodiment in the natural world: "The heavens declare the glory of God and the firmament shows forth God's handiwork."[42]

41. Polanyi and Prosch, *Meaning*, 92.
42. Psalm 19:1 (translation mine); Poteat, *Philosophical Daybook*, 5.

5

Radical Embodiment in Light of the Science and Religion Dialogue

In creating humankind God sculpted "the earth being," according to the etymology of "Adam," the Hebrew word for "humanity" used in Genesis 2. The portrait of humankind painted by the scriptures of Judaism, Christianity, and Islam regards the human person as a psycho-somatic unity. Scientific evidence increasingly points to the truth that human beings are fundamentally embodied in nature, contrary to the Greek-influenced mind-body dualism that has reigned for most of Western theological and philosophical history. In this chapter I will highlight the significance of our embodiment relative to evolutionary biology and to the nature of consciousness in light of cognitive science and neuroscience.

As argued in chapters 1 and 3, radical embodiment entails a radical, inalienable correlation between subject and object, between perceiving self and thing or world. This is to say that human perception and bodily engagement correlatively define and are defined by the world. Before applying this principle directly to contemporary currents in science, I will cite some key points of Merleau-Ponty's treatment of this principle to both review and amplify previous exposition. The picture that controlled both sides of the dualistic debate of modernity assumed that reality was determinate—already fully specified either in our minds or by the environment—quite apart from our bodily engagement with the world. It was this discarnate picture that Merleau-Ponty doggedly attacked in *The Phenomenology of Perception* with thick descriptions of scientific experiments and of both ordinary and extraordinary examples of human and animal perception. The touchstone running through Merleau-Ponty's corpus (pun not intended though noticed) is this: every human perception—and by extension every human act of reflection—involves a correlation of 1) our attention and our embodied effort to make sense of the world and 2) input and givenness from the world. This correlation is radical; it is the surd behind which we cannot venture. As Merleau-Ponty concludes after considering the case of a brain-injured man's deficiencies in perceptual knowledge:

> Consciousness is being towards the thing through the intermediary of the body. A movement is learned when the body has understood it, that is, when it has incorporated it into its "world," and to move one's body is to aim at things through it; it is to allow oneself to respond to their call, which is made upon it independently of any representation.[1]

And as he writes of "the cogito" near the end of the work:

> There is vision only through anticipation and intention, and since no intention could be a true intention if the object towards which it tends were given to it ready made and with no motivation, it is true that all vision assumes in the last resort, at the core of subjectivity, a total project or logic of the world which empirical perceptions endow with specific form, but to which they cannot give rise.[2]

For Merleau-Ponty then the world has a structure, a logic, whether we exist to experience it or not. But he deliberately distinguishes between the "thing" that "calls" to us to help in the project of its definition versus "the object" which is supposedly—but in reality never can be—fully constituted apart from our bodily engagement. Nor conversely is the self "aware of itself as absolutely transparent, and as the originator of its own presence in the visible world."[3]

One can find analogues to this principle of the partial openness of objects to determinateness by another in realms and processes of physics that are presumably independent of any consciousness: 1) on the subatomic quantum level, in keeping with Heisenberg's uncertainty principle, particles and energy appear to inhabit certain probability ranges unless and until they are measured or otherwise come into contact with another physical reality 2) Einstein's theories of relativity

1. Merleau-Ponty, *Phenomenology*, 138–39.
2. Ibid., 404–5.
3. Ibid., 405.

entail that the temporal interval between events depends on the relative speeds of frames of reference—there is no absolute space or time fully constituted apart from the event or encounter. Note that the openness is only partial: the potential quantum states fall within boundaries and whether a given event is subsequent or consequent to another does not change for any frame of reference. We might hypothesize a general principle: each physical reality has a certain "for-itselfness," that is, an integrity that "pushes back" relative to other realities, even as it is partially constituted by other realities. Theologian Paul Tillich had a similar intuition when he wrote that every reality resists being "treated as a mere thing, as an object which has no subjectivity."[4]

As indicated in Chapter 1, Whiteheadian process philosophy for its part claims the "unit occasion of experience" as the basic constituent of actuality. This metaphor or concept, however, seems to privilege the subjective/mind side over the objective/physical. The object is (reduced to) an earlier subjective experience which is only partially "prehended" by a present subject. Subject and object become the same in essence, and any distinction between them becomes just a matter of time and perspective.

But for radical embodiment subjectivity and objectivity correlate simultaneously. Each reality has/is both "inside" and "outside" in relation to other realities, with the degree of emphasis on internality versus externality relative to context. As Merleau-Ponty asseverates, "Inside and outside are inseparable."[5] The contextuality of inside/outside plays out with respect to the body itself. When I look at my arm it is relatively external compared to when I reach with it for a bowl of food. When I think about the synapses that occur in my brain as I type this sentence, my brain becomes very objectified, external, "third-person," and abstract in comparison to my subjective experience of the meaning of this sentence. In truth I can never get outside my phenomenal or experiencing body in any absolute or concrete sense. It is the surd into which I cannot penetrate beyond a certain point nor from which I can extract myself. Conversely, when a blind person walks with a cane or when I drive a car, the cane and car become internalized extensions of the body rather than external objects to which one attends.

4. Tillich, *Systematic*, 1:173.
5. Merleau-Ponty, *Phenomenology*, 407.

To play a bit more with the mutual defining of environment and human or animal in perception, we can consider effects on or alterations to the environment. When one encounters an object tactilely, the effect is tangible and obvious. However, in the more subtle cases of vision and hearing, effects also occur. Certain light waves and sound waves are stopped or captured by the body and its organs of perception and are processed in varying ways depending upon which organism we consider (while other waves are reflected or refracted). Thinking about how different animals engage their environment in perception and movement sets the stage for our next topic.

In their book, *The Embodied Mind*, cognitive scientists Francisco Varela, Evan Thompson, and Eleanor Rosch deftly extend the theory of the correlation of sensorimotor capabilities and the environment, claiming support from biologists Richard Lewontin and Susan Oyama: The mutual defining or determination of a perceiving/acting subject and the world applies to the evolutionary process itself. Here the concept of organism as self-organizing and emergent biological system crucially comes into play, as evolving organisms and environment mutually specify each other. The label that the three affix to their theory of evolution is "natural drift." A self-organizing, dynamic biological system has an integrity that puts pressure on the environment, so to speak, even as the environment puts pressure on it. This notion dissents from the dominant neo-Darwinian concept of optimal fit. This latter notion lays all the influence, all the causative power, on the side of the environment: the environment defines the organism but the organism exercises no effective specification upon the environment. We might observe that relative to Cartesian dualisms, optimal fit opts only for the objectivist and empiricist side in reductionistic fashion. Varela and company note various difficulties with standard neo-Darwinian theory.[6] Pleiotropy is the linkage of genetic traits. Optimal fit however should work against pleiotropy: maximal independence of traits would provide maximal flexibility to adapt to each environmental change. Relative stability of species over time also creates problems for optimal fit. Exemplars of such stability include the stasis of certain species—species that remain unchanged through eons of tremendous environmental change—as well as the phenomenon of punctuated equilibrium. This latter concept

6. Varela et al., *Embodied Mind*, 180ff.

points to the evolutionary record of major changes coming only after a "critical mass" of environmental change causes a tipping point. The all-pervasive influence posited by optimal fit does not fit well, though, with punctuated equilibrium: rather one would expect ongoing gradual changes corresponding to ongoing changes in the environment (as well as major changes in periods of sudden, climactic shifts).

As an alternative to optimal fit, natural drift proffers adequate fit. Biological organisms, as self-organizing systems, have their own integrity that pushes back against and partially determines the environment. Therefore, the evolutionary adaptive requirement is the less stringent one of adequacy, rather than that of optimal bending to each and every environmental modification. As Varela and crew put it, "The environment of course puts constraints or pressures on 'viable trajectories,' but at the same time the organism's perception, motor, and cognitive capabilities partially create its world, its environment."[7] As with individual cases of movement and perception mentioned above, we may first think of very tangible ways that a species modifies its environment, such as beavers building dams, various mammals digging tunnels and burrows, and birds constructing nests. On this score, we modern human beings have so modified our environment through culture that we have inured ourselves to many of the usual evolutionary pressures, while with the same stroke we have put unusual environmental pressures on countless other species. Less obviously, species also find—and create—their niches by the unique structures of their perceptual organs. Self-organizing organisms select (partially but really) which input from the environment to attend to, even as the environment also does real "natural selection." So bats specify their environment by attending to sound waves in their manner, indeed producing the sound waves they perceive in correlation with their environment. Animal species specify their worlds visually in differing ways: The three kinds of cones we humans possess make us tripartite in our color vision, while some other species have two, four, and perhaps even five types of cones.[8] Thus different species attend to differing frequencies of electromagnetic radiation in diverse ways. Additionally, genetic mutations themselves do not follow completely random trajectories: they occur more frequently when organisms un-

7. Varela et al., *Embodied Mind*, 185ff.
8. Ibid., 181–82.

dergo stress from the environment. The above cases, with the exception of human beings, relate to instinctual behavior. The Baldwin effect, however, ventures into the spontaneous choices of animals and, though controversial, has received recognition by some biologists for over a century. It refers to the phenomenon whereby the learned choices of animals might affect natural selection: for example, individuals choosing to eat elevated vegetation selects for proto-giraffes. The bottom line is this: the self-organizing and emergent capabilities of biological organisms and networks mutually or correlatively specify and evolve with an environment.

Jean Staune has noted that European scientists, not needing to defend against significant cultural influence by Intelligent Design proponents, have shown much more openness to possible evolutionary forces besides the environment working on random genetic mutations.[9] Stuart Kauffman has advocated for the self-organizing properties of organisms in evolutionary history.[10] Mathematician Ian Stewart has contrasted the circumscrihed nature of the actual distribution of genetic mutations in accordance with the non-linear equations associated with dynamic complex systems versus all the mathematically possible mutations.[11] Others, such as Christian de Duve, Simon Conway-Morris, and Michael Denton, while not choosing the rubric of self-organization, have argued that the constraints of the laws of bio-chemistry make life and self-conscious organisms far from a random development.[12] Finally Anne Dambricourt, referencing fractals and strange attractors in self-organizing systems, claims to discern an internal process of embryonic development with respect to the neural tube over 60 million years, leading to human bipedality.[13] The reality of biological self-organization does not hinge on the truth of Dambricourt's very controversial thesis, though any truth to her bold assertion would constitute striking evidence of it.

9. Staune, "Darwinism, Design, and Purpose." See also, Polkinghorne, *Faith, Science*, 71–75.

10. Kauffman, *Origins of Order; Reinventing the Sacred*.

11. Stewart, *Life's Other Secret*.

12. De Duve, *Vital Dust*; Morris, *Crucible of Creation*; Denton, *Nature's Destiny*.

13. Dambricourt, *Légende maudite*.

Embodied Consciousness

We will now transition from a focus on evolutionary biology to an embodied model of consciousness informed by neurobiology and cognitive science. As adumbrated in Chapter 3, Nobel Laureate Gerald Edelman and best-selling author Antonio Damasio have advanced embodied-biological models of mind, arguing that body-minded consciousness involving intrinsic values has been evolutionarily adaptive. For both, consciousness arises from continuous mappings in the brain of the body, involving both spatial orientation and feeling, and of the natural and social environments—in correlation, as informed by past mappings. These neural patterns then correlate to conscious "images" or "representations." Note that neither uses "representation" in a Cartesian manner, that is, as a repetition or mimicking of an already fully constituted physical or mental reality. Instead their theory traverses the same wave-length as Merleau-Ponty and Varela. As Damasio pens, "Rather than mirroring the environment around it, as an engineered information-processing device would, each brain constructs maps of the environment using its own parameters and internal design, and thus creates a world unique to the class of beings comparably designed."[14] Further summarization of Edelman and Damasio's theories will occur in the course of my arguments.

Both Edelman and Damasio contrast their biological model with functionalist computational models. "Functionalism" within the discipline of cognitive science typically refers to understanding the human mind and its properties, including consciousness, in terms of information processing in analogy with modern computers.[15] Or as Edelman bluntly puts it, functionalism entails that "either the brain is a computer or the computer is an adequate model for the interesting things that the brain does."[16] Historically computational models have been discarnate, plying the mind side of Cartesian dualism. Edelman and Damasio's harshest words target serial Turing machine models, from what Johnson and Lakoff have labeled "first-generation" cognitive science.[17] Such computational models represent the purest form of functional-

14. Damasio, *Feeling*, 322.
15. Peterson, *Minding God*, 55.
16. Edelman, *Remembered Present*, 29; *Bright Air*.
17. Johnson and Lakoff, *Philosophy in the Flesh*, 75ff.

ism, where hardware, material, structure, and process matter not at all, subordinated to the final product of the software program. As long as a system functions to produce a given result, it is functionally equivalent to any other system yielding the same result. So in Alan Turing's disembodied theory a huge digital computer has human intelligence, if it could type out statements that sounded as human as statements typed by an out-of-sight person. Such first-generation models are antithetical to the actual structure and working of the human or animal mind.

Yet despite their explicit excoriation of functionalism, Gregory Peterson, in his fine work, *Minding God: Theology and the Cognitive Sciences*, labels Edelman and Damasio's approaches as functionalist. Though Peterson does concede that Edelman and Damasio do not rely "as heavily on computational models as does cognitive science," he still categorizes their approach as functionalist because it centers on information processing.[18] In response to my paper for a panel on that book, he also stated that their biological approach is not only functionalist (in that it involves matter structured and sequenced in a certain way) but likely also computational, in that the brain's processes probably can be simulated on a Turing machine.[19] Edelman and Damasio would disagree on the possibility (let alone probability) of Turing machine simulation of the brain. On the wider issue of defining "functionalism," Peterson's general definition in terms of matter structured and sequenced in a particular way strikes me as overly broad. What in our world is not structured matter in some sense? The only alternative to functionalist models of consciousness here would seem to be idealistic, immaterial ones. Moreover, I judge that Peterson applies his narrower definition of information processing too broadly by lumping embodied biological models under it. Of course I do not deny that the brain processes information. But that fact in and of itself does not get us very far. Many non-biological systems and non-conscious as well as conscious biological systems process information. At least if we accept William James' characterization of even mystical states as noetic, all conscious states probably involve some kind of cognition. My bottom line is this: Just because some configuration of matter and energy involving information processing parallels processes of the embodied human or animal

18. Peterson, *Minding God*, 57.
19. Peterson, "Symposium."

body does not make it conscious. Given the reality of self-organizing systems with emergent properties, we do know that certain very complex biological systems with very particular configurations of matter and energy possess consciousness. We have no compelling reason to think that very different forms of matter and energy will possess the same emergent property. Are today's alchemists those of the Artificial Intelligence community who expect consciousness to arise, as if by magic, from non-organic matter performing a computer simulation of certain biological processes?

Second-generation connectionist models come closer to imitating the structure of living minds. In and of themselves, however, they are still discarnate. Before examining problems of connectionist or parallel distributed processing (PDP) vis-à-vis biological models of consciousness, we need to say more about their nature. Second-generation cognitive scientists noticed differences between the brain's structure and function and those of a Turing machine. The relevance of brain structure to function and the relevance of the environment were also acknowledged. Practically speaking, Turing-type computers failed to solve relatively simple human problems.[20] The second generation has advanced to parallel processing, where a task is subdivided to multiple processors operating simultaneously. In turn, a unit's task is organized into neural networks. As Peterson notes, here the distinction between hardware and software becomes blurred, because output depends on the configuration of the strengths of individual nodes, as does the distinction between programmer and program, given that the computer may learn.[21] Thus current cognitive science models the brain/mind in terms of parallel distributed processing (PDP) or connectionist computation. However, as Edelman stipulates, connectionist computers do not necessarily qualify as "selectional," where the computer makes selections and learns based on its own values.[22] More specifically non-selectional

20. Peterson, *Minding God*, 38.

21. Ibid., 40.

22. Edelman, *Bright Air*, 226–27. Even human memory is selectional. In Damasio's terminology, memory involves "dispositional representations, containing not a picture per se, but a means to reconstitute 'a picture.'" A representation of Aunt Maggie's face, for example, holds "the firing patterns which trigger the momentary reconstruction of an approximate representation of Aunt Maggie's face" (*Descartes' Error*, 102). This contrasts with computer memory as playback or replica. Similarly, writes Edelman, human memory involves an apparently open-ended set of connections between subjects and

models still require a programmer/operator and initial programming that specifies inputs and outputs (as opposed to real-life inputs which carry no preassigned meanings). Thus, learning is instructional, determined by the program, rather than selectional, determined by the organism—the latter of which appears to involve the indeterminism of choice. In Edelman's judgment, such initial programming specifies not just values but responses. Indeed, the assigning of so-called values to nodes of the network appears to be more quantitative than qualitative: these values are also called weights, with each node bearing a certain numerical value. Nevertheless, Edelman believes some connectionist robotics can boast truly selectional learning.[23] Instead of preassigned weights, a robot was programmed to prefer light rather than darkness and touching objects over not touching—preferences Edelman classifies as values. Moreover, the Massachusetts Institute of Technology Cog project, involving a robot that mimics the human body in certain respects, carries such preferences further. I take issue with Edelman, though, that these computers genuinely qualify as selectional. Cog does not internally "select" its basic values but rather the programmer does. Such preferences programmed from the outside seem a far cry from biological values that evolve immanently through the organic materiality and life processes of nature. Even if one concedes that Cog learns selectionally, I think Edelman has conflated necessary with sufficient conditions: selectional learning may indeed be necessary for consciousness but hardly sufficient. While Edelman views such robotics as a first step in the possible construction of a conscious artifact, on this issue I find him in discord with the fundamental thrust of his biological model.

At bottom the human mind is, in terms of structure as well as of input, analogue; the most basic unit, the neuron, is capable of a multitude of different states. By contrast a computer is digital; each gate is either on or off, assigned a value of "0" or "1". Peterson mentions another difference between the brain and current computers: "computer neural networks have no analogue to neurotransmitters."[24] Finally, Edelman

---

a rich texture of previous knowledge, not adequately represented by computer science terms like storage and retrieval (*Bright Air*, 238); instead it is "a process of continual recategorization" (ibid., 102).

23. Edelman, *Bright Air*, 188ff.

24. Peterson, *Minding God*, 40.

identifies a physiological factor that individualizes a brain: cells migrate and many cells die, especially during early brain development.[25]

I mention these factors to suggest the complexity of the human brain compared to even PDP computers. First-generation computing was theoretically simple. Not coincidentally cognitive science identified with Chomsky's theory of an innate human language module or what Fodor has labeled a language of thought.[26] A computer program is most conducive to rule-governed syntax that corresponds to objects or relations in the world defined by necessary and sufficient conditions.[27] However, as Edelman declares, "the world . . . is an unlabelled place"[28] and Darwinism spells the death knell for any essentialism.[29] Serial central processing computers could not begin to approximate how humans and animals categorize or form body schemas and pre-linguistic perceptual and mental images. But second-generation selectional connectionist and embodied computers have stretched beyond the limitations of first-generation processing and can begin to approximate human and animal functioning. Yet that they will ever reach the complexity of humans and animals in perceptual categorizing is quite questionable.

Wittgenstein's philosophy suggests the immense complexity of categorizing. He theorized that "some categories have *degrees* of membership but no clear boundaries and others may include more central or prototypical members."[30] Eleanor Rosch's research has confirmed Wittgenstein's theory of family resemblances.[31] For instance, *red* has fuzzy boundaries but central members are 1 on a 0-1 scale, while *bird* has sharp boundaries but some members are more prototypical.[32]

What of embodied artificial intelligence as with Cog, which allows for development of some body schemas and perceptual imaging? Anne Foerst has suggested that such a project attempts to collapse the differences between computational and biological models by

25. Edelman, *Bright Air*, 69. See also Damasio, *Descartes' Error*, 260.

26. Fodor, *Language*.

27. Edelman, *Bright Air*, 228–29.

28. Edelman, *Remembered Present*, 28; *Bright Air*, 99.

29. Edelman, *Bright Air*, 234, 239.

30. Ibid., 235.

31. Wittgenstein, *Philosophical Investigations*, 67, 77, 108, 164, 179.

32. Rosch, *Cognition*.

constructing a robot with "a body that is as humanlike as possible."[33] Commendably the Cog website issues this caveat: "Since we can build only a very crude approximation to a human body," there is the potential "danger that the essential aspects of the human body will be totally missed."[34] The fact that Cog lacks a flexible spine permitting "analogue" movement as well as legs enabling movement of the whole body through space may be quite significant. Thus, we must recognize not only the complexity of the computational "brain/nerves" part of a human or animal, but also of the motile body in organic connection, for gauging how complex a robot must become to approximate human or animal conscious functioning. In comparison to animals and humans, any artificial intelligence may well remain a relatively formal and closed system of symbols and rules.

Speaking of organicity, a first crucial point in distinguishing an embodied-biological model is precisely that human beings are living organisms—breathing, motile, eating, sexual organisms, not primarily knowers or information processors. As suggested above, an embodied-biological model differs from functional or computational models due to the intrinsic values of a self-organizing system. Organisms do not just process information; they specifically process information according to biological values. To refer to the above-mentioned "for-itselfness" or proto-subjectivity of any reality, biological systems take this to a new level with their emergent properties. Ursula Goodenough and Terrence W. Deacon speak of biological systems in terms of "third-order emergence": "genetic and epigenetic instructions place constraints on second-order systems and thereby specify particular outcomes called biological traits."[35] That we refer to an organism as *self*-organizing points to an integrity or integration, a for-itselfness, which allows us to recognize its values. As Goodenough and Deacon put it: "third-order emergence defines the onset of telos on this planet and, for all we know, in the universe. Creatures have a purpose, and their traits are for that purpose."[36] By contrast a strictly computational model cannot recognize the inherent values of an organism, because the organism's symbolic or semiotic

33. Foerst, "Cog," 100.

34. MIT, "Overview."

35. Goodenough and Deacon, "From Biology," 820.

36. Ibid., 821.

activities must be reduced to uninterpreted and uninterpretable cause and effect.

This points to a key principle of biological systems and their emergent properties for which computational models fail to account: The whole is different—and more in terms of complexity—than the sum of its parts. That is, the self-organizing whole has new properties that the parts individually do not possess. This principle constitutes one reason I doubt that biological information is simulative on a Turing machine, for the latter's serial processing appears to reduce the whole to the "linear" sum of the parts, to the neglect of global properties. I would note that no scientist today claims a literal linearity in biological systems. But in recognizing global properties, I reject the minimalizing position of John Holland that the emergence of complexity is reducible to nonlinear "computational relations between localizable elements and agents in their immediate environments."[37] Instead I posit a thorough correlative relationship of the parts working on the whole and the whole working on the parts in a manner that allows for global properties. That the *whole* possesses properties greater than the sum of the parts will play a crucial role in the remainder of this chapter.

The second crucial point is that human beings, along with many animals, are *conscious* living organisms. I take consciousness itself to be an emergent property of some self-organizing biological systems. It is no supernatural ghost but is an integrated property, new and different in comparison to the individual properties of its component processes, far more than just a linear sum of these components. One analogy I offer for the plausibility of this interpretation is the difference in the make-up of the atoms of adjacent elements in the periodic table: adding one proton and one electron results in tremendous change in the physical properties of an element, rather than in the augmentation of previous properties in some linear or near-linear fashion. In a related generalizing vein, Ian Barbour remarks how the energy configurations, including wave functions, of atoms constitute a whole that is much different from those of its constituent parts when acting independently; similarly on the next level, the energy patterns of a crystal formation differ markedly from those of its constituent atoms when separated.[38] While allowing

37. Gregersen, "Levels of Complexity."
38. Barbour, *When Science Meets*, 81–82.

for the novelty of consciousness to emerge, my biological-embodied model also offers continuity between non-conscious and conscious organisms. Consciousness is the becoming aware of values or interests, such as nourishment and hydration, which non-conscious organisms possess. Indeed, the reason we intuitively recognize the purposes of non-conscious organisms is because we consciously experience them in ourselves.

Values

Speaking of values, a tremendous difference or cluster of differences between embodied models of biological consciousness and functional-ist models has to do precisely with *values*. Both Edelman and Damasio envision a central role for values as manifested in emotions and feel-ings, in the evolutionary emergence of consciousness. Damasio is espe-cially captured by feelings, with all three of his book titles advertising "emotion" or "feeling." With respect to the correlation between body states and the world, both Damasio and Edelman are well aware of the animal or human's desire to experience pleasurable feelings and avoid unpleasant ones—the hedonistic element, as Edelman puts it. Embodied-biological creatures obviously enjoy an assortment of values or pleasures—gustatory, olfactory, tactile, kinesthetic, auditory, visual, sexual, etc. However, embodied biological values are not limited to these fairly obvious states relating to hunger, thirst, sex, perceptual or kines-thetic beauty, or to avoidance of danger. Another type recognized by Edelman and Damasio is (more or less) homoeostatic biological value. Both emphasize that most homoeostatic bodily functioning—as well as most brain functioning—is inaccessible to consciousness. (This is a very different version of the unconscious or subconscious than Freud's discovery of repression.[39]) Homoeostatic awareness does not have the same precision as perception. Nevertheless, while a significant portion of visceral input occurs in non-mapped brain structures, "plenty of vis-ceral input is mapped well enough for us to detect pain or discomfort in identifiable areas of the" body. Additionally, "input from muscles and joints . . . ends up in topographically mapped structures,"[40] while rela-

39. Damasio, *Descartes' Error*, 106–8, 187–89; *Feeling*, 297ff.; Edelman, *Remembered Present*, 101, 194ff.; *Wider Than the Sky*, 87ff.

40. Damasio, *Descartes' Error*, 151.

tively stable maps of general body structure provide "the basis for our notion of body image."[41]

Indeed, despite their relative imprecision compared to sense perception, such *background feelings* of our body states constitute for Damasio the key to the core consciousness of animals and humans, as broached in chapter 3.[42] Core consciousness is the nonverbal sense of self that at least all mammals possess (which Damasio distinguishes from the self-consciousness that humans attain through language—Edelman uses the parallel terms "primary" and "higher-order" consciousness). Here Damasio separates such background feelings from stronger emotional states, from the primary and social emotions. While we do not normally focus on these background feelings, their absence strikingly suggests their crucial nature. In working with anosognosiac patients, as noted in chapter 3, Damasio has observed persons unable to experience background feelings, thus unable to sense their current body state.[43] While their retention of linguistic ability allows them an outdated understanding of their identity, they report irrationally on current motor defects and they evidence inappropriate affect about the state of their health. As Damasio suggests, these patients' self, unable to plot current body signals on the ground reference of the body, is no longer integral.[44] Such a person is incapable of minding the body.

With respect to the positive effects of their presence, Damasio theorizes that these background feelings contribute to consciousness in their role as "primordial representations of the body" which "provide a core for the neural representation of self"[45]; indeed they cut to "the very core of your representation of self."[46] Moreover, adds Damasio, background feelings frame the very feeling of being alive, "the feeling of life itself, the sense of being."[47] Regarding the brain in a vat thought experiment, Damasio urges that such literal disembodiment "would re-

41. Ibid., 152.
42. Damasio, *Descartes' Error*, 150ff.; see also, *Feeling*, 285–87.
43. Damasio, *Descartes' Error*, 62ff.
44. Ibid., 154–55.
45. Ibid., 235ff; see also, *Feeling*, 37, 110, 285–87.
46. Damasio, *Descartes' Error*, 151; see also, 237.
47. Ibid., 150.

sult in suspending the triggering and modulation of body states that . . .
constitute . . . the bedrock of the sense of being alive."[48]

Shaun Gallagher condemns functionalists, and even some non-
functionalists like John Searle, for Cartesian disembodiment precisely
in their acceptance of brain-in-a-vat consciousness as equivalent to
the real thing.[49] Nevertheless, he appears to fall into a related Cartesian
dualistic trap, when he rejects Damasio's notion of homoeostatic/back-
ground feelings as neural representation of the self. Instead, Gallagher
posits a clear distinction between "body image," as involving conscious
representations, and "body schema" as "a system of sensory-motor ca-
pacities that function without awareness or the necessity of perceptual
monitoring."[50] Indeed, Gallagher goes on to assert that "posture and
the majority of bodily movements operate in most cases without the
help of bodily awareness."[51] However, sometimes I become aware of a
part of my body that begins to hurt or become fully conscious of the
motions of my body in walking, which hitherto I had performed on
"automatic pilot." I do that seamlessly, without a start, without the need
to reorient myself—at least when I function normally as an embodied
being. That fact seems to me to suggest that Damasio's model, which
gives full due to background, marginal, subliminal, or tacit feeling and
awareness, comes closer to reflecting reality than Gallagher's. I find be-
side the point Gallagher's citation of persons with intact "body image"
but with significant gaps in their "body schema," which for example
may result in a person failing to comb the hair on the left side of the
head.[52] The assumption under Damasio's model that this person would
have subliminal awareness of the feelings of the head does not compel
Gallagher's conclusion about this type of neurological damage: namely,
that the person must use such awareness, if existent, in more conscious
acts of attending to the appearance of that part of the body (acts in
which the relevant parts of the body become an external object to the
person, relatively speaking). Gallagher is correct that we have no consciousness or awareness of much that happens physiologically within

48. Ibid., 228.
49. Gallagher, *How the Body Shapes*, 134–35.
50. Ibid., 24ff. See also, 135.
51. Ibid., 28.
52. Ibid., 24–25.

our bodies.[53] But then neither Damasio, Edelman, nor I dispute that. That being said, Polanyi probably overstates the case when he ventures "to extend the scope of tacit knowing to include neural traces in the cortex of the nervous system."[54]

I would add to Damaio's model—or at least more clearly state— that our normal sense of being alive includes not only feelings of our body states but also the sense of being oriented to the world. Apart from the particular goods we realize and harms we try to dodge, our normal bodily orientation to the world of itself involves positive feeling and value.

Furthermore, I would challenge Edelman in particular for undue circumspection regarding the scope of feeling and realization of value in the world. Edelman emphasizes that only mammals—and probably reptiles when warm enough—are conscious.[55] While it is probably best to use the term consciousness in the ways Edelman and Damasio do, the issue of whether animals without a central nervous system have feelings remains a very open scientific question. My hunch is that some degree of sentience or feeling reaches way down in the animal kingdom. Evidence exists that neurons evolved from protozoans—one-celled aquatic navigators —which both oriented themselves to the flow of their environment and attempted to realize particular goods.[56] While process notions that every cell (and indeed every integrated unit of reality) has feeling is speculative in the idealist tradition, that neurons or configuration of neurons in lower species possesses some sentience is not at all far-fetched.

I will conclude this section on homoeostatic values and body state feelings with a comparison to computer models: While some computers can now be programmed to "prefer" continuation of their power supply, continuous monitoring of the state of their machinery or hardware—let alone subjective feel of said machinery—is alien to computer models, even connectionist/PDP or "selectional" ones. The Cog website for its part notes that "a robot must have some notion of energy consumption

53. Ibid., 29.
54. Polanyi, *Tacit Dimension*, 15.
55. Edelman, *Bright Air*, 123.
56. Hunt, *Nature of Consciousness*, 96–106.

to successfully create humanoid movement."[57] "Meso: A Biochemical Subsystem," though, is only in the idea stage at present. Furthermore, whether an embodied artificial intelligence can move from simple kinesthetic monitoring to the complex and continuous monitoring of states of the human body—which seems requisite for consciousness—is questionable. Plus, subjectivity itself remains at issue, as the just-mentioned continuous monitoring is necessary but may not be sufficient.

Damasio's negative comments on the possibility of a conscious artifact further convey the difference between a functionalist computational model and the intrinsic values inherent to self-organizing subjectivity in a biological model:

> (T)he artifact's internal states may even mimic some of the neural and mental designs I propose here as a basis for consciousness. They would have a way of generating second-order knowledge, but without the help of the nonverbal vocabulary of feeling, the knowledge would not be expressed in the manner we encounter in humans and is probably present in so many living species. Feeling is, in effect, the barrier, because the realization of human consciousness may require the existence of feelings. The "looks" of emotion can be simulated, but what feelings feel like cannot be duplicated in silicon. Feelings cannot be duplicated unless flesh is duplicated, unless the brain's actions on flesh are duplicated, unless the brain's sensing of flesh after it has been acted upon by the brain is duplicated.[58]

The Nature of Consciousness

At this point I want to address directly the issue of explaining or making sense of the nature of consciousness, first scientifically and then metaphysically or theologically. Peterson charges that Edelman and Damasio do not make much progress in advancing a scientific explanation. He refers to the (ultimate?) nature of consciousness as "the hard question." According to Peterson, in developing their theory of the bodily scene as central to consciousness, Edelman and Damasio have addressed only "the easy problem." That is, "(h)aving explained the possible neurological basis for the scene, consciousness is said to be explained as well."[59] In

57. Adams, "Meso."

58. Damasio, *Feeling*, 314–15.

59. Peterson, *Minding God*, 54.

a related vein, Peterson notes that not all biological "representations and self-representations are conscious." Edelman and Damasio's theories fail to clarify "why we should expect representational or self-knowledge states to give rise to the subjective character of consciousness at all."[60] Peterson attributes this alleged avoidance of the hard question to the simple fact that current neuroscience lacks the means to treat it.[61] In fact, Edelman and Damasio do get specific about the benefits for survival and flourishing of *conscious* representation and self-representation that surpass those of unconscious representation: Consciousness allows for continual monitoring amplified by attention and interest, thus lending salience to select stimuli.[62] Damasio adds that consciousness allows a greater capacity to manipulate images or representations.[63] Edelman notes how higher order consciousness allows for modeling the world, planning, and comparing outcomes free of real time.[64] Hunt counts himself among a number of psychologists who regard consciousness as an adaptive "capacity involving the direction, choice, and synthesis of nonconscious processes."[65] Damasio for his part also offers a very empirical argument for consciousness' utility through observing the consequences of its absence in diseased patients: even its temporary suspension results in "inefficient management of life"[66] for persons suffering from epileptic automisms,[67] akinetic mutism,[68] or advanced stages of Alzheimer's disease.[69] For example, in epileptic automism, the person engages in complex behavior, such as drinking from a glass, or a sequence of complex behaviors that involve wakefulness and manipulation of perceptions and motor images—but no consciousness. What is lacking is motivated emotion, an "identifiable person with a past and

60. Ibid., 66.

61. Ibid., 54.

62. Edelman, *Remembered Present*, 92ff.; Damasio, *Descartes' Error*, 229ff.; *Feelings*, 124–26, 168ff.

63. Damasio, *Descartes' Error*, 261; *Feelings*, 24, 124–25.

64. Edelman, *Remembered Present*, 92.

65. Hunt, *Nature of Consciousness*, 26.

66. Damasio, *Looking for Spinoza*, 207.

67. Damasio, *Feeling*, 96ff.

68. Ibid., 101ff.

69. Ibid., 103ff.

an anticipated future." There is no "core self," no core consciousness.[70] Thus according to Damasio, background feelings and the core sense of self that arises from them serve powerfully to bring coherence to our behavior. To perhaps belabor the obvious here, where unconscious representations continue in these diseased states, something substantive is lost along with consciousness. Consciousness evolves from a certain type of integration, but once emergent it constitutes an integration bringing further integrative effects.

In maintaining that consciousness does have biological utility, Damasio and Edelman would seem to oppose a physicalist reductionism where consciousness is an epiphenomenon of the neural substrate, which alone has utility. At this point we need to delineate possible relationships between the neural substrate of the brain (and the body) and consciousness. To do so, I will tweak some of the language often associated with emergence. "Weak emergence" will refer to consciousness as an emergent property without any causal effectiveness. That is to say that only the neural substrate or correlate—quite apart from the qualia of consciousness—exercises any causal function or effectiveness. Consciousness, so to speak, just comes along for the ride and has at least no utilitarian function or value. Interestingly enough, despite earlier work cited above on biological utility, Edelman appears to default to this position in his latest book, *Wider Than the Sky*, assuming it represents the only view compatible with the closed system of cause and effect to which he subscribes. Edelman's official position therein is that consciousness (C) is a simultaneous, entailed property of neural activity involving high-order discriminations (C'). Technically C' does not cause C, while C' is the only aspect of the brain that exercises causality.[71] C as a mental element that "reflects a relationship" "cannot exert a physical force."[72] Thus consciousness is not "causal," not "efficacious."[73]

I will refer to the next option as "closed strong emergence." It views consciousness as an emergent property with tangible causal effects, but with its causal effects in every way inseparable from (though not reducible to) its component parts. That is to say that the total causal effects

70. Ibid., 98ff.
71. Edelman, *Wider Than the Sky*, esp. 76ff.
72. Ibid., 78.
73. Ibid., 3, 78, 116.

of the parts and the emergent whole comprise a package. *If* the causal properties of the parts could be isolated and engaged apart from causal properties of the emergent whole, they would be less complex and less efficacious. However, on this view they cannot. Therefore, as a closed system, each state of consciousness and neural substrate in conjunction with the environment determines the subsequent state. This I take to be the view of Jaegwon Kim.[74] Based on the following contortions of *Wider Than the Sky*, I also judge this as the option actually most compatible with the trajectory of Edelman's thinking: Edelman expounds that C' necessarily entails C, so that the "Zombie hypothesis" is untenable— that is, no non-conscious humanoid could perform all the functions of a conscious human.[75] However, given Edelman's metaphysical assumptions, about which I will write more below, apparently no scientific answer exists as to why C' states entail C states (just as there is none as to why green looks green or why something rather than nothing exists). That is, the laws of nature happen to be such that C states constitute an attendant property of C' states, but as far as science is concerned they could have been otherwise. Furthermore, one seemingly could imagine a possible universe where causally effective C' states occur without any C states—a Zombie universe with somewhat different physical laws than our own. One could then at the same time imagine that in Zombie universe, C' states provide continual monitoring and salience with respect to attention and interest sans consciousness. Except . . . Edelman goes on to "speculate" on the evolutionary adaptive advantages of "the relationship of entailment between C' and C": C states communicate information about C' states to the individual animal and to others which would not happen otherwise.[76] Edelman's speculation implies that C' states without consciousness could not in any possible universe have the same causative effects as such states with consciousness. So the adaptive utility is part of the package a la Kim's closed emergence.

I will push the envelope and endorse a third option (one that Damasio at least does not rule out): open strong emergence. Here consciousness as emergent property exercises a measure of independent causal effectiveness, the power of some indeterminate free will.

74. Kim, *Supervenience*.
75. Edelman, *Wider Than the Sky*, 80, 145–46.
76. Ibid., 76ff., 81.

Of course, consciousness always depends on its component neural correlates for its very existence. On this model, however, a given neural substrate and its attendant consciousness may be compatible with more than one subsequent state, with the emergent property of consciousness tipping the balance, a case of "top-down" causation. Some interpret the results of Benjamin Libet's well-known experiments to gainsay the possibility of free will: the "readiness potential" of subjects arbitrarily to move a finger precedes seemingly spontaneous action by one-half second or more. However, Libet also discovered that humans do have the power to consciously veto the brain's signal of readiness potential. Moreover, a readiness potential for the veto itself does not precede that decision. Nor, as Glenn Statile notes, does the decision of a major-league batter to swing on a certain plane involve such a readiness potential—and that choice occurs in one-sixth of a second or less. Finally, the complexity of actual human deciding and acting calls into question the relevance to the issue of free will of readiness potential for non-contextual simple motor movements: morally relevant and other more complex (series of) actions involve contexts and time durations radically different from Libet's situations.[77] In addition to citing Libet's experiments, Daniel Wegner argues the illusionary nature of free will by compiling examples where humans mistake what or who controls our actions, such as hypnosis or feelings of automatism as in consulting a Ouija board.[78] Here, though, we have a case where the abnormal or even pathological becomes the standard for judging what happens in normal functioning, even as we will see below regarding our sense of self in Thomas Metzinger's thought.

Physical reductionistic models of consciousness oppose radical embodiment from the objectivist-empiricist side of Cartesian dualism. (Note that scholars may ply both this side and the idealist computational side in different aspects of their thought.) Technically such a reductionist rejects the very idea of emergence. However, a weak emergentist who disclaims any value to consciousness—even the serendipitous or coincidental value of subjectivity coming along for the ride—falls into the same camp. Consciousness here loses its integral connection to our bodily engagement with our natural and social worlds. Instead,

---

77. Statile, "Libet's Loophole." See also, Gallagher, *How the Body Shapes*, 237–39.

78. Wegner, *Illusion*.

consciousness becomes an epiphenomenon or illusion. Patently this model alienates us from our bodies and our embodiment in the world. Natural selection implicitly or explicitly becomes an external programmer that tricks us, while the putative program is the genome. Steven Pinker spells it out: "The mind is a system of organs of computation, designed by natural selection to solve the kinds of problems our ancestors faced in their foraging way of life, in particular, understanding and outmaneuvering objects, animals, plants, and other people"—and nothing but that.[79] (Also notice how the individual-competitive receives emphasis over the social-cooperative dimension here.) All that matters is survival. What is real is the functioning that optimizes chances of survival. Values or feelings that the animal experiences are epiphenomena, not real like the correlative physical process (dualistically separated from subjective experience). As it were, natural selection and the reductively physical fool the animal into cooperating with biological process conducive to survival through illusory values or pleasures. Note how in this model the external environment totally specifies or determines the organism; this model misses the mutual specification or partial self-determination by the conscious organism according to its intrinsic values. Various commentators have spotted an incongruity in the hypothesis of consciousness as epiphenomenal: despite its illusory character nature has selected consciousness. In my and Damasio's judgment the "communication" that is consciousness, "the very feeling of you—as an individual being involved in the process of knowing of your own existence and the existence of others,"[80] has obvious consequences and effects. It must be causal or efficacious in some sense (at least in the mode of closed strong emergence)—or it would fail to be adaptive. To play on words, embodied consciousness *functions* in a sense transcending the usual functionalism: It makes a difference in the world that a non-causal epiphenomenon, fiction, or illusion cannot. Speaking for much of the Artificial Intelligence community, two of Cog's builders, Brooks and Stein, declare "that phenomena such as consciousness are illusory."[81] Damasio's neurological research appears to belie such a reductionistic claim.

79. Pinker, *How Mind Works*, 21.
80. Damasio, *Feeling*, 127.
81. Foerst, "Cog," 104.

Related to the epiphenomenal question is the degree of integration or lack thereof in consciousness, whether the common-sense view of an integrated self is itself an illusion. Rodney Brooks, chief architect of Cog, portrays a connectionist robot as the model for animal consciousness: "Out of the local chaos of" the "interactions" of the activities of the various "layers," "in the eye of the observers, a coherent pattern of behavior emerges"—but only in the eyes of the observers, not in any animal or human self.[82] Varela and company, committed to a Buddhist metaphysics of no-self (anatman), likewise take the notion of an integrated self to be illusion. From cases of psychopathology, including schizophrenics who look at themselves in the mirror and exclaim, "I do not exist," Metzinger argues that we humans superimpose a sense of (a non-existent) self.[83]

Against the above claims, I argue for the reality of a conscious integrated self from the perspective of radical embodiment. Clearly I do not support a unitary self—which would be the type of self we might expect if the mind were a central processing Turing machine. Rather I contend that connectionist biological consciousness is sufficiently integrated to warrant speaking of a self. Though of course it does not decide the issue, I would first of all point to the very term "self-organizing" systems. We intuitively assume a sufficient degree of integration that we use the term "self" for non-conscious biological and even non-biological natural systems. Furthermore, those who think of natural selection as fooling consciousness assume an integrated biological organism with interests (like eating and reproduction) served by such trickery. Even those who carry out the logic of epiphenomenalism to its conclusion—that there is nothing even to be tricked—cannot, and to my knowledge do not, deny that biological organisms possess the integration of homeostatic and metabolic interests. Finally, as much of Damasio's research has involved brain-damaged subjects, I judge his interpretative approach to be more fruitful than Metzinger's: rather than taking pathology as indicative of the true nature of normal states, Damasio uses pathological cases to ascertain what they lack in comparison to our normal consciousness of self, as we have seen above.

---

82. Brooks, "Intelligence," quoted in Varela et al., *Embodied Mind*.
83. Metzinger, *Being No One*; Apple, "Mind as Representational."

Related to the question of the reality/efficaciousness/value of consciousness versus its illusionary/epiphenomenal nature is the issue of whether first-person knowing entails any substantive difference from third-person knowledge. Michael Polanyi's concept of tacit knowledge helps in fathoming why reductionist "solutions" to the first person-third person problem prove misguided, as well as why we humans so readily come up with discarnate models of human nature, whether functionalist, computationalist, linguistic constructivist, or reductive physicalist. As highlighted in earlier chapters, Polanyi argues that most of our knowing is tacit. First-person knowing always involves subsidiary or tacit elements, in the first instance elements of our body in interaction with the world, which we subconsciously rely upon as we *focus* upon a particular meaning or goal.[84] Recall the example of a blind person walking with a cane. When a person first learns to walk like that, one attends to the tactile sensations of one's hand. But soon one's focal awareness turns to navigating one's world; the hand's sensations have become tacit. Whether we talk of our "original" bodies or the extensions of our bodies represented in tools and language, we indwell the bodily meaning of our perceptions and movements, our speech, and our subconscious and perhaps some unconscious brain processes, even as we attend to our world.

By way of contrast Paul Churchland represents the reductionist dismissal of first-person subjectivity. He takes on those like philosopher Thomas Nagel who claim that a full understanding of consciousness involves knowing what it is like to be a certain animal. For example, Nagel claims that a full third-person account of bat neurophysiology cannot tell us what it is like to navigate by echolocation, and that an expert neuroscientist completely color-blind cannot know the experience of red.[85] According to Churchland such assertions of something more or different for first-person versus third-person knowledge confuse knowledge

---

84. Whether all such tacit elements can in principle (though not practically) be made explicit is debatable (for example, see Zhenhua, "Tacit Knowledge: Wittgensteinian Approach," "Tacit Knowledge: Knowing"), though I alleged in chapter 1 and argued in chapter 4 that our radical embodiment means they cannot. But even if they can, the key point here is that third-person knowledge, by making focal or explicitizing the tacit, changes its very meaning.

85. Peterson, *Minding God*, 58–59.

with perspective, thus committing a category error.[86] So for Churchland the external observer with full knowledge of the functioning of an organism's brain would possess all the knowledge that the organism possesses. From a Polanyian perspective, though, the reductionist commits the category error. The error results from failure to notice that third-person knowledge makes focal or explicit what is tacit for the organism, thereby changing its meaning, its very character. An everyday example occurs when one focuses on the sound of a word by repeating it: the word becomes strange to our ears as its contextual meaning evaporates. In this manner "(s)ubsidiary awareness and focal awareness are mutually exclusive."[87] Damasio concurs that ever-accumulating third-person knowledge will not "be helpful at all to experience the world" as I myself do.[88] Edelman avers that first-person experience is not "completely negotiable" by any third-person account.[89]

Therefore, contra Churchland first-person knowledge is *not* the same knowledge as third-person, only from a different perspective. Once again reductionism fails to see that the whole is more or different than the sum of the parts. We might say that in purportedly explicitizing tacit knowledge, reductionism linearizes or sequentializes the global meanings inherent in self-organizing systems, in this case the holistic meanings inherent in embodied-biological consciousness. A thought experiment by Edelman provides backing for a Polanyian perspective: Imagine a homunculoid inside a person's brain who comprehends all the representational activities of its neural substrate. Edelman concludes that because the homunculoid "does not have the animal's body," it "cannot fully recapture the content of that privacy"[90]—in Polanyi's language the homunculoid cannot indwell that body. David Gelernter, sharing many of the theories about consciousness of Damasio and Edelman, develops his opinion that no artificial intelligence will likely achieve consciousness. Sympathetic to Searle's "Chinese Language Room" thought experiment, he nevertheless finds it more complicated and round-about

86. Churchland, *Engine of Reason*, 195–208.

87. Polanyi, *Personal Knowledge*, 56.

88. Damasio, *Feeling*, 305–6.

89. Edelman, *Wider Than the Sky*, 63, 74–75.

90. Ibid., 74–75.

than necessary.[91] Instead he asks the question, "*What is it like to be a computer running a complex AI program?*" He answers, exactly like a computer running any other program. The computer keeps executing digital commands (0 or 1) until the program ends. He finds it absurdly unlikely that doing such low-level operations at a certain rapid speed will itself yield subjectivity or that accumulating a critical mass of software elements will do the same. Rather, for perspectival consciousness to emerge as a property requires the chemistry and physics of neurons in a body.

For the embodied-biological model, perspective is indispensable and inalienable: we always know from some particular, embodied perspective. Values or pleasure always achieve realization in the first-person (or "first-animal" for creatures with only "primary" [Edelman] or "core" [Damasio] consciousness rather than "higher order" or "self" consciousness), in the subjective, in the intentional, in the body—never in the third-person, the general, the disembodied. That value or meaning is intrinsic, inherent to our embodied being in the world, forms the crucial difference for Edelman and Damasio. As argued in chapter 3 language, key to human higher order consciousness, is not a preprogrammed syntax arbitrarily paired with intrinsically meaningless signs; rather "symbolic structures are meaningful to begin with,"[92] since they arise from our bodily structure, orientation, and values. Embodiment and the inherent meaningfulness of embodied existence make all the difference in the world.

This bears profound implications for our knowing other embodied animals. The Cog website stipulates that a humanoid robot must "attribute beliefs, goals, and desires to other individuals" and notes that recognizing such intentions as different from one's own is instrumental in a child's self-recognition.[93] Yet if Cog or a descendent fails to realize core subjective consciousness—which I do not foresee for such non-biological intelligence, it will not recognize subjectivity in others and its capacity to attribute distinct embodied perspectives will be minimal at best.

91. Gelernter, "Artificial Intelligence." (See n. 47, Chapter 3, for a description of the Chinese Language Room thought experiment.)

92. Edelman, *Bright Air*, 239.

93. Scarsellati, "Theory of Mind."

If reductionistic functionalist accounts refer directly to the body at all, it is the body in the abstract, in the third-person, the body as a configuration of matter and energy that nature blindly programs to survive. It is not your, my, or their valuing, smelling, burping, laughing, crying, walking, or dancing body. Such functionalist models entail a fundamental alienation and absconding from one's body, from one's own embodied existence in the world. In these models the body at best hides in the background. This sharply contrasts with an embodied-biological model where background feelings of our body states figure crucially for consciousness itself. Thus functionalist models are finally discarnate. It is no coincidence that physicalist reductionistic models typically complement discarnate idealistic computational models.

Metaphysical and Theological Ruminations

Given that Damasio and Edelman's work centers on the nature of consciousness, with consciousness understood as inherently meaningful, it is not surprising to discover theological and metaphysical implications. But we need clarity on where science ends and the trans-scientific begins. While we have seen above that, contrary to Peterson's contention, Damasio and Edelman do offer scientific explanations, they both indicate that the hard question, the issue of the ultimate nature of consciousness, in principle transcends the purview of science. Edelman characterizes the situation this way: Attempting a supposedly scientific explanation of "qualia," the subjective feel of experience, "is as speculative as a scientific explanation of why matter exists. As scientists we can have no concern with ontological mysteries concerned with *why* warm feels 'warm.'"[94] Damasio too speaks of "mystery"[95] and voices skepticism about "solving *the* consciousness problem."[96] Thus, both believe that science can establish the biological feasibility and utility of consciousness, not its ultimate nature or purpose.[97] A corollary would follow: why the laws of nature permit consciousness, rather than disallow it, is a theological or metaphysical rather than scientific question.

---

94. Edelman, *Remembered Present*, 167–68; see also 138–39.
95. Damasio, *Feeling*, 12, 26ff.
96. Ibid., 26.
97. Damasio, *Descartes' Error*, 125–26.

The stage is set then for constructive ramifications of an embodied-biological model beyond the scientific. Before my own ruminations I will note Damasio's intimations regarding such ramifications: In describing consciousness as the feeling of what happens when we perceive or make any image, he goes on to declare that "consciousness was invented so that we could know life." Damasio acknowledges that his "wording is not scientifically correct, but I like it."[98] In discussing the evolution of emotions, he opines "it is as if nature decided that life was both very precious and very precarious."[99] So Damasio senses some purpose behind the evolution of consciousness.

Now for my turn. As just above a universe inconducive to any consciousness or sentience is theoretically conceivable. Indeed, developers of the anthropic principle have delineated many conceivable universes inhospitable to any life. Given that some representational states are unconscious, we may imagine a world with forms of animal life devoid of any consciousness. So what are we to make of the fact that our universe has been conducive to the evolution of embodied minds? While from a physicalist viewpoint any evolutionary utility for consciousness may degrade its possible metaphysical value, I view it conversely. That the universe is such that consciousness exists and enhances the chances of biological survival and flourishing constitutes evidence of a teleological character for a purposive universe and a purposive ultimate source of that universe. Whether one believes in a personal creator of the universe as I do or in a transpersonal source such as the over-arching cosmic order of T'ien in Confucianism or the "Way" of Taoism, probably most religious and philosophical traditions have held that a purpose of the universe is for humans—and often other creatures—to experience value. Thus, consciousness or mind has had a place in the world, has "belonged" in the cosmos, for most religious and metaphysical traditions. For a biological model, though, not consciousness per se but embodied consciousness belongs. It is embodied consciousness that enhances the survival and flourishing of embodied beings. Thus, an embodied-biological model coheres with an incarnational theology or metaphysics. Incarnational existence is created as good by God or "bodies forth" through meaningful ordering by a transpersonal ultimate.

98. Damasio, Feeling, 31.

99. Damasio, Looking for Spinoza, 30.

Another angle supporting the purposiveness of embodied consciousness from the perspective of the universe and/or its ultimate source is the *surplus* of meaning or value. That is, animals and humans enjoy values—particularly aesthetic values and in the human case intellectual values—extraneous or serendipitous in terms of biological survival. Perhaps such values that transcend immediate survival issues related to recognition of sustenance or of danger or to sexual reproduction still have a less direct biological utility: the more values and interests an animal finds, the more incentive it has to live, to want to survive. Recent work on the emotion of wonder ties in to this notion of the value of interest and fascination that goes beyond satisfying immediate needs.[100] To whatever extent that increased chances of survival pertain and this argument from serendipity loses force, the argument for the purposive nature of the universe if consciousness of values is adaptive, correspondingly gains strength. Of course, one could also regard the surplus value as attendant side effects of a complex brain (and body). Yet that the universe allows such complexity itself carries teleological implications.

I have stated that biological values indisputably exist. We have been discussing the larger issue of whether they exist on purpose relative to the universe and its possible source. I would note that the question of the whole in relation to its parts figures crucially here. From a Polanyian perspective, if one just focuses on the parts of the universe more or less in isolation—as reductionistic approaches do, one will necessarily miss any holistic meaning. To grasp any overall meaning to the universe entails focusing on a wider meaning to which the parts only subsidarily testify, for which they serve as clues. One must then have a kind of faith or intuition through which one indwells the wider meaning in order to see it.

Functionalist models of consciousness reinscribe the mind-body/matter dualism expounded by Descartes. As they focus on computer models of information processing, they ply the "mind" side: a discarnate mind utilizing neutral, indeed value-free, reason. An extreme manifestation of this attitude comes in the hope of immortality through downloading human information and presumably human consciousness onto

---

100. Fuller, "Spirituality in the Flesh"; "Wonder."

machines, as religious belief meets science fiction.[101] Robert Geraci, in an issue of the *Journal of the American Academy of Religion*, expounds the thought of two contemporary gurus of "apocalyptic Artificial Intelligence," who see better, more machine-like human bodies (or cyborgs) as a way station to becoming "disembodied superminds"[102] or *"software, not hardware"*[103] (emphasis original). Mary Midgley astutely cites a seminal figure in this line of thought:

> The advantage of containing no organic material at all ... would be increasingly felt. . . . *Bodies at this time would be left far behind*. . . . Bit by bit the heritage of the direct line of mankind—the heritage of the original life emerging on the face of the world— would dwindle, and in the end disappear effectively, being preserved perhaps as some curious relic. (Emphasis hers).[104]

On the other hand, to the extent functionalist models of consciousness reflect a reductionistic model of biological utility, they ply the "matter" side in strict materialist or physicalist fashion: mere matter is the only "objective" reality, so consciousness, feelings, and values become only epiphenomena. Again Polanyi's notion of tacit knowledge helps us understand why some models of consciousness go astray. Given the usually *tacit* bodily nature of all we do, know, and think, it becomes easy to forget or ignore our inalienable bodily indwelling in favor of discarnate models that deny our lived and lively phenomenal bodies. Anne Foerst proposes that, in good postmodern fashion (albeit rather dualistically opposing objectivity with symbolic/performative/ existential truth), we can accept diverse stories about human nature, including both the assumptions of the machine-like nature of consciousness by the Artificial Intelligence community as well as theological intuitions of deep value to human life.[105] But how can one accept two stories if they outright contradict each other at crucial points— indeed when they diverge on whether animal and human experience has value? Reductionistic assumptions that consciousness/subjectivity is illusionary, epiphenomenal, and without intrinsic value run counter

101. Geraci, "Apocalyptic AI."

102. Moravec, "Letter from Moravec," 20; Geraci, "Apocalyptic AI," 154.

103. Kurzweil, *Age of Spiritual Machines*, 128–29; Geraci, "Apocalyptic AI," 154.

104. Midgley, "Soul's Successors," 65–66; Bernal, *World, Flesh, and Devil*, 56–57.

105. Foerst, "Cog," pp. 103ff.

to the scientific theories of Damasio, Edelman, and others, not to mention theological anthropologies permissible under their theories. If we are to achieve integration, it cannot come from attempting to bring together incommensurate stories. Rather integration must enter on the ground floor of animal and human nature and consciousness. Radical embodiment and its embodied-biological model offer a way to bypass discarnate and dualistic models of consciousness: Mind and body come intrinsically integrated, for certain animal and human bodies arrive together with embodied consciousness in the course of evolution. Thus, the experience of embodied values on the one hand and biological survival and flourishing on the other stand mutually implicated with and mutually integral to each other. Embodied minds belong in this world, and we earth beings can normally feel at home here.

6

The Postmodern Spirit and the Status of God

PRECEDING CHAPTERS HAVE TOUCHED ON THE NATURE OF DIVINITY. In this chapter I propose to focus on the status of the concept of God, particularly in Western theology, in light of the postmodern spirit. I will identify three pertinent options, arguing for the superiority of one of these. Before proceeding with that identification, I will rehearse three entailments of the postmodern spirit especially important for the purposes of this chapter:

1) Human knowledge is always mediated, contextual, and constructed (at least in part).

2) Humans and animals live in interconnection with one another and with the world. Persons never exist simply or absolutely distinct from one another and the environment; we are also a part of one another and our environment. Where self ends and other begins is not clear-cut but relative to context.

3) The body of course figures crucially in all our knowing and relating. For radical embodiment, body is not split from mind, nor is it reductively physical, but rather exists as correlative with consciousness. A person persists as a mindbodily continuum. "Mind," as awareness of and attempting to make sense of things, and "body," as that with which we have and relate to a world come radically interrelated and correlative, never simply distinguishable, and both come into play at some level in all our acts.

The Three Types

I find in contemporary Western theology three types of response that take seriously the postmodern spirit regarding the viability of the concept of God. In brief they are: 1) minimalist conceptions of God; 2) denial or virtual denial of the concept of God, the "death of God"; and 3) fairly traditional conceptions of God.

Given the wariness of the postmodern spirit about grand claims to knowledge, it comes as no surprise that some theologians offer minimalist conceptions of "God." One such thinker, a senior statesman on the theological scene, Gordon Kaufman, has moved from more traditional understandings of God. In his seminal work in theological minimalism, *In Face of Mystery*, Kaufman identifies God with "serendipitous creativity."[1] He opts against attributing to God personality, consciousness in any sense, intentionality, or agency.[2] This contrasts sharply with earlier work that characterizes divine creativity in terms of an overarching "act."[3] Kaufman even expresses an unwillingness to assign any actual transcendence to God, finding it sufficient to identify God with, or as wholly within, the cosmic process.[4] Some countervailing tendencies, though, crop up, where some transcendence attempts to enter through the back door, as when Kaufman speaks of God as "ground(ing),"[5] "underlying,"[6] "behind,"[7] "unifying,"[8] "expressing itself,"[9] or "working"[10] in and through all processes, all reality.[11] In this minimalist project Kaufman hopes to reconstruct the idea of God, so that

1. Kaufman, *In Face of Mystery*, esp. 264–80.

2. Ibid., 268–72, 329.

3. Kaufman, *Systematic Theology*, 50–56.

4. Kaufman, *In Face of Mystery*, 271–72. Officially transcendence is either unknowable—the ultimate mystery (415) or merely formal—"the (imagined) ultimate point of reference" (327).

5. Ibid., 296.

6. Ibid., 330.

7. Ibid., 297, 418.

8. Ibid., 418.

9. Ibid., 296, 417.

10. Ibid., 297, 330, 339, 415.

11. Kaufman's follow-up, *In the Beginning . . . Creativity*, further elaborates his idea of God as serendipitous creativity, but continues the dictum of its existing within the observable universe—with inklings of transcendence.

both theists and nontheists who find the universe conducive to life and its fulfillment can find common ground on an ultimate concept.

In a vein similar to Kaufman, Sallie McFague declares in *Models of God* that all Christianity claims "with any assurance" about ultimate reality is its supportiveness of life and its fulfillment. She parenthetically adds—claiming more than Kaufman—that this power is "personal,"[12] but without ever elaborating upon its meaning or significance. Anything beyond that reveals something about how human beings do or should understand themselves, their society, and their world, but reveals nothing more about God.

I should note that such minimalist conceptions of God do not break onto the current scene as a complete novelty. For example, in the 1940's Henry Nelson Wiemann developed a process perspective that equated God with the growth of value in the universe. Similarly, pragmatist John Dewey defined God as the process of human beings interacting with the larger environment, ever creating new values. I claimed in Chapter 1 that the shift from a modern to a postmodern age has been a gradual and ongoing one that began in the nineteenth century. If this contention bears some truth, it should not surprise us that minimalist conceptions are not brand new. Even some scholars writing as mainline Christian theologians in the 1940's and 1950's offered minimalist ideas of God similar to the above, namely, Bernard Loomer and Bernard Meland, like Wiemann from the University of Chicago. What appears as new today is that mainline Christian theologians with the renown and influence of Kaufman and McFague proffer such minimalist models.

The above kinds of minimalist conceptions of God have appeal in avoiding both modern absolutism and relativism (the latter again following from the failure to realize absolute knowledge and presence). They also resonate with the postmodern enjoinment to respect otherness, by granting that other religious—and secular—traditions accord with the most basic Christian or metaphysical claims. These conceptions do retain something of the basic Western notion of God; this concession, though, begs the crucial question of whether they retain enough of that meaning to qualify as a development of, rather than an alternative to, this God-concept.

12. McFague, *Models*, x.

Minimalists can point to the negative theological tradition and to a traditional idea that we can only know God in relation to us, but not in Godself. On the other hand, thinkers of the *via negativa*, in affirming the divine infinity, unity, and transcendence have claimed much more than the minimalists of today. Parenthetically, I do wonder whether McFague would spend so much time developing symbols for God, if she fully believed these tell us nothing about the nature of ultimate reality but only serve a socially useful purpose.

More traditional conceptions of God provide an explanation of the universe—regarding it as caused by a reality in some meaningful if symbolic sense "conscious," intentional, agential, and integrated—while minimalist conceptions attempt only or mainly to describe the universe. For those who find the universe amenable to some ultimate explanation, minimalist ideas will obviously fall short.

That the large majority of contemporary theistic believers would find minimalistic ideas to fall short of what they mean by "God," I advance as an uncontroversial assertion. (However, I might add that Jewish believers probably contain a significant proportion open to minimalist ideas, while mainline Protestant believers contain a significantly higher proportion than evangelicals.) However, the question of whether most future believers in the Christian and Western traditions will understand "God" in terms of "minimalist" conceptions awaits a verdict—and minimalist thinkers argue that in light of the postmodern spirit this constitutes precisely the direction in which modification of the concept of God should proceed.

I have indicated that minimalist ideas respect alterity in granting the truthfulness of basic claims of other religions and worldviews. However, the truthfulness granted represents that of a generalized and demythologized sort. More particular and traditional claims of other religions receive no acknowledgement from the least common denominator approach of minimalism, even as most of the particular or traditional claims of Christianity are jettisoned. Differences among other religions may not garner sufficient respect, even as Christianity's or Judaism's own particular claims—how they differ from other religions and each other—also may not. I sense that genuine dialogue will get short-circuited in a leap to a least common denominator.

The second type of response holds that the absence of any absolute possession of truth or of the self by humans entails the absence of any absolute reality. On the plane of logic, this "death of God" or radical position is in error, as indicated in Chapter 1. Granting the contextual relativity of all human existence and meaning does not rule out the possibility of an absolute being or reality. The absence of any absolute human connection to the Absolute does indeed follow from a consistent upholding of the contextual and mediated quality of all human knowing; but whether an absolute reality exists and can be known—relatively of course—does not at all follow from such contextuality.

In fairness to radical thinkers, they do not explicitly assert the logical entailment of the denial of absolute human meaning with the death of God. Rather God's reputed death is more an outgrowth of the spirit of this age. An underlying assumption prevails here: that God functions as a projection of human desires and values. Then as notions of human absoluteness gradually fade, so eventually fades away the affirmation of God.

Of course, like a vampire in a horror movie or, perhaps better, a revived Marvel Comics superhero, God does not die so easily. We have already noted the immanentist and pantheistic tendencies of radical postmodernism when it comes to divinity, especially in Chapter 1. Some radical postmodernists themselves have acknowledged that the concept of God, indeed in its transcendent dimension, continues to have a hold on them. In this regard we have encountered, particularly in Chapter 2, the difference, the alterity that refuses capture by any of our language, perceptions, or other constructions. To the extent radical thinkers recognize such possible notions of divinity, I detect some similarity with the minimalists: God or divinity persists within the world or as a (mysterious and penultimately transcendent) aspect of the universe. The radicals are slower in identifying the divine with a positive aspect of the universe, such as creativity or that which works for the fulfillment of life. And given that divinity either constitutes all that exists or that which defies any definition, we should expect just such reticence. However, when radicals celebrate an ideal of justice, which challenges all structures of dominance and oppression, we do obtain something positive, albeit through the back door, through radical postmodernism's own *via negativa*. This then provides some parallel to minimalism's uplifting of the divine as that which works for the fulfillment of all life.

We arrive now at the third type, those acknowledging the postmodern spirit, yet retaining a relatively traditional idea of God. However, before an initial positive description of that type, I will first say a word about the postliberals and then about process theology. As argued in earlier chapters, postliberals self-consciously claim imbuement with the postmodern spirit. However, I concluded that they utilize postmodern logic defensively, in order to hold on to an absolutistic notion of revelation not in keeping with that postmodern spirit. In addition, as suggested in Chapter 1, they cling to a traditional notion of a transcendent God not informed by the postmodern spirit.

In *Varieties of Postmodern Theology*, David Griffin recommends process theology's conception of God as especially appropriate to the postmodern spirit. Certainly the temporality and interconnectedness, correlativity, and sociality of life that the postmodern spirit affirms find counterparts in the process version of God's nature: God possesses a genuinely temporal dimension in relating to the world and is affected by creatures in some sense a part of God. On the other hand, as argued in Chapter 1, its notion of divine (and all) causation owes more to modern idealism than to the postmodern spirit. Furthermore, despite its commendable emphasis on sociality, its theory of divine causality ironically ends up as individualistic, indeed atomistic. God affects only individual occasions of experience, through their prehension of God as attractive object, without God having any direct effects on larger spans of physical and social reality (albeit God does attempt to influence the myriad creatures to make decisions conducive to an integrated and social world). Certainly this third type can take much of value from process theology but must also demur at some important points.

Various thinkers have offered conceptions of God traditional in affirming divine ultimate creativity, ultimate power, omniscience, and transcendence in the sense of some distinctness with respect to the world, while like process theology also upholding divine temporality and responsiveness/reciprocity with respect to the world. (For example, Nicolai Berdyaev, Pierre Teilhard de Chardin, John MacQuarrie, Hans Jonas, and Matthew Fox.) I would want to push this tendency by developing and promoting an explicit and full-fledged panenetheistic understanding of God, which I will argue is most appropriate vis-à-vis the postmodern spirit.

The Inevitability of Metaphysics

Preliminary to that, however, some metaphysical and epistemological issues demand attention. Some will presume that, given the limitations on human knowing acknowledged by the postmodern spirit, either the minimalist or radical perspective has credibility, while more traditional conceptions of deity can no longer elicit a plausible defense. I will argue otherwise.

To lead into these considerations, I will venture an observation relative to our preceding discussion. All three types share an emphasis on immanence in comparison to the relative emphasis on transcendence of classical theistic models. The radicals do away with transcendence—except for perhaps the trace of *différance*, the minimalists allow just a hint of it, while "traditionalists" affirm a more substantial measure of transcendence. On one level, minimalist and radicals may evidence cognitive humility; however, to rule out transcendence and make the ultimate more or less equivalent to the (processes of the) universe marks a definitive stand that claims much. Granted, any transcendent aspect of the ultimate may indeed be more difficult to know compared to an immanent aspect more immediately connected to observation of the universe. Nevertheless, to effectively deny the reality of a transcendent dimension strikes me as far from humble. A more humble position would be to say that we can neither affirm nor deny anything regarding divine transcendence; nor can we say much, if anything, about immanent ultimacy or deity, nor about the purposes or integrity of the universe, due to our ignorance of the relationship, if any, of divine immanence to transcendence.

The above hints that the eschewal of metaphysics by radicals and some other thinkers is hardly humble—nor finally successful. Far from being impossible since Kant's critique, metaphysics while problematic remains inevitable, whether admitted or not. Every position or worldview involves beliefs and assumptions about the ultimate nature of reality and the nature of ultimate reality. To state the impossibility of metaphysics itself claims something very significant about the nature of our universe—namely that the universe is so constituted as to make impossible knowledge about the ultimate nature of things.

Radical postmodernists get rather specific in "knowing" assertions about the unknowability of things, claims not merely epistemological but metaphysical as well: for example, 1) the impossibility of cognitive closure, 2) no reality exists besides interpretation/ representation/construction or the difference that defies all representation.[13]

As suggested in Chapter 1, for the postmodern spirit some gap or distancing between referent and signifier always pertains. Radical postmodernists infer from this the instability of all meaning, while moderates decide for the adequacy of most signification. Given this gap, especially in relation to God, some more traditional thinkers like Jean-Luc Marion and Walter Kaspar try to side step metaphysics by speaking of God in terms of "love" and "freedom," rather than of "being."[14] Indeed, as Marion expounds, the excess or "saturation" that is God breaks all the bounds of mere being.[15] Whatever the value of such moves, these theologians still maintain an infinite and ultimate reality, necessary and absolute in some sense, who/which creates the world. Clearly definite metaphysical commitments come into play here, even if some of the terminology has more of a "biblical" than a "philosophical" provenance. What has proven impossible and wrongheaded is the Enlightenment absolutism which assumed we could establish neutral, universal metaphysical beliefs to which all "reasonable" people must subscribe. Given the plurality of metaphysical perspectives, radical postmodernists and postliberals finally opt for incommensurability, as argued in Chapter 1. Of course, the very notion of the ultimate incommensurability of worldviews itself involves a serious metaphysical commitment. To conclude this section, those who take atheistic, agnostic, or minimalist positions regarding (ultimate) reality should not have their (often unclaimed) metaphysical commitments automatically granted a privileged status.

The (Un)Knowability of God

Having argued for the inevitability of metaphysical commitments, I will now consider the issue of the (un)knowability of other non-divine beings, which may have some relevance to the question of the (un) knowability of God. As we have seen in chapters 1 and 2, in one of its

13. As suggested in Chapter 4, in light of the inexhaustibility and temporality of life and of creaturely fallibility, for the postmodern spirit no *absolute* closure pertains. Yet most creatures achieve *adequate* cognitive closure and determinacy most of the time, according to an embodied moderate postmodern perspective.

14. Marion, *God without Being*; Kaspar, *God of Jesus*.

15. Marion, *In Excess*.

aspects radical postmodernism posits our immersion in our constructions, interpretations, representations of reality. In some tension with
this immanentism with respect to meaning stands radical postmodernism's emphasis on the indeterminacy, shiftiness, self-deconstructing or
self-oppositional nature of meaning: the "otherness," even if unacknowl-
edged, of all meaning, including the otherness within the self. (What
can tie together these two tensive aspects is a lack of transcendence or
freedom with respect to meaning: we are buffeted by a constantly shift-
ing interplay of the presence and absence of meaning—except perhaps
when by grace we somehow manage to resist dominant constructions.)
Given that radical postmodernism favors absence of meaning over presence and stresses irreducible and unalterable alterity, and given its immanentism, it definitely has solipsistic tendencies. However, in practice
it has not denied our having some knowledge of other human beings.
If the postmodern insight that perception, language, and symbolism
never act as purely, transparently, or simply representational does not
preclude knowledge of other beings, then one cannot legitimately preclude knowledge of God based solely on that insight. Instead, one must
make a specific argument why God is uniquely unknowable, why the
one sometimes called the wholly other must remain the (perhaps non-
existent) epistemologically wholly other.

God, of course, has traditionally functioned as an ontologically
and epistemologically exceptional case of meaning—without going so
far as to deny the possibility of some knowledge of God. Some thinkers
have chiseled a sharp distinction between God in relation to us (somewhat knowable) versus God in God's own self (unknowable). John Hick
with his Kantian-influenced contrast between the phenomenal and
noumenal with respect to God[16] and Robert Neville with his distinction
between God as expressed in creation and God as "utterly indeterminate" apart from creation[17] serve as contemporary examples. Martin
Heidegger probably represents the most influential contemporary
thinker to rely upon such a distinction, in his case that between Being
and particular beings.[18] Heidegger's distinction entails a "differentiating

16. Hick, *God Has Many Names*, 42ff., 83–87, 71–92.
17. Neville, "Depths of God," 8.
18. Heidegger, *Identity and Difference*.

process which simultaneously connects them and holds them apart."[19] Traditional theology, on Heidegger's critique, has identified God with Being, while understanding Being as analogous to beings; thus ontotheology has (incorrectly) placed God within the grip of the differentiating process.[20] If God is instead understood as prior to the differentiating process, then a "glancing revelation" becomes our only hope for knowing God. Regarding such glancing revelation as impossible, many interpret the upshot of Heidegger's critique precisely to be the impossibility of knowing God.[21]

I myself cannot accept a too sharp demarcation between a transcendent (God in God's self) and an immanent (God for us) aspect of the divine. Such dualism smacks more of the modern than the postmodern spirit, seemingly an extension of subject-object dualism. Modernity's controlling picture spawned the problem of knowing other minds by its privileging of self-reflexive subjectivity. However, in normal experience, from infancy on, we learn about self and others correlatively through our and their embodiment. So in general we have no reason to privilege our own subjectivity and intentionality, while doubting that of others.

My thesis, first advanced in chapter 3, contends that we likewise know God through our—and God's embodiment in the world. If we concede the dualism between God in relation to the world and in Godself we have already lost the epistemological ballgame to the agnostic and atheistic interpreters of Heidegger. For if God in relation to the world—divine immanence can disclose nothing about God's self or nature, that is, nothing at all about the value and purpose of creation for God, then indeed we have no right to postulate anything transcending the processes of the cosmos. But if we allow the possibility of some continuity or connection between God in relation to world and God's self and intentionality, knowledge about the world (divine immanence) may yield some knowledge of the divine self or nature as more than world. Granted there obtains a distinction between the subjectivity-objectivity correlation in the world on the one hand and that which comes prior to creaturely subjectivity-objectivity on the other. Yet I see no justification a priori to preclude knowing something about the initiator of the

19. Godzieba, "Ontotheology to Excess," 8.

20. Heidegger, *Identity and Difference*, 70–72.

21. Godzieba, "Ontotheolgoy to Excess."

"differentiating process of being" by means of those processes of being. Panentheism in particular (which I will shortly more fully expound) provides a model which partially differentiates or distinguishes God from creation, while not subjecting God to the differentiating process in the way the creatures are, for God initiates, encompasses, and optimally governs that process; thereby God assumes positions both immanent in and transcendent of that process. Precisely because God comes prior to that process, it can be part of God and God can be part of it.

Some radical postmodernists, such as Charles Winquist, have issued a more particular disclaimer of the possibility of knowledge of God. They have maintained that theological claims stand wholly within a culture and language, and so cannot hope to refer to any transcendent reality.[22] (Of course, this assertion partakes of the immanentist tendencies of radical postmodernism, which if taken to their logical conclusion would mean imprisonment within any and all of our constructions.) This strikes me as a rather weak argument. Language and culture change continually, yet we find ourselves quite capable of partially transcending a given version of these in grasping new versions. Moreover, as argued in Chapter 4, I hold that we can have some understanding of other cultures and religions (albeit we do not understand these exactly as natives do). Furthermore, I submit that we can have some understanding of meaning for animals who clearly do not grow up immersed in human language and culture. In various contexts, I adequately understand the cries of our cats, as communicating a desire to lick out the milk from the bottom of my bowl of cereal, to have their supper served, or for me to lie down on the bed so she can climb on my chest and get petted. Conversely, fascinating stories of parrots and a dog who have mastered a significant human vocabulary, even creatively and meaningfully using their knowledge in new contexts, have appeared in the media, as well stories of complex non-linguistic communication with and imitation of humans by dolphins.[23] These stories suggest that even non-primate animals can sometimes transcend their own biological and cultural spaces to come to know human others in striking ways. If we (and other animals) can partially transcend our cultural-linguistic frameworks to know something of these various others, I contend that

22. Winquist, "Silence of the Real."

23. Associated Press, "Parrot Dies"; Barash, "Animal Intelligence"; Kirby, "Parrot's Oratory"; Morell, "Inside Animal Minds."

no a priori reason exists to gainsay that we may do so with respect to ultimate reality.

I have attempted to refute epistemological and metaphysical arguments and question-begging assumptions against the possibility of metaphysics generally and, in particular, a more than minimalist theistic metaphysics. Hopefully having succeeded in clearing the decks for those who would develop modified traditionalist understandings of God, I next offer my attempt.

A Panentheistic Concept

Panentheism literally means "all [is] in God." It attempts to do justice to both divine transcendence—that God is "beyond" or more than the world—and divine immanence—that God is "in" the world. Panentheism maintains that the world and its creatures form a part of God. To expand on that, panentheism holds that the world exists in God, included in the divine life, but that the reality of the individuals or the structures of the universe or of the universe as a whole do not exhaust the divine reality. Thus God is all-inclusive or all-encompassing with respect to being. Strictly construed, and so I construe it, this entails that all divine relations are internal relations, that is, relations between God as integrated whole and the creatures as included parts. Charles Hartshorne, the principal theological interpreter of the progenitor of process thought, Alfred North Whitehead, aptly argued for the logic of such panentheistic inclusiveness: "if we deny the inclusiveness of the divine unity, we will either have to admit that relations between God and the lesser minds belong to no real individual, no real substance, or have to admit a super divine individual to which they belong."[24]

Note that some distinguishing between the divine and the world is crucial here. While the universe is part of God, God and the universe do not form an undifferentiated whole. Panentheism draws definite distinctions between God as the including whole and the non-divine parts considered in themselves. Ontologically, certain properties of divinity, such as aseity ("self-existence") or necessary existence and all-encompassing attributes such as omnipresence, omniscience, and ultimate power, apply to the including whole but definitely not to the creaturely included parts nor to the universe itself. In another aspect of

24. Hartshorne, *Man's Vision of God*, 295.

distinction between the divine and the world, panentheism insists on their mutual freedom and on indeterminism: Spontaneity and freedom in the universe mean that antecedent causes do not fully determine present events and actions, so that even God cannot fully predict or foreknow the future; creatures have real choices.

As panentheism attempts to find an optimal correlation of divine transcendence and immanence, I and other panentheists find it helpful to compare it with other options. It contrasts with traditional Western theism in this latter's emphasis on the distinctness and externality of the world with respect to God. Traditional theism tends to picture God as a distinct individual, separate from the creatures, analogous to the way humans usually are regarded as distinct from each other; God is one Person and we are other persons. Enlightenment deism, with its view that God created but does not involve Godself with the world, represents an extreme of this picture, as does so-called "classical theism," with its affirmation of various alleged divine attributes stemming from ancient Greek philosophy—immutability, impassibility, and eternity (in the sense of timelessness). Even as panentheism resists the tendencies of traditional theism simply to distinguish God from the creation, so it resists the tendency of pantheism to reduce the divine to the world—to its creatures, its structure, or to the universe as a whole. Pantheism literally means "all (is) God or divine," that is, everything at least in its true essence partakes of divinity. One could say that panentheism attempts to get as close to pantheism as possible in stressing the intimate relationship between God and nature, while still insisting on clear distinctions between them. Pantheism, though, tends to a (quasi) materialistic or (quasi) substantialistic picture of divinity: Entities in the world share the divine essence or substance to a greater or lesser degree. Therefore, any distinction between the divine as a whole and the constituents of the universe is a matter of degree rather than of kind. In addition, since everything exists as a mode or attribute of God, pantheism typically denies indeterminate freedom.

Regarding the intimate connection, the immediacy of presence, of the divine to all that exists (surpassing the closeness of any creature to any other creature and even to itself), I have delineated two aspects of panentheism, a passive and an active one.[25] Formally, the passive as-

25. Neils Gregersen has distinguished between "dipolar or Whiteheadian" and "expressive" varieties of panentheism, paralleling my passive and active aspects. He,

pect entails that *everything* that happens in the universe fully registers with the divine, makes a (lasting) difference to the divine. Given my preference for a personal model of divinity in analogy to animal and human consciousness, I prefer to write in terms of divine knowledge and compassion. At the same time, I realize that divine reality differs quite dramatically from creaturely reality. In recognizing the anthropomorphic dangers of attributing conscious personhood to the divine, Hartshorne and Paul Tillich described God as "not less than conscious" or superconscious. With that caveat in mind, I would characterize the passive aspect of panentheism as God's knowing and having compassion for all that exists without externality, mediation, or loss. However, God's knowledge and valuation comprise more than the creaturely experiences and their attendant individual valuations, which are fully included in the divine experience; that is, God's valuations do not reduce to the individuals' values or their sum. So God directly knows all that happens, all the joys and sorrow, the goods and ills of this world; and all of these affect the divine beatitude.

For a full-fledged panentheism I maintain the necessity of an active aspect of divinity as well. Formally, this would entail that all creaturely power and activity in some sense exist as a part of divine power and activity; the divine is all-encompassing in terms of power. This means that our power and activity always remain in intimate connection to divine power. Our power in some sense comes from the divine power. Given panentheism's insistence, though, on appropriate distinctions between the divine and the world, we cannot equate our power with divine power. Such distinctions cut both ways. We cannot reduce divine power to our powers or their sum, for divine power transcends all creaturely power. At the same time divinity does not determine our decisions for us. Instead, the divine empowers us in our possession of some indeterminate freedom. Given my preference for a personal model, I see God as intentionally holding back from using divine power in a wholly deterministic way. So God empowers all that exists without externality or mediation (that is, there is no third thing between the divine and creation); or if one prefers, God's empowerment of some genuine indeterminacy and freedom of choice and action in the creaturely realm

---

however, regards them as incompatible forms, while I maintain their compatibility and indeed their necessity for a full-fledged panentheism ("Three Varieties," 21, 27–34, 292 n. 36).

constitutes the only "externality" or "mediation" that pertain. And absent such ongoing and continuing divine empowerment, the universe would vanish into nothingness.

Having just advocated the active aspect of panentheism, I recognize the controversial nature of whether an immediacy of divine power can be construed so as to safeguard genuine creaturely indeterminate freedom. Whitehead, Hartshorne, and those process thinkers who have followed in their metaphysical footsteps have rejected creation from nothing and its entailment of immediate empowerment of existence,[26] precisely because of their belief that it would controvert creaturely freedom by enveloping, smothering, and destroying it. Instead they have opted for an ultimate ontological independence of creaturely occasions of experience, thus echoing Plato on matter (and individual souls). (Low-level unit occasions of experience exist apart from God, and without divine guidance would lead a rather chaotic existence. Divine influence, though, through the "initial aim" presented by God to each occasion enables the growth of order and complexity, while the absence of such influence could possibly lead to the demise of all creaturely occasions of experience.[27]) Let me offer an argument for the compatibility of indeterminate creaturely freedom and divine immediate empowerment. Process thought holds that *individual* unit occasions of experience, each with some measure of indeterminate freedom, exist contingently (though God will always have some world). It agrees that we individually do not cause this indeterminate freedom. We find ourselves with the freedom, capability, power to decide; but we co not create our freedom to be creative. What does? According to Whitehead "creativity" functions as "the category of the ultimate,"[28] as "a metaphysical principle belonging to the nature of things" of which everything else is an instantiation.[29] Indeed, even God as well as the world "are in the grip of the ultimate metaphysical ground, the creative

26. Contemporary Christian theologians typically understand the deeper meaning of creation from nothing to conflate with divine sustaining creativity or preservation, rather than a matter of whether the universe came into existence once upon a time. In other words it refers to the utter contingency of a world always in need of divine power for its existence.

27. E.g., see Cobb and Griffin, *Process Theology*, 64–66.

28. Whitehead, *Process*, 31.

29. Whitehead, *Adventures*, 236.

advance into novelty"[30] (though God in a primordial non-temporal de-cision determines the possibilities, sets the limitations and conditions, for the creative process[31]). However, what guarantees that the ultimate ground of actuality for process thought, the principle of creativity, must allow for creaturely indeterminate freedom? Just calling it "creativity" is not enough. One unsympathetic to the idea of such freedom could postulate that, given creativity's ultimacy, it determines all the details of the processive advance into novelty—what appears new to us is not new for this ultimate ground. Given that for me the divine functions as the ultimate ground of possibility and actuality, why cannot and should not that divine power allow for indeterminate creaturely freedom? What prevents the divine from so doing or being? (especially if one grants that no impediment would exist for an ontologically independent real-ity of creativity to allow for freedom); what power outside or beyond divinity so constrains it? If one believes in a transpersonal divine, one might say that it lies in the nature of the divine to engender indetermi-nate freedom. If one opts for a more personal God, one might say God so chooses. Thus, I maintain that God does not make all decisions, but respects the integrity of secondary causes, allowing chance to operate (as in quantum events and in the intersections of diverse agencies) and allowing free finite agents to decide. God "holds back" or limits divine power in not making creatures' decisions, instead empowering and al-lowing them to choose among and carry out possible options. Finally, to echo Hartshorne's above comment on the need for a truly all-inclusive reality, if divine power does not include all power, who determines the conditions for interaction between God and the metaphysical principle of creativity? To borrow a Tillichian phrase, we would have to look for a "God above God"[32] (and above "creativity").

I have placed myself as a postmodernist advocating a fairly tradi-tional model of God with a strong sense of divine transcendence and ultimacy. Some theologians like John Polkinghorne and Keith Ward balk at joining the ranks of panentheists, in part because for them its notion of God compromises divine transcendence, sovereignty, and purity.[33] I

30. Whitehead, *Process*, 529. See also, *Science*, 179; *Adventures*, 236.

31. Whitehead, *Science*, 178–79; *Process*, 522.

32. Tillich, *Courage*, 182–90.

33. Ward, "World," 67–72; Polkinghorne, *Science and Creation*, 53.

have already addressed one aspect of the concern with sovereignty, by positing an active aspect which contrasts with process theology's rejection of creation from nothing and its reliance finally upon divine persuasion alone, both of which preclude analogizing any Aristotelian type of efficient causation to God. What of the charge that panentheism subjects God too much to the evils of the world? Because of this concern, Polkinghorne only supports an "eschatological panentheism"[34] (a phrase originally coined by Tillich[35]) or in Neils Gregersen's typology a "soteriological panentheism"[36]—that is, only when creation reaches final perfection can it be said to reside "in God." While I grant that much in our world happens contrary to the perfect divine will, my own sense of divine ultimacy and sovereignty will not brook any separation of God from anything that now exists, even in its fallenness or imperfection. And given this intimacy between the divine and the world, I cannot imagine that God and the divine beatitude will not suffer some negative effect from the evils that befall God's creatures. I do maintain that the divine ensures the actuality of more good than evil in the world at any given time, so I stand with process theology in its endorsement of ever-increasing divine beatitude through God's temporal dimension. Moreover, with respect to moral purity, I find severely deficient a God unaffected by the sufferings of the creatures.

If some theologians have felt that panentheism itself compromises divine sovereignty, transcendence, and ultimacy, they find even more troubling the metaphor of the world as the body of God. Arthur Peacocke represents one theologian endorsing panentheism but demurring from any suggestion of the world as God's body (though he has written approvingly of the feminine, womb imagery panentheism encourages).[37] Of course, any metaphor for the divine includes moments of both affirmation and negation, in recognition of both similarity and dissimilarity of the divine to the creaturely reality invoked. Hartshorne, who employed for the God-world relationship the analogy of the human mind to the cells of the human body, clearly delineated aspects of the analogy in need of qualification to preserve divine perfection or

34. Polkinghorne, *Faith of a Physicist*, 64.

35. Tillich, *Systematic*, 3:420–22.

36. Gregersen, "Three Varieties," 21, 24–27.

37. Peacocke, "Articulating God's Presence," xiv, 150–52; *Theology*, 158–59.

unsurpassibility: 1) God does not have an external environment outside of the body of the world with which to contend.[38] 2) Divine embodiment in no way threatens God's existence, which is necessary.[39] 3) In contrast to our limited knowledge of our own cells, God omnisciently encompasses the world's actuality.[40]

As long as we acknowledge those aspects of the metaphor requiring negation, I find the metaphor of the world as God's body most appropriate given panentheism's emphasis on divine immediacy: A human or animal has a (comparatively) direct awareness and a (comparatively) direct control of many of the actions of its body. Accepting Damasio's concept of background feelings adds to the scope of our bodily knowledge, in that we are aware of much of our body at some level every waking moment. Of course, for the divine the registration or awareness of whatever happens in the universe is always full, never marginal. That points to the importance of internality for panentheism and for the metaphor of the world as God's body: While parts of our body are internal both physiologically and in terms of tacitly indwelling them in knowing and acting, at the same time they are somewhat external to our *conscious* embodied mind. This will not do for the divine. Indeed, our limitations on the amount of content to which we can focally attend comprise part of our finitude. To paraphrase St. Augustine, God loves each individual as if she or he were the whole universe and the whole universe as if it were one person. (In their better moments—when emphasizing divine immediacy and upholding genuine creaturely freedom, Augustine and some other classical theologians sound like closet panentheists.)

I have focused so far on the perfect internality and immanence of the divine with respect to the world as its body. There is a sense in which such immanence coincides with transcendence in the divine case, in that it implicates divine unsurpassibility in relation to omniscience, ultimate power, and immortality. But I need to talk more directly about divine transcendence. To lead into that I must first address human transcendence. For *radical* embodiment, we do not transcend our bodies in any thorough sense. Yet we can educe some relative transcendence. We can

---

38. Hartshorne, *Man's Vision of God*, 178–79, 187, 200; *Natural Theology*, 97–98, 100.

39. Hartshorne, *Man's Vision of God*, 180–81.

40. Ibid., 178, 184–85; *Natural Theology*, 97–98, 100.

decide upon different ways to place our bodies in the world, to take action with our bodies. Furthermore, some of the actions we can take can
change our bodies physiologically or in terms of our phenomenal habit
bodies. And of course in our imaginations we can take on very different
bodies and live in very different worlds. Finally, insofar as we consider
the human body in terms of its component parts taken separately or
reductively, we do transcend our bodies in the sense that embodied
consciousness constitutes an emergent property. Sallie McFague hand-
ily identifies alternatives vis-à-vis divine embodiment: "Pantheism says
that God is embodied, necessarily and totally; traditional theism claims
that God is disembodied necessarily and totally; panentheism suggests
that God is embodied but not necessarily or totally."[41] (Interestingly,
Kaufman decries "the idea of God as essentially an autonomous ego
utterly distinct from and independent of all other agents,"[42] yet does not
indicate why a panentheistic or other non-minimalist organic conception of God cannot adequately address this and other shortcomings of
the classical model.) Thus for radical embodiment the divine is analogous to the human in terms of some transcendence and freedom with
respect to the body. However, as I will spell out in the next chapter, only
the divine in some aspects absolutely transcends its body.

Having indicated that panentheism insists on some freedom of the
divine with respect to its body, by way of contrast I will note that pantheism typically does not. First of all, it tends towards determinism with
respect to the world. Moreover, divine freedom would seem to presume
an integrated divine reality clearly more than the universe, its constituents, or its structure. This pantheism does not provide, as it tends to
reduce divinity to the elements, the rational structure, or the whole of
the universe. Nevertheless, Grace Jantzen represents a contemporary
pantheist who emphasizes the trope of the body of God.[43]

---

41. McFague, *Body of God*, 149–50. McFague's three categories do not exhaust the
terrain. Some forms of pantheism with acosmic tendencies, such as advaitic Hinduism
which parallels classical theism with its divine immutability, impassibility, and eternity,
call into question how real divine embodiment is. Also, some forms of non-traditional
theism may admit some internal relations of God with respect to the world, yet refuse
panentheism's claim that *all* is in God.

42. Kaufman, *In Face of Mystery*, 332.

43. Jantzen, *God's World*.

The universe does manifest interconnectedness and some mutual influence—given the universality of natural "laws," given that any forces of gravity and electromagnetism have an effect, however slight, throughout the universe, and given that some quantum effects defy localization. Nevertheless, the universe does not possess the interconnectedness and mutual influence of the parts of a biological organism, a literal "body." So we recognize another negation in our metaphorical use of the world as God's body. Relative to this negation, the panentheistic model provides the advantage of a transcendent dimension of divinity that serves as an additional integrating factor for the universe, which the pantheistic model does not. Finally, while McFague has done much valuable work in developing and enriching the metaphor of panentheism, her minimalism described earlier and her declaration that "God is many, not one"[44] undermines the integrity of the divine that includes but transcends the universe according to panentheism.

In its refusal then to simply distinguish God from, or simply equate divinity with, the world and in its extension to affirm God's embodiment in the world, panentheism offers a fairly traditional vision of God compatible with the postmodern vision of human beings and, I believe, compatible with the nature of reality and ultimate reality. Indeed, while aware of appropriate qualifications, we should affirm our actual world as the body of God. As evidence of the embodied nature of human rationality and meaning continues to mount, the resonance of the world as God's body represents too valuable a resource to ignore or deny.

A Postmodern Epistemology: The Embodiment of God

I have argued against the a priori, carte blanche unknowability of God—as well as offered a panentheistic conception of God which I believe will prove epistemologically defensible. The postmodern spirit, however, must discount certain traditional sources for knowledge of God. As argued in Chapter 3, if we apply to God the denial of any human absolute, direct, or unmediated knowledge, then we must deny the validity of the following: 1) revelation in the sense of a supernatural or self-authenticating intentional action or communication from God, 2) mystical experience as a direct awareness of the very consciousness or essence of God.

44. McFague, *Body of God*, 155.

The modern spirit has led many to rule out tangible supernatural activity in the physical world. The notion of some direct divine presence or communication to human interiority, though, has encountered less suspicion. However, if the logic of the postmodern spirit prevails, this notion too must fall. As suggested in Chapters 1 and 2, some thinkers in the tradition of Barthian neo-orthodoxy, including the postliberals, have attempted to distance themselves from supernaturalism, while still maintaining—if not explaining—the absolute, self-authenticating character of divine revelatory activity. This too must fail according to the postmodern spirit.

While mystical experience may have pragmatic validity as a mode of consciousness that attunes one to the truth of the interconnectedness of all reality, to interpret it as directly induced by God or as a tapping into the very mind or consciousness of God cannot succeed on post-modern criteria. By way of contrast, as indicated in Chapter 1, much influential modern theology, affected by Romanticism and/or ideal-ism, has included some form of a direct or mystical awareness of God: Tillich's "mystical a priori," neo-Thomism's implicit awareness and love for God, and Whitehead's "initial aim."

If under the postmodern spirit we bar any absolute or unmedi-ated human connection with God, then I submit that how we know God should not differ in principle from how we know other realities. As I have advocated throughout this project, the best instantiation of the postmodern spirit vis-à-vis knowledge means bodily knowing. All our knowing comes through our and others' embodiment in the world. Therefore, as suggested in Chapter 3, whatever knowledge we obtain of God will come from our and the divine embodiment in the world.

Even as we know of the reality and intentions of others through the processes and actions of their bodies, so the world's processes and activities may be interpreted as the body of God that gives us knowl-edge of the divine reality and purposes—including the intention that sentient, valuing, conscious life exist. We might then regard the universe as a body supporting life, providing order—or better a proper mix of regularity and chance, and creating beauty. Some of this knowledge will be relatively reflective, such as that of 1) the Big Bang and the evolu-tion of stars, planets, and life 2) the balance of atmospheric compo-sition, pressure, and movement, of composition and temperatures of ocean, land, and air, etc., which provide an environment conducive to the preservation of life. Some of this knowledge will come in a more prereflective manner, such as an intuition of divine purpose in gazing at the beauty of a sunset or in the experience of pregnancy and birthing. This paragraph means to be suggestive rather than exhaustive as to how we might discern God as embodied in the world. One's sense of God and the world here must be cumulative and integrative or holistic. Obviously the universe contains many instances of evil. The theist will likely interpret this as an inevitable dimension of powerful, yet fragile, processes that assure the good of the whole. The theist then will have an overall evaluation of the world as good and purposeful, though taking into account the many negativities of existence. Clearly, interpreting the universe as the (good) body of God resonates with traditional teleological arguments for God's existence. (The intimacy of the connection of God and world represents the main innovation of panentheistic and bodily models over external classical forms.) Chapter 7 will offer more argumentation for God's existence, combining teleological and cosmological arguments.

Patently my model of knowing divine intentions through the actions of God's body focuses on general processes, as suggested in Chapter 3. It relates to "general" rather than "special" providence and revelation. Someone might want to argue that particular events, including those observable in the physical world, such as the crossing of the Red Sea by the Israelites, constitute actions of God's body through which we discern divine intentions. Given that my model entails learning about divine purposes cumulatively, I indeed affirm that some events, persons, or texts may paradigmatically reveal God's nature; but I cannot accept them as special actions by God. Let us construe them as not involving supernatural intervention (as with Peacocke and Polkinghorne's versions of top-down causation or those theologians who hypothesize God's control of macro-events through determining quantum indeterminacies). Still it seems to me that creaturely indeterminacy and freedom must be confined within narrow bounds, if present at all, to maintain divine agency and responsibility for these particular events (beyond God's general activity and empowerment of every event). And then the question remains, why is God especially responsible for fore planning and causing these particular events, but not all other events, especially those involving tremendous evil? In sum, I regard models of divine control of specific events as backdoor attempts to reinscribe divine interventionism in supposedly more "natural" forms, rather than allowing the creation and its creatures the freedom to develop according to its nature and their choices.

We cannot legitimately doubt that we know persons' intentions through their bodily actions. While we may err in our reading of particular actions and intentions, practically speaking we cannot generally doubt this kind of knowing—and certainly not the existence of other embodied persons—unless, theoretically, one creates a philosophical problem under the influence of the absolutist spirit of modernity or, practically, suffers from emotional illness.

Is our knowing through God's embodiment nearly so certain? Alvin Plantinga has labeled beliefs in the existence both of other minds and of God as "properly basic."[45] Clearly many in secular society and in nontheistic religions doubt the existence of a personal God. And many of the former doubt the reality of any divine reality. Even as a confirmed theist, I would hardly claim for my purported knowledge of God's existence the obvious and indubitable nature of my knowing the existence of other persons. Yet I claim the embodiment of God in the world as a plausible metaphor, intuition, and inference. I will write more about this plausibility in the concluding chapter, which follows.

45. Plantinga, "Reason and Belief." John Apczynski has made, I think, a convincing case that "proper basicality must be understood as within a particular historical tradition of inquiry, in Plantinga's case, the Reformed tradition of Christianity ("Belief in God"). Yet I would want to ask about the models of knowing that historically have led to belief in God as properly basic in that tradition. One model has involved belief in absolute and self-authenticating supernatural revelation. Another model, controversial as an interpretation of Calvin and the Reformed tradition, posits a direct "awareness of divinity," albeit obscured by sin (Plantinga, "Reason and Belief," 65). Of course, both models come under suspicion by the postmodern spirit. Another model involves discerning God's existence and intentions through observing the world, which I obviously accept as a viable option, though not as "properly basic" in the sense of our knowledge of other embodied persons.

7

Radical Embodiment and Transcendence

The Absence—and Presence—of God

A corollary of God's radical embodiment is that the trope of "the absence of God" in radical postmodernism and in post-Holocaust theology (not to mention the Christian mystical tradition) can and must be taken seriously. No, God does not disappear into the universe a la 1960's "death of God" theology or some versions of radical postmodernism. I believe that the embodied panentheistic formulation I have advanced can account for a certain experiential sense of divine absence, while at the same time allowing for the reality and presence of the divine.

Clearly my model—and various other models as well—postulates the absence of particular, distinguishable actions or events in which God or divinity is especially or uniquely agential or causal. Given the embodied, mediated nature of knowledge, the transcendent dimension of divinity—the aspect constituting more than our universe—is never immediately given. So we can expect no supernatural revelation or intervention, as I have indicated before. However, informal surveys in my classrooms suggest that at least most people in the United States have wished for some direct sign from God to confirm God's existence or to recommend a direction for their life (in conducting these surveys I have been one of the many raising a hand). The same surveys included a second question whose results indicate that most people do not believe they have received such a sign. Obviously many have felt the absence of God in the sense of particular, distinguishable actions or communications. This feeling of absence, of course, becomes the most acute and painful in situations of individual and mass physical and/or psychological trauma or death.

Due to the all-encompassing nature of the divine, to the immediacy of the universe to divine cognizance and power on my panentheistic conception, no particular event, experience, or action in the world
can be simply distinguished from God and the divine life. Thus a sense
pertains in which the divine is both nothing (in the literal sense of "nothing," no particular thing) and everything. God is neither uniquely nor
exhaustively identifiable with any of the particularities of this world,
while at the same time divinity immediately includes and identifies
with all the particularities of the cosmos.

On my model the including whole immediately apprehends the
included parts. However, the converse does not hold. The creatures,
the parts, have no immediate or mystical awareness of the divine consciousness, or better, super-consciousness, of the transcendent aspect of
deity, or of the whole as more than the included universe. We have no
immediate knowledge of God's immediate apprehension or empowerment of us, of our unmediated presence to the divine. Probably this is
precisely what we should expect with a panentheistic model. Because
the divine does not constitute a clearly distinct reality or cause, because
nothing resists our immediate presence to God, there obtains nothing
particular of divine inclusion to distinguish (from what we experience
of ourselves and of the universe). Nothing particular of divine inclusion
stands external to us, or different from us, for us to perceive. We represent an immediate part of the divine, but the divine does not similarly
constitute an immediate part of us, even in attenuated form.

As I have maintained, whatever knowledge we have of the divine comes mediated, as does our knowledge of creaturely others. In
the case of other creatures, particular aspects of the world, particular
embodiment(s) enable knowledge. In the divine case, the whole universe as embodiment enables knowledge. This entails mediation and
interpretation of a different order than our knowledge of particular or
fragmentary entities. It constitutes a holistic or integrative interpretation that makes a judgment based on whatever knowledge one possesses of the whole universe—of course always a partial knowledge. To be
sure many particular experiences and elements inform such judgments
(for example, in Chapter 6, I mentioned particular processes conducive
to life). However, none of these in themselves should be taken as immediately, uniquely, or singularly decisive in revealing God—though of
course some elements will stand out as more significant or indicative

than others. Rather they figure as part of a contextual interpretation of the universe and the one embodied in the cosmos. If one disallows the possibility of divinity acting or revealing its nature in exclusive, particular ways, then one must make a judgment as to the absence or presence of God based upon an overall assessment of the nature of our universe.

Having just elaborated upon my contention that the theist may infer or intuit something of divine intentions, purposes, ends, directions, and/or care for this world through divine embodiment, I will contend that the theist may also affirm transcendence in the sense of a divine reality and life beyond our universe. Nevertheless, its contents— whether other universes or non-worldly aesthetic values—must remain beyond our ken. The divine does not grant us immediate awareness of any universe beyond our own nor of any transworldy contents of the divine reality or mind. At least in this life, we are finally immanent in this world, our transcendence always dependent upon and relative to the forces that give us life and consciousness, always dependent upon and relative to our embodiment. Such constitutes the radical truth of our embodiment, of our existence as "Adam" —the earth being, or in recognition of the evolution of our cosmos, the radical reality of our composition from stardust, of our existence as a child of the universe. Only the divine possesses a transcendence in some sense absolute.

Why Divine Transcendence and Ultimacy?

But why hold out for any sense of divine transcendence with respect to our universe? Perhaps the only divine transcendence is a relative one, where the divine has a reality and perspective *in relation to the universe* transcending that of its component parts individually or in sum, but nothing more. To the extent we take the metaphor of the world as God's body rather literally, that would constitute the maximum transcendence possible. Or maybe the universe itself, as a totality, represents whatever divinity that exists?

Here we venture into the realm of the ancient Greek philosopher Parmenides, who raised the question of why there is something rather than nothing. We venture into the questions and concerns that gave rise to the so-called cosmological argument, or argument from contingency—why does a cosmos, which appears to be contingent in its particulars and as a whole, exist at all? Today philosophers and theologians recognize that no argument can "prove" whether the universe requires a necessary cause, and if the universe does, what the nature of that cause would be. Whether an argument about ultimate causes works depends on the assumptions, traditions, and worldviews of individuals and cultures. (However, as Hartshorne aptly noted, such arguments can clarify one's assumptions and commitments and clarify what is at stake.[1]) Rather it is a matter of what explanation of the universe's existence one finds most satisfactory, a matter of where one does not feel the need to press on and ask, "But what caused that?" Or to put it negatively, it is a question of the most plausible ultimate mystery, of the surd which we cannot get behind. Of course, some apparently have not felt any need, or have given up on the need, to ultimately explain the universe. Some of these we might classify as "atheists" in the broadest sense: those who feel no reality exists which could explain the universe's existence; it exists by ultimate chance or as a brute fact. Others we might classify as agnostics, who regard any ultimate cause of the universe as a completely impenetrable mystery.

For me a satisfactory explanation of the universe, or of why anything exists, must address the relationship of possibility to actuality. That is, of all possibilities, why have only certain possibilities as to the nature of our universe achieved actualization? If we do not address this issue, we concede that the existence of our particular universe comes down to ultimate chance or brute fact. I submit that a satisfactory explanation of the universe must postulate a reservoir or source of all possibility. Whitehead felt this need and posited the primordial nature of God as the principle of limitation: In a non-temporal decision God determined which possibilities out of all potentiality would be available to our universe. As suggested by previous discussion, I believe Whitehead compromised the status of the divine as truly the source of all possibility. For realities—unit occasions of experience—come into existence through the principle of creativity and then receive more particular possibilities from which to choose. This seems to imply that this ultimate principle of creativity, along with God, serves as a source of possibility for unit occasions which become actual. Thus we have one source for inchoate realities and another that allows for their definition.

1. Hartshorne, *Natural Theology*, 29–33.

For me the divine serves as the one reservoir of all possibility and thus the ultimate source of all actuality. In this I accept something of the basic sentiment and intuition of the cosmological argument: a reservoir of all possibility makes sense, and this reservoir in some sense is necessary. On the other hand, I do not regard this idea as an absolute, a priori, truth. To imagine a counterfactual, if all that existed were a twelve-inch cube, I would have to concede the falsity of the cosmological principle: this insignificant cube exists by chance or as brute fact. Thus, I see a need to pair cosmological and teleological sensibilities. The complexity and in my judgment overall goodness or value of the universe—the assessment of the universe as a whole as evidence of divine embodiment—reinforces the cosmological principle: *this* universe makes sense as a limitation or choice out of all possibilities rather than as brute fact or as ultimately due to chance.

In Chapter 6, I noted elements of negation in claiming the metaphor or analogy of the world as the body of God, in order to protect divine ultimacy. The above discussion has implications in this regard. For humans and animals embodiment comes first: All our possibilities stem from our embodiment in the world. Clearly the opposite pertains to my conception of divinity: Possibility ontologically precedes any actualization or embodiment of possibility in the divine case and only in the divine case.[2]

Overcoming Objections to Divine Transcendence and Ultimacy

Findings in the physical and psychological sciences—or rather interpretations thereof—rule out any divine transcendence or ultimate divine causality, according to some thinkers. I find their conclusions quite question begging. Edward Slingerland emphasizes the cruciality of human embodiment and draws on some of the same sources as I do.[3] Nevertheless, after acknowledging the reality of emergence in biological organisms, he declares that all explanations are by nature reductive.[4] As

2. One of the reasons Arthur Peacocke rejected the metaphor of divine embodiment is its entailment that God creates God's body in contradistinction from the human case ("Articulating God's Presence," 150).

3. Slingerland, "Study of Religion," 378. See also 387–92.

4. Ibid., 384–87.

my material on self-organization in chapter 5 suggests, I take exception to this dictum. Many scientists who maintain a robust theory of
emergence, such as Stuart Kauffman, take strong exception. Kauffman
characterizes emergent properties in the biosphere as unpredictable
in principle.[5] As a general rule, properties of component parts or their
sum provide only a partial explanation of the emergent properties of
the whole. Instead, one has to take into account the emergent properties
themselves for a fuller explanation. Regarding the matter of a divine
cause of the universe, to insist on the reductive nature of all explanations disbars this possibility from the start (construing the parts of the
universe and/or their sum as divine themselves would be the only way
to allow divinity under this reductive rule).

In a somewhat related vein, Donald Braxton argues that the self-
organizing qualities of matter militate against any transcendent (or I
would add any overall immanent) directionality or purpose to the universe.[6] Philosophical speculation about a cause of the universe other
than an intelligent agent—such as that the universe came into existence
through a process of vegetation—go back at least to Hume.[7] The self-
organizing capabilities of matter ontologically do precede the particular
products of such self-organization, including biological organisms. And
one can speculate about the existence of a self-organizing reality that
gives rise to our and other universes—a random universe-generating
machine and some versions of string theory bank on precisely that. Yet I
am not satisfied. I ask, what caused the existence of the universe-generating machine or the eleven-dimensioned strings and their properties,
which purportedly birth multiple universes? Braxton's assertion then
thoroughly begs the question of whether these self-organizing qualities
of nature just exist by ultimate chance or brute fact, or whether they
may manifest some overarching divine purpose (if we accent the metaphor of transcendence and more personal models) or underlying divine
directionality (if we accent that of immanence and more transpersonal
models). Hume himself offers tantalizing ruminations concerning teleology. Commentators agree that *in general* the character Philo speaks
for Hume in his *Dialogues concerning Natural Religion*. After driving

5. Kauffman, *Reinventing the Sacred*, 31–43.

6. Braxton, "Naturalizing Transcendence."

7. Hume, *Dialogues* (Part VII *in toto*), 61–67.

off the blowhard Demea (who holds dogmatically to a classical portrait of God)—Philo concedes to Cleanthes that the teleological argument works. While the matter still generates controversy, I judge that Philo speaks for Hume at this juncture. Though the argument does not meet the Enlightenment standard of absolute proof a la science and mathematics (which fueled Hume's skepticism), Philo/Hume indicates that the world does intuitively strike one as the product of some sort of intelligence or reason.[8]

Mark C. Taylor, in the latest manifestation of his post post-structuralist, constructive phase, proffers a metaphysics bearing significant similarities to my own with its emphasis on reality as self-organizing and emergent.[9] Taylor, though, comes down on the same side as Braxton, concluding that no transcendence in the sense of a purposive or directional ultimate cause lies behind these self-organizing processes. Self-organization itself serves as the ultimate principle, so it is self-organization all the way down, so to speak. (Taylor does come to the empirical conclusion that "history" does manifest a "discernible trajectory" of increasing complexity and "connectivity."[10]) Furthermore, the "immanent transcendence," of which he sometimes writes, means that the divine is especially associated with the open, de-structuring disfiguring ("transcendent") element within these self-organizing processes that allows for the emergence of the new.[11] The reader at this point may sense that from the perspective of radical embodiment, Taylor still incorporates too much of Derridean deconstruction.

Taylor's theory of religion in *After God* also bears similarities to my own, focusing on its provision to human life of meaning and purpose.[12] With respect to reality and life in general, as well as to religion and other particular aspects of them, Taylor posits an interplay of the structuring and figuring of complex meaningful wholes, on the one hand, and the de-structuring and disfiguring of the same, on the other. Formally, these two function dialectically as equals, though as above Taylor sometimes

8. Hume, *Dialogues* (Part XII), 107–14.

9. Taylor, *After God*.

10 Taylor, "Refiguring Religion.," pp. 117–18.

11. Ibid., 41, 127, 311.

12. Ibid., see esp. 12.

reveals a preference for the destabilizing side.[13] I take issue with that preference. Radical embodiment grants a certain priority to the side of the stability of complex wholes. First, consider our bodies, complex biological organisms. Of course, all the processes and actions of one's body are temporal. While the homeostatic processes of one's body are far from literally "static," they presume significant stability and generally succeed in maintaining the integral stability of the organism. Even as one grows in youth and declines in old age, the basic structures of one's organs of perception and thought, means of motility, and internal organs normally remain relatively stable. Likewise, with one's bodily actions: these too involve continual change through time. Yet they also presume a basic stability of one's embodiment in the world. With the exception of some of the effects of aging and of some diseases that can strike at any time, none of this on-going change entails de-structuring and disfiguring. Of course, disorderly, chaotic conditions far from equilibrium led to more complex reality in the birth of biological organisms. But now that human organisms have emerged, in each generation we strive to avoid chaotic conditions far from equilibrium in terms of the overall relationship of ourselves with our environment—for when we fail major disease or injury or death results.

Taylor sometimes appears to equate the destabilizing side of things with the truth that any complex reality defies complete representation.[14] Perhaps here Taylor remains too tied to the primacy of linguistic metaphors in post-structuralism. As Polanyi especially has demonstrated, that we cannot specify all the elements of a whole does not necessarily entail any lack of structure or a hidden destabilizing force. (Of course, the temporality of life means that the whole of one's experience and interpretation ever changes to a greater or lesser degree.) Conversely, we can represent in great depth some instances and causes of de-structuring and disfiguring, such as some human diseases and some failures of human institutions (though of course we never achieve absolute knowledge of these or anything else). On one level, Taylor recognizes that all our creativity assumes certain constraints. Nevertheless, he identifies the de-stabilizing element with Schelling's *Unvordenkliche*, that which is

13. Ibid., 345.
14. Ibid., 119–27, 304ff.

prior to all subject-object differentiation and particularity.[15] This seems to presume that in our own creativity we partake of this undifferentiated, "infinite," "virtual" reality, which Taylor especially associates with the divine. And only because of the "virtual presence" of this reality can we be creative. Interestingly, his position parallels that of Radical Orthodoxy, which as indicated in Chapter 4, maintains that only the infusion of the inexhaustible divine saves the world from the exhaustion and death it would otherwise suffer. Taylor also associates this de-structuring, undifferentiating element with the experience of the sublime, which he equates with the experience of unlimited possibility.[16] While we do not possess the divine as structured particularity, still in Taylor's scheme we may end up with a "having of the divine" more in keeping with the modern than the postmodern spirit. For radical embodiment, we and our world in no sense have direct dealings with that aspect of divinity that serves as the reservoir of all possibility, of that which is prior to embodiment. All the activity and creativity of emergent complex realities happen within structures. These structures do not specify all relevant possibilities. Here I reject Whitehead's Platonic model that views all the possibilities contained in God's primordial nature as particular and definite. Instead I hold with Hartshorne that possibility is indefinite, although falling within certain ranges. As I asserted in Chapters 3 and 4, a genuine inexhaustibility and even infinity pertains to human action and creativity. At the same time, limits circumscribe this creativity: we and our world are ultimately finite. To appropriate a mathematical analogy, the real numbers between 1 and 100 are infinite, yet clearly fall within a range. As complex organisms encountering complex wholes we bring relatively indefinite, indeterminate possibilities into definition. All of this happens, though, post-differentiation, within a differentiated world. The absolutely or strictly undifferentiated is not part of our world. For radical embodiment, we humans can take joy in the great openness of future possibilities—of possible future embodiments. But only the divine can in any sense experience absolutely unlimited possibility.

Given his metaphysics, Taylor approves of physicist Lee Smolin's speculation that the laws of the physical universe evolve through self-

15. Ibid., 119–21.
16. Ibid., 123–24.

organization and natural selection.[17] Indeed, in the first fractions of a second of the Big Bang, four fundamental forces of the universe and their inter-relationships did emerge. Given our ignorance regarding dark matter/ energy and why the rate of expansion of the universe is accelerating, I certainly will not rule our that some important laws or regularities of the universe do change. Nevertheless, the evidence we have so far suggests that the self-organizing properties of the physical world rest and rely upon stable natural laws and regularities which do not change at all, or at least not in any observably significant way: these include quantum mechanics; special relativity; general relativity including gravitation; nuclear, atomic, and molecular inter-relationships, involving nuclear and electro-magnetic forces.

As indicated earlier, Taylor's framing of his theory of religion dialectically pairs the structuring and disruption of meaning. In an interview, however, Taylor does confess that he prefers the aspect of religion that creates "insecurity."[18] I believe I discern some shortchanging of the side of structure and stability in his framing of the theory: Taylor pens that religion "figure(s)" structures and "lend(s) life meaning and purpose."[19] I have granted that religious traditions construct or create meaning—but only partially. Religion, at least when valid, also finds or discovers meaning or incipient meaning. This is so for radical embodiment because of the meaningful structures of our bodies that correlate with structures of the world. In keeping with a preference for the destabilizing side, Taylor regards "infinite" or "endless restlessness" as the proper relationship of self to world, which the best forms of religion cultivate.[20] Radical embodiment again insists on the temporality of our lives as we achieve new values in new situations. However, it sees the best forms of religion as those that cultivate a sense of at-home-ness in the universe where we rely on a relatively secure base as we venture forth to meet and create meaning in our social and natural worlds. (By contrast Taylor associates at-home-ness only with monistic worldviews which deny difference and the new.[21])

17. Ibid., 322–23.
18. "Q & A with Taylor."
19. Taylor, *After God*, 12.
20. Ibid., 38, 41, 345.
21. Ibid., 37–39.

In Chapter 3, I briefly addressed the question of whether our human tendency to attribute animate intentionality or agency to events should discredit belief in some ultimate divine cause of the universe. Psychological and cognitive studies have clearly shown that even infants distinguish between animate, intentional, "self-moved" bodies and inanimate objects. Also, evidence exists of an evolved human tendency to over-ascribe agency or teleology in some contexts. My own life experiences make me quite aware of people's tendency to posit a purpose or reason behind events which seem to me to involve chance and contingency. I have polled classes on whether their birth and the future day of their death stems from chance or from a pre-set divine plan. (As I anticipated, students are more inclined to think their birth involves chance than their death.) Many, often a majority, believe their dying falls under divine control. Certainly for many the thought of chance impinging upon something as important as their demise is scary. As a pastor, I have witnessed many bereaved persons comforting themselves by appealing to some (perhaps hidden) divine reason behind an untimely death. Of course in that context I have refrained from correcting what I regard as their mistaken theology.

Clearly my embodied panentheistic model does not involve God determining or controlling particular events. Have I, despite some human tendency to over-ascribe agency, managed to live my life in accordance with that model? Once during seminary, I recall thinking that a certain trajectory of my life may have happened because God wanted it to. In the many years since then with all their ups and downs, I have never entertained (at least consciously) the idea that God caused the relevant events to happen.

Before cutting to the chase, I will consider other evidence Slingerland offers to support the robustness of our tendency to ascribe agency to non-intentional realities. In particular he cites computers and computer animated graphics.[22] I will add a recent study showing that the more human-like the computer animation, the more likely it is to activate areas of the brain dealing with social interaction/mental state attribution.[23] I respond, but of course we attribute intentionality to characters in stories, cartoons, plays, movies, etc. However, we normally

---

22. Slingerland, "Study of Religion," 395–96.
23. "Do We Think Machines Think."

do so with a so-called "suspension of disbelief." Although we do feel some of the same emotions, and some of the same areas of our brains do activate, in response to fictional events as to real ones, studies—and experience—tell us that we naturally respond more strongly to the real thing. And contrary to Slingerland's summary of our relationship with computers, I have never felt that a computer was out to get me. Rather, my frustration multiplies precisely because I realize this is just a dumb machine, rather than a person with whom I can converse and thus perhaps find a solution to my problem.

What should we conclude? First I refer back to a fundamental assumption of postmodernity: the cruciality of context. As biological organisms attempting to orient ourselves to the world, we seek causal explanations, both physical and social. At the same time, this biological attempt at orientation entails that we want *true* explanations. After our tendency to over-detect agency causes us to worry about a possible danger lurking in the bush, we often then determine no danger exists. In this determination we may or may not figure out what caused the initial rustling. And we usually manage to do quite fine if we do not find a particular explanation or cause. Of course, we normally assume a proximate physical cause led to the rustling, whether or not we pinpoint it. Now in the case of the universe itself, we cannot similarly assume that it must have some cause. Yet neither can we just assume that it must not. Recent research pertains here, supporting the existence of two decision-making systems of mammalian brains operating at different speeds in different contexts.[24] (I would add the caveat that per Damasio's work these parts of the brain work together in the broader contexts of our lives.) The faster sub-cortical system would manifest the stronger tendency to over-detect agency. The slower, more reflective, in certain ways more accurate, cortical system would thus tend to serve as a corrective to over-active agency detection. In short, as I intimated in Chapter 3, I find quite simplistic the conclusion of some that the human tendency to over-detect agency in some contexts disproves or makes entirely unlikely the existence of an ultimate cause of our universe.

Notice that my above argument for the divine as the ultimate reservoir and limiter of all possibility does not, at least not directly or obviously, hinge upon the divine being *consciously* "intentional" or "pur-

24. "Will Our Future Brains."

posive." It does depend upon the limitation of possibilities being more than random, based on some combination of orderliness and openness to complex change. To say more than this easily gets into language that normally connotes conscious evaluation: this limitation involves a "reason" or "reasons," that which is "interesting," a "choice" or "decision." Perhaps to describe this limitation as "directional" is the best we can do for a metaphor not so typically associated with consciousness. To speak of a "*telos*," or "end" may also work.

This brings me to certain Eastern religions that I interpret to embrace belief in ultimate divine causality, while eschewing belief in a personal, conscious God. In my understanding, Ti'en of Confucianism, the Tao of Taoism, and "sunyata"—the emptiness which is the source of all fullness, the formless source of all forms—in Mahayana Buddhism all function as ultimate divine cause of the universe. Indeed, Taoism and Mahayana Buddhism could be labeled panentheistic, in contrast to other more dualistic or monistic Eastern religions and strands. The world is construed as within the Tao or sunyata; the world "bodies forth" from the Tao or sunyata. Only here the transcendent—in the sense of a divine reality more than or beyond its manifestation in/as the universe—is modeled as transpersonal or formless rather than as personal with attributes. Clearly these religions do not believe that our world exists solely by chance—direction, teleology, or reason in some sense applies. Slingerland for his part dismisses the possibility of any larger or overall direction or purpose to the universe: Some modern Westerners harbor "a more diffuse, non-theistic sense that what we are doing 'matters'—a conceit that makes no sense unless we project some sort of abstract, metaphorical agency onto the universe."[25] He attributes this projection to the sphere of social interaction, specifically the human need for social approval. I would mention again that our basic biological drive for orientation to our world involves both the social and physical—and perhaps in the human case orientation and explanation beyond our physical and social universes. Slingerland's dismissal appears to apply not only to those with the vague sensibility he cites, but many Eastern believers as well as some Western religious naturalists who see the universe or aspects of it as divine, as involving some non-theistic directionality. These folks do attribute precisely some meta-

25. Slingerland, "Study of Religion," 396.

phorical agency or causality to the universe or to the overarching (again traditionally more Western) or underlying (more Eastern) source of the universe. That these Eastern believers and Western religious naturalists have deliberately rejected metaphors of personal agency for their version of ultimate reality constitutes an argument against Slingerland's assumption that the need for social approval lies behind all belief in an ultimate or overall direction or purpose to the universe.

Before a final word about Eastern vis-à-vis Western religions, I will offer a specific version of the teleological argument. I submit that the existence of sentient, conscious, intentional beings in the universe is better explained by the existence of a conscious, intentional—or, better, super-conscious or not less than conscious—divine source, than either by the universe as a whole or by a transpersonal cause greater than the universe, *if* these are construed as thoroughly and strictly non-conscious. The absolutely non-conscious ultimately causing the conscious strikes me as incongruous. At the same time, like McFague, Kaufman, and many other theologians, I want to avoid idealism or anthropomorphism. Billions of years of life on earth have preceded the few million years of hominid life, and hundreds of thousands of species of sentient life share this planet with us. Therefore, I believe we fall into arrogance and absurdity to claim that the existence of other life is just for our benefit or that we are infinitely more valuable than other animals. Comparatively, the degree of complexity of experience, emotion, thought, and morality makes a human individual more valuable than a non-human one. But that hardly means other animals have no or little intrinsic value. To the extent we have lost a sense of life's sacredness, we will not regain it by devaluing animals—with whom we share much in embodied experience, emotion, and values according to this project; but rather by deeming all sentient life as sacred. What of the large swath of space and time apparently devoid of sentient life?—and even if many other planets teem with such life, still most of space-time does not. Here some type of panpsychism a la process thought has appeal—though we may well never possess any means to know whether fundamental particles might have some small degree of sentience. Nevertheless, even if we cannot embrace panpsychism, I judge that the value of life on earth and the other places it probably exists justifies belief in the directionality or teleology of a universe and its source, which act to make life possible.[26]

As suggested in chapter 6, my embodied pantheistic model posits that everything that occurs in the universe registers with, makes some difference to, affects the divine. I defend this idea by contending that the divine as the ultimate source of all potentiality and actuality has the capability to remain in touch with the whole universe (and all other universes if any exist). Indeed, if the divine serves as the ultimate power behind or within all things, I find it implausible that anything of the universe is external to the divine (save, in some sense, the indeterminate freedom of choice and spontaneity of creatures). Negatively, positing the externality of the world to the divine implies, to again invoke Tillich, a "God above God," who includes and empowers both this penultimate divine and the universe, setting the conditions and structures for the interactions of these relatively external beings. If everything registers with the divine and a directionality exists favoring some order and complexity—and in turn value, then to apply the analogy of care or love to the divine does not seem to represent too much of a stretch. It matters then to the divine, to the divine will, to achieve the optimum of value over disvalue or suffering among embodied creatures. If so, this may constitute an argument in favor of a personal and conscious divine—or, better, not less than personal and super-conscious—over a non-personal, non-conscious model of divinity. To my knowledge, the Eastern religions I have mentioned do not say much concerning the fate of humans and animals as mattering to divinity—although bodhisattvas or buddhas with compassion to end all creaturely suffering, understood as incarnations of sunyata or the Buddha nature, could provide

26. On my embodied pantheistic model of the divine, as indicated before, I do not posit direct or particular communication from the divine. A corollary follows for me from that and from divine creative direction or intention manifest in the processes of nature—which result in only a small percentage of creatures having the reflectivity to imagine the divine: Though God is in some sense personal for me, I do not believe the divine intends to have a "personal relationship" with the creatures, at least not in the usual sense of that phrase, as specific back and forth communication. Rather God communicates through the overall divine embodiment and intends fulfillment of our lives through our own embodiment in our physical and social worlds, with the divine serving as the ultimate backdrop and context of our lives. That being said, I do believe that the directionality or intentionality of the divine does include the likelihood or even certainty that *some* creatures will possess the reflectivity to ask and answer questions about the divine.

a counter-example. Then again, the dearth of examples may just reflect my ignorance.

To conclude consideration of East and West in relation to the divine: Though I have been writing about the divine in relation to us, our inability to know anything of the divine beyond that, of the divine "in itself," cautions against over-confidence about our models of divinity. In Chapter 6, I suggested that panentheism denies the distinctness or separateness of the divine with respect to the creatures usually associated with personhood. Just above I have labeled some Eastern ways as panentheistic. If such Eastern concepts of the divine are interpreted as more "transpersonal" than "impersonal," much of the difference between East and West falls away. I definitely consider Eastern religions regarding the world as basically good, as well as some forms of religious naturalism, as allies with the Western religions in upholding directionality or teleology with respect to incarnate life. They contrast with religions that might deny the basic goodness of embodied life and with modern viewpoints that regard life as a matter of ultimate chance or brute fact (including Gordon Kaufman's, even if his "serendipitous creativity" or my colloquial rephrasing, "happy chance," gives a positive spin to ultimate randomness). While at this point I favor the metaphoric power of imaging the ultimate source of embodied existence as (super)conscious and (super)personal, especially in relation to what happens to us and our world as mattering to the divine, greater Eastern circumspection on this score deserves our respect.

Given Sallie McFague's affirmation of a divine (personal) power and spirit supportive of life, what should we make of her position regarding general providence, to use a traditional theological term? I think she concedes too much in her unwillingness to endorse divine "causality" or even "directionality," let alone "intentionality," with respect to the universe as a whole or its evolutionary forces. McFague and I appear to share a complementarity/commensurability model of the differing roles of science and theology (or metaphysics): Science describes and explains physical events and causes, while theology makes religious or metaphysical judgments or constructs that transcend, but should not contradict, scientific evidence.[27] Assuming that basic model, I find no warrant for McFague to bar theology from considering an

27. McFague, *Body of God*, 146–47.

ultimate intentionality, direction, or cause behind evolution. Of course, evolutionary science deals only with "local causes";[28] but it is precisely the province of religion or metaphysics, *not* science, to deal with ultimate, global causes—or the lack thereof. McFague wants to avoid—as do I—the "God of the gaps" trap into which theology too often has fallen in the past. It is indeed misguided to purport that specific evolutionary events correspond to and prove specific divine creative intentions. However, the issue of any ultimate cause or purpose behind or within the existence of fundamental "laws" or processes of this evolving universe is a legitimate one. As indicated in Chapter 6, McFague also undermines her affirmation of a divine personal power, and of an integrated pantheistic reality able to include and empower the reality of the universe, by her declaration that God "is many, not one."[29] On a pantheistic model, we best describe the divine as "many in one" or "many and one," rather than as simply "one" or as "many, not one."

A Resurgent Dualism?

Regarding human nature some thinkers, including Slingerland, have paired an alleged innate Cartesian or disembodied dualism with hyperactive agency detection. In their eyes, this pairing further explains—and discredits—the supposed human tendency to invent allegedly disembodied supernatural causes. For radical embodiment, this provides some challenge. While these thinkers share with me a conviction that in reality humans are not/do not have disembodied spirits, at best their hypothesis would make that much harder the task of disabusing people of a harmful picture of human nature. At worst these thinkers reinscribe dualism, consigning humanity to bifurcation and perpetual conflict, between the supposed scientific and metaphysical truth of a reductionistic physicalism on the one hand and an inescapable (at least for most of us) folk psychology of disembodied spirits on the other.

From my perspective of radical embodiment, a reductive physicalism does not overcome dualism; rather it just opts for one side of the binaries. Genuinely overcoming dualism entails giving just due to body and mind, object and subject. It involves correlation of aspects, a "double aspect monism" if you will, rather than a monism of physical

28. Ibid., 145.
29. Ibid., 155.

objects. Slingerland seems to begin with hope of such an overthrowing of dualism: "the mind is the body, and the body is permeated through and through with mind."[30] However, he ends up with a version of "weak emergence," where mental qualities constitute only a convenient way to talk about brain states.[31] He concludes that the fundamental nature of consciousness is the same as that of everything else in the universe—a configuration of matter and energy, just more complex than most: "human beings, like all of the other entities that we know about, appear to be robots all the way down, whether we like that idea or not."[32] But we do not like that idea! Here is where dualism re-enters. Part of us wants to know the truth, however unpleasant (a part which I view as continuous with our biological desire to accurately orient ourselves)—in this case, the alleged physicalist truth that we are just things.[33] However, to quote Jack Nicholson's character in *A Few Good Men*, another part of us "can't handle the truth."[34] For evolution has designed us not to think of ourselves and others as mere things (even though we are). Or as he puts it in a subtitle, "We are robots designed not to believe that we are robots."[35]

Slinglerland accentuates the dualism by equating this human proclivity to view our subjectivity as real with belief in *disembodied* souls or minds. For him human religious longing that a part of human persons survives death represents the main evidence.[36] Cognitive psychologists Paul Bloom and Jesse Bering also advocate an innate disembodied or Cartesian dualism. They have conducted or cited several psychological experiments that they believe support their position. In addition, Bloom in his popular trade book, *Descartes' Baby*, and Bering in a major article

30. Slingerland, "Study of Religion," 378.

31. Ibid., 388–90.

32. Slingerland, "Study of Religion," 392.

33. Ibid., 400–402. Interestingly Slingerland cites the movie, *The Matrix*, where most humans live as brains in a vat but do not know their true state. Earlier I cited Damasio and Edelman, who contend that the absence of a body means that a brain in a vat could not duplicate embodied experience. Though Slingerland does not specify the disembodied state of such brains, I would opine that what the heroes fighting the Matrix, and viewers identifying with them, find unacceptable is not just the deception, but also the disembodiment.

34. Ibid., 392–404.

35. Ibid., 394.

36. Ibid., 394–95.

in *Behavioral and Brain Sciences*,[37] cite anecdotal evidence of movies
where people switch bodies and/or of the ways people talk about their
brains, as well as religious belief in life after death and in supernatural
agents. I find all of this heavily interpreted—and heavily influenced by
a disembodied picture of human beings present to a greater or lesser
degree in Western philosophy from ancient times, given new impetus
by Cartesianism in modern times, and still all too alive and well in these
postmodern times.

Relative to the question of innate dualism, I find it helpful to distinguish two hypotheses, as I stated in an e-mail to Bloom: Hypothesis
one—Humans innately distinguish between animate, sentient, intentional embodied beings and inanimate things.[38] Hypothesis two—Humans
innately distinguish between souls/minds and bodies (or to elaborate,
between disembodied souls and mindless bodies; the assumption here
is that souls can exist in separation from any body). At my college re-
union around the time *Descartes' Baby* was coming out, I asked Bloom
whether the results of the relevant psychological experiments clearly
favor (a shortened version of) Hypothesis two over Hypothesis one. He
answered in the negative. In a recent e-mail he indicated that he finds
more "compelling the thesis of mind-body dualism for interpreting the
results of the most significant experiment(s), by Bering and Bjorklund,
than the animate-inanimate distinction. Specifically he writes that the
fact that most young children believe that a dead mouse's mental states
continue while its biological states do not "strongly suggests that kids
think it has no body but still has a mind."[39] In contrast, my hunch is
that the believing children imagine that the mouse's psychological
states continue in a different body in another world. To my knowledge,
however, Bloom never explicitly evaluates this proposition vis-à-vis
that of inherent mind-body dualism. Similarly in his above mentioned
article, Bering begins with this assertion: "By stating that psychological
states survive death, one is committing to a radical form of mind-body

37. "Folk Psychology." This issue contains Bering's article, many commentaries, and
Bering's responses to them (453–98).

38. Gary Fuhrman refers to his version of this as a "primary dualism" in his review
of *Descartes' Baby.*

39. Bloom. E-mail to David Nikkel.

dualism."[40] Thus I see both Bloom and Bering as begging the question relative to my interpretation.

But let us examine the Bering-Bjorklund research. I would first of all exhort anyone interested in these issues to read for oneself the article on this rather elaborate series of experiments.[41] To summarize, they conducted three experiments with varying configurations of preschool, kindergarten, early elementary, older elementary, and/or adult participants, each in succession involving more, and generally increasingly specific, questions, in response to a depiction of an alligator eating a mouse. General results showed that most younger children believed that psychological states of the mouse continued, while older elementary children and adults believed that most such states did not. While this article grants the difficulty of separating evolutionary from cultural mechanisms,[42] Bering and Bloom conclude that, if cultural learning were the only influence, belief in continuation of psychological states should *increase* with age (due to the impact of religious traditions).[43] At the same time Bering judges that the growing biological knowledge about death that comes with age does work to *decrease* such belief [44] (I would note that such knowledge would combine natural developmental and cultural influences). To explain the actual decrease with age in continuation belief, I would add one more factor, a cultural one, which Bering and Bloom ignore: the influence of the traditional Christian position that humans experience an afterlife, while animals do not. My sense is that many American adult believers in a human afterlife harbor some doubts about pets surviving death, and even greater doubts concerning wild animals. At the same time I can imagine parents simply telling their young child that deceased grandpa is alive in heaven and/or that a dead pet or feral animal is alive in another world, without sharing their own relevant distinctions and ambivalences. Bering does "note that only a very small percentage of children used any eschatological" language,

40. Bering, "Folk Psychology," 453.

41. Bering and Bjorklund, "Natural Emergence."

42. Ibid., 218.

43. Ibid., 230; Bloom, "Is God an Accident?" 6.

44. Bering and Bjorklund, "Natural Emergence," 218–19.

including "heaven," during the experiments, though he concedes that "this is not compelling evidence . . . in its own right."[45]

Let me get more specific about the experiments' results. Ruling out cultural influence, Bering and Bjorklund asseverate, "It seems strangely counterintuitive that" younger children "stated that dead agents did not need to drink water but answered that it was possible for dead agents to be thirsty,"[46] regarding this as evidence for innate mind-body dualism. Yet if these children were strict dualists, they would realize that a truly disembodied soul would not feel thirsty. On the other hand, young children who believed that mouse now existed in another world with a different body—probably at least partly under the influence of culture—might more plausibly think that mouse could feel thirsty. Of course, Bering and Bloom could object—rightly—that this argument assumes reasoning too precise for the capabilities of young children. But then the burden of proof, I think, falls back on them as to why they insist on the precision of the hypothesis of innate mind-body dualism, rather than on the more general distinction between animate and inanimate. Overall the experiments yield a pattern of decreasing belief with age in continuation of both biological and psychological states. Experiment 3 differentiates the questions about states into six categories: biological, psychobiological (e.g., being thirsty), perceptual, desire, emotional, and epistemic.[47] While late elementary children show a decrease in continuation belief in all six categories compared with kindergarteners, changes in the biological category (save one question) are fairly dramatic, and those in the psychobiological quite dramatic. Changes in the perceptual category are not that dramatic, because kindergarteners already show a relatively high rate of disbelief regarding such continuation. Finally, changes in the categories of desire, emotional, and epistemic, while significant, are not that dramatic. This means that a significant proportion of the older children believe in continuation with respect to several questions in each of these latter three categories. Moreover, a significant proportion of adults believe in continuation with respect to at least one question in each of the three categories (though the uneven results of comparison between older children and adults do evidence an overall

45. Ibid., 230.
46. Ibid., 224. See also, 229–30.
47. Ibid. See esp., Table 4, 226.

pattern of decrease in such continuation belief). I find all of the results of Experiment 3 consistent with the following: For those who entertain the possibility of an afterlife world for dead mouse, their picture of the nature of that world sharpens *with age*, including beliefs that afterlife denizens have more accurate knowledge about certain matters and that good predominates over evil more so than in this world (Bering and Bjorklund do notice participants' greater likelihood to attribute positive than negative feelings[48]). In a related vein, adults' much higher disbelief that mouse still wants to go home or still hopes to get better at math perhaps reflects their picture of an otherworldly existence where mouse is already at home and does not need math. I found particularly striking that 64% of adults responded that dead mouse "still loves his mom" (compared with 80% of late elementary and 94% of kindergarten children). I would guess that this high percentage reflects a combination of two factors: 1) Love is strongly connected to beliefs about afterlife worlds, even for some generally unsure about animal survival (which probably reflects cultural influence). 2) Some adults who disbelieve that mouse is consciously experiencing love of mom in the present might still hold that once love has existed, in some (inchoate) sense it can never die. (For some of these latter adults, this principle might also apply for the emotions of sadness and anger. On the other hand, given the usual positive portrait of a possible afterlife world, that 100% of adults disbelieve that mouse is "still scared of the alligator" should not surprise us). To cut to the chase, I find nothing in the results of this significant series of experiments to favor innate mind-body dualism over an animate-inanimate distinction or dualism, if you prefer. In this context of afterlife belief, the latter plays out in belief in animate existence with *a different body* appropriate to another world.

Regarding understanding of the relationship of our brains to ourselves, Bloom has a piece under review entitled, "Developing Intuitions about Which Personal Properties Are Associated with the Brain,"[49] and in *Descartes' Baby* relates a conversation he had with his then six-year-old son Max. I do not find it at all surprising that adults and children resist identifying themselves with their brains in what I view as a reductive way. Rather they regard themselves as a *full-bodied*, whole self, not

---

48. Ibid., 228.
49. Choe, Keil, and Bloom, "Developing Intuitions."

particular brain processes taken in isolation. For example, Max resists making his brain responsible for value-laden experiences such as "dreaming, feeling sad, or loving his brother."[50] I agree with Gary Fuhrman that "Max is simply giving a *holistic* explanation [emphasis his].... As a budding philosopher, Max seems more like a young Merleau-Ponty than a Descartes." Also apropos is his reference to Damasio's somatic marker theory of emotions.[51] While feminist philosopher Mary Midgley makes this remark in relation to philosophers of mind, I believe it also applies to most cognitive psychologists and cognitive neuroscientists:

> What is ironic, however, about this ostensible rejection of 'dualism' by most contemporary philosophers of mind, is the persistence in their thinking of shades of the Enlightenment ghost they thought they had routed. For, when they discourse about the "mind/body" relation they rarely consider anything in that "body" below the level of the neck. Either they focus exclusively on the mind's relation to the brain, or more generally, on its relation to the physical world *tout court*. Flesh and bones (and, unsurprisingly, women's minds) are still relatively neglected subjects in the field.[52]

What about the transferability of bodies and consciousness in popular culture, as in the movie *Freaky Friday* or in Voldemort taking over someone's body in the *Harry Potter* stories? Already in Chapter 3 in connection to shamanism, I referred to our ability to imagine what it would be like to be another body. That comes with our embodiment and our reflective, imaginative abilities. I would stress that in such popular instances no one exists or acts (whatever that might mean) in a disembodied state—when depicted they always have a body of some sort. Plus, suspension of disbelief operates here. I dare say that if someone claimed in real life that a demon or evil person/spirit had taken over a friend's body, almost all of us would be incredulous, especially if the friend behaved more or less normally. And if the friend behaved quite unusually, most of us would suspect a psychological problem. Even for those of us who entertained the possibility of some type of possession, we might suppose that the demon has some kind of body, but a body that allows it to possess human or animal bodies. As I will expound

---

50. Bloom, *Descartes' Baby*, 200.

51. Fuhrman, Review of Paul Bloom, *Descartes' Baby*.

52. Midgley, "Soul's Successors," 66–67.

below, primal and ancient peoples typically believed that good and bad spirits had bodies, albeit different from ours. The mistake I believe Bloom, Bering, and Slingerland commit in their speculation is this: They take these imaginative scenarios and picture viewers as Cartesian philosophers who attempt to explain abstractly and logically these strange happenings—instead of recognizing these persons as embodied beings who naturally imagine in bodily ways.

As just mentioned, primal and ancient animistic belief and belief in gods, goddesses, and spirits entailed embodiment in nature or in some kind of anthropomorphized—or animalized—body. Of course, these embodied spirits do not suffer all the limitations that humans and animals endure with their bodies. And their bodies may be hidden from us or even invisible to our ordinary vision. Not only did primal and ancient people typically depict deities as embodied, they believed the actual divine bodies bore some analogy to their representations. While ancient Judaism prohibited representation of God (the historical reality of which happened much later than depicted in Hebrew biblical narrative), it did not explicitly deny, and in some scriptural passages specifically refers to, God's body. The underlying rationale was that the greatness of God and the divine body in comparison to human or animal bodies would countenance no visual representations. The complete disembodiment and immateriality of God in learned Jewish and Christian theology resulted from a long journey strongly influenced by Greek philosophy, particularly of the Platonic and Aristotelian varieties. (Even Stoicism, influential in the ancient world and in some respects on Judaism and Christianity, affirmed some materiality to the divine, even in its pure state of Fire.) Some forms of Hinduism came to view the divine Atman/Brahman in itself as pure consciousness, with incarnations as lesser states of reality and value for at best penultimate purposes. Yet divine embodiment has hardly died in Hinduism as a whole—far from it.

Likewise, most of the pre-history and history of religious belief in life after death does not actually support disembodiment. Primal religions typically believe in an embodied world in some spatial relation to our present one—though unreachable until we die—and better than our present one, without all the evils. The clichéd "happy hunting ground" represents one version of this. As ancient agricultural civilizations developed, afterlife beliefs typically changed: In some cases afterlife belief died, in many others an unhappy picture of the afterlife emerged. I attribute this change to the dominance of agriculture in these cultures and in their controlling pictures about life: just as dead plants, dead human bodies are buried in the earth. While new plants come from the soil and nourish new human life, human individuals do not revive from the grave. Typically, afterlife belief focuses on an Underworld, where people are mere shades or shadows of their former selves, as in the Hebrew concept of Sheol. Note that the dead do have a body, albeit a shadowy one. While they do not suffer complete disembodiment, I sense that the lack of full-blooded, full-bodied life constitutes precisely the most unsatisfactory aspect of existence in Sheol or Hades. The unhappy nature of such an afterlife takes some of the steam out of the argument for a human compulsion to believe that some (disembodied) part of us survives. Annihilation appears a better prospect than "life" after death in Sheol.

Finally I would note that resurrection of the body represents the most original version of life after death in the Western monotheisms of rabbinic Judaism, Christianity, and Islam. The influence of Greek philosophy, especially (neo)Platonism, has complicated the picture in Western theology, introducing a disembodied soul—at least until the Judgment Day—with which to contend. Nevertheless, I suspect that for everyday believers in an afterlife from these religions, the vast majority imagine themselves in heaven with a perfect body, reunited with departed family and friends whose transformed bodies they immediately recognize.

Our fundamental distinction between animate, sentient, intentional beings and inanimate objects does provide an entry, an opportunity for disembodied or Cartesian dualism. But such dualism is a cultural choice that overcomes a deeper pre-reflective tendency to imagine ourselves *as embodied*—both in counterfactual situations in this world and in an assumed afterlife to come, as well as to so imagine any extraordinary intentional agents. And that is precisely what we should expect if we human beings indeed are radically embodied.

I will offer a final word about Slingerland's dualism of a reductive physicalism and an inescapable idealism. What if I am wrong and the universe and life are ultimately matters of blind chance or brute fact? I think we can articulate a less vicious dualism, one that does not assume we are mere things who (fortunately) cannot accept this metaphysical reality. On Slingerland's view, the universe provides no metaphysical imprimatur on the value of sentient organisms. Fine, for the sake of my argument. Due to evolutionary psychology, we seek social approval from the universe as a whole, or its source, but cannot get it. The existence of sentient beings issues totally from serendipity, from happy chance. Given that the existence of any and every thing here bears no relation to the value of anything, the universe can then tell us nothing about the deepest value of anything, nothing about metaphysical value. Therefore, others and I judge sentient beings to be of intrinsic value in themselves unlike non-sentient realities—and the universe is in no position to tell us otherwise. Life is sacred. Thus, in metaphysical reality, human beings and animals are not mere things—for through my embodied experience, I sense the intrinsic worth of sentient individuals. Slingerland appears to assume that science—or his interpretation thereof—dictates the metaphysical truth of our thingness, when science itself cannot make such value judgments. Of course, it would be nice if the universe and its source endorse the value of sentient beings—and I of course have argued that they do. It would indeed be nice to have an ultimate confirmation that we do belong here. But as I have argued in this book, especially in Chapter 5, at least we do belong here penultimately: We have evolved as embodied, conscious beings adapted to survive and even thrive in our physical and social worlds, adapted to realize diverse and genuine embodied values—perhaps ultimately due to chance or, as I have argued, perhaps not.

Radical Embodiment and an Afterlife?

Before completely concluding this project, let me address the issue of any life after our existence as evolutionarily adapted biological organisms, given the focus of this final (eschatological?) chapter on transcendence, especially as I have dealt with the nature of afterlife belief in this section. Do we then transcend our embodied life in this world as experiencing subjects after our biological death? The whole tenor of my development of radical embodiment—that all our values stem from our embodiment in this universe—implies the probability, the presumption of a "no" answer to this question. On the other hand—and I would be untrue to my role as a theologian if I did not offer the other hand, according to my theological mentor Ronald Williams—might other dimensions to this universe or another realm unconnected to it provide a suitable environ-ment for human and animal embodiment upon death? I will explore ideas of the afterlife from two interlocutors for this project, psycholo-gist Harry L. Hunt and theologian Paul Tillich, both of whom intend to endorse embodied, rather than disembodied, existence in eternity. For Hunt consciousness and time are co-implicated in "the whence-whither flows and pulsations of perception,"[53] following Gibson's theory of space and time as "inseparable aspects of a single, seamless, ecologi-cal array."[54] Cognitively speaking, Hunt hypothesizes that the "extreme transformation of duration" into an eternal now associated with LSD and deep meditative experiences involves the following: the pulses of consciousness become indistinguishable from the gaps between them, yielding a state of luminous glow. The sense of change "ceases, while ongoing self-referential consciousness, synesthetically translated" con-tinues. This experience entails a sense of "the openness of the horizon."[55] Hunt then relates such experiences to near-death and actual death experiences. He states that from a first-person perspective, "we really cannot die," either passing out or "with immediate awareness retained or reappearing," becoming one with eternity. "Pragmatically speaking," he concludes that we should trust our subjective experience and hope for such an afterlife.[56]

I have problems, however, both with Hunt's justification for, and the nature of, his version of an afterlife. Other subjects who remain in this life have objective evidence that the bodily basis for such experi-ences does cease. To evaluate the nature of this afterlife, I will note a similarity of my embodied understanding of mystical experience and Hunt's understanding of extraordinary experiences, including that of death: It features an *openness* in some sense to all reality. Hunt refers to it in terms of infinite space and eternal temporality.[57] By way of con-trast, I take the right interpretation of mystical and related experiences to be openness to future embodiment. Embodiment in infinite space and time equals embodiment nowhere (unless one is the divine em-

---

53. Hunt, *Nature of Consciousness*, 249.

54. Ibid., 244.

55. Ibid., 252.

56. Ibid., 256.

57. Hunt, *Nature of Consciousness*, 252.

bodied in everything which comes to be). It is empty.[58] For non-divine individuals embodiment means particular embodiment—in this life and, if such exists, the life to come.

Tillich's picture of the afterlife has some affinities to Hunt's. Tillich does warn that positive literal language can say little about the afterlife, instead needing to yield to "poetic imagination." He does write of the absence of "time and change" in a fulfillment where all aspects of our embodied earthly life—not just our minds—are elevated to the Eternal Presence.[59] What appears to be missing in Tillich's picture, as in Hunt's, then, is any real passage of time, which an embodied afterlife would seem to demand.

Process luminaries Whitehead and Hartshorne reject subjective immortality in favor of an "objective immortality," where God lovingly remembers all that transpired in our lives, forever enriched by the good in our own lives and the good that we have contributed to others. I have always found this idea very attractive, apart from the question of subjective immortality. My embodied panentheistic model of divinity provides that all we do registers with the divine. And given the ultimacy of the divine as the source of all possibility and actuality, it makes sense that the divine will never lose this memory—for what external power could wrest it away. So the value of our lives to ourselves and others furnishes everlasting value to the divine life, which will always find new embodiments—and just perhaps through the creativity of the divine, we will find new embodiments beyond this life. In any case, the divine source and goal of all our lives beneficently has made provisions for what is best for us, as it has made for us a home.

Coda

William James wrote of our legitimate need to feel we belong to the universe—to feel at home in the universe if you will, that the universe in some manner conduces to the fulfillment of our needs and values. With this book I have argued that we human beings as embodied creatures can normally and rightfully feel at home in this universe—and

---

58. While Taylor's version of the sublime referred to above stays far away from any notion of eternal afterlife, its sense of absolutely unlimited possibility seems to issue in a similar emptiness of embodiment nowhere.

59. Tillich, *Systematic*, 3:412–14.

that this universe and the ultimate reality within and behind it value our lives. If the reader is not yet convinced, I will close with a Jamesian pragmatic argument. All we know comes through our embodiment in the world. Critical reason, I have acknowledged, has a legitimate and important role to play in various contexts. Yet, for critical reason, which stems from our embodiment, to question the very meaningfulness of that embodiment seems finally to represent the epitome of hubris in the modern spirit. From which disembodied no place does it attempt to make such an assessment?

As James penned, "What, in short, has authority to bar us from trusting our religious demands?"[60] James claimed the right to supplement the universe's physical order "by an unseen spiritual order which we assume on trust, if only thereby life may seem to us better worth living"[61]—a trust that "our inner interests" have a "real connection with the forces that the hidden world contains."[62] Radical embodiment claims that our normal background feelings of integral bodily presence and our normal tacit sense of meaningful bodily orientation and engagement with our world resonate with a universe and a divine reality that mean for us to be here and to find fulfillment. Finally, the question comes down to this: Will we trust our embodiment in the world?

---

60. James, *Will to Believe*, 56.
61. Ibid., 52.
62. Ibid., 55.

Bibliography

Adams, Bryan. "Meso: A Biochemical Subsystem for a Humanoid Robot." Online: http://www.ai.mit.edu/projects/humanoid-robotics-group, 2004.

Aichele, George. "Literary Fantasy and Postmodern Theology." *Journal of the American Academy of Religion* 19 (1991) 323–37.

Allen, Charles W. "The Primacy of *Phronesis*: A Proposal for Avoiding Frustrating Tendencies in Our Conception of Rationality." *Journal of Religion* 69 (1989) 359–74.

Apczynski, John V. "Belief in God, Proper Basicality, and Rationality." *Journal of the American the American Academy of Religion* 60 (1992) 301–12.

Apple, James. "Mind as Representational Analysis: Bridging First and Third Person Accounts." Paper presented to the American Academy of Religion Annual Meeting, San Antonio, TX, November 2004.

Ariely, Dan. *Predictably Irrational: The Hidden Forces That Shape Our Decisions.* New York: Harper Collins, 2008.

Associated Press. "Parrot Dies after Life of Service to Science." September 13, 2007.

———. "Study Finds Sex Reassignment Fails, and Nature Prevails." November 10, 2001.

Barash, David P. "Animal Intelligence." *Chronicle of Higher Education*, August 17, 2007, B10–11.

Barbour, Ian G. *When Science Meets Religion.* San Francisco: Harper Collins, 2000.

Beardslee, William, David Ray Griffin, and Joe Holland. *Varieties of Postmodern Theology.* Albany: State University of New York Press, 1989.

Bering, Jesse M. "The Folk Psychology of Souls." *Behavioral and Brain Sciences* 29 (2006) 453–62.

Bering, Jesse M. and David F. Bjorklund. "The Natural Emergence of Reasoning about the Afterlife as a Developmental Regularity." *Developmental Psychology* 40 (2004) 217–33.

Bernal, J. D. *The World, the Flesh, and the Devil.* London: Kegan Paul, 1929.

Bernstein, Richard. *Beyond Objectivism and Relativism: Science, Hermeneutics, and Praxis.* Philadelphia: University of Pennsylvania Press, 1983.

Bloom, Paul. *Descartes' Baby: How the Science of Child Development Explains What Makes Us Human.* New York: Basic, 2004.

———. E-mail to David Nikkel, July 18, 2008.

———. "Is God an Accident?" *Atlantic Monthly* 296 (2005) 105–12.

Bock, Jerry. *Fiddler on the Roof.* New York: Crown, 1964.

Boroditsky, Lera. "How Does Our Language Shape the Way We Think?" *Edge*, 12 June 2009.

Bowler, Mike. "Learning Ability for Language Strong in Babies." *Baltimore Sun*, August 19, 2001.

Boyer, Pascal. *The Naturalness of Religious Ideas: A Cognitive Theory of Religion.* Berkeley: University of California Press, 1994.

Braxton, Donald M. "Naturalizing Transcendence in the New Cosmologies of Emergence." *Zygon* 41 (2006) 347–63.

Brooks, Rodney A. "Intelligence without Representation." *Journal of Artificial Intelligence* 47 (1991) 139–59.

Brown, Delwin. "Beyond *Boundaries*: Toward a Radical Historicism in Theology." *American Journal of Theology and Philosophy* 18 (1997) 167–80.

———. *Boundaries of Our Habitations: Tradition and Theological Construction.* Albany: State University of New York Press, 1994.

Brown, Delwin, and Sheila Greeve Davaney. "Theology and Tradition: Rethinking the Connection." Paper presented at the American Academy of Religion Annual Meeting, New Orleans, November 1996.

Bryson, Joanna J. "Embodiment *vs.* Memetics." Online: www.citeseer.ist.psu.edu /697496, 2006 .

Burkert, Walter. *Creation of the Sacred: Tracks of Biology in Early Religions.* Cambridge, MA: Harvard University Press, 1996.

Butler, Judith. *Bodies That Matter: On the Discursive Limits of "Sex."* New York: Routledge, 1993.

Cannon, Dale. "Longing to Know If Our Knowing Really Is Knowing." *Tradition and Discovery* 31 (2005) 6–20.

Caputo, John. "The Good News about Alterity: Derrida and Theology." *Faith and Philosophy* 10 (1993) 453–70.

———. *The Prayers and Tears of Jacques Derrida.* Bloomington: University of Indiana Press, 1997.

Cassirer, Ernst. *An Essay on Man.* New Haven, CT: Yale University Press, 1944.

Cavell, Stanley. *Must We Mean What We Say?* Cambridge: Cambridge University Press, 1976.

Chodorow, Nancy J. *The Power of Feelings: Personal Meaning in Psychoanalysis, Gender, and Culture.* New Haven: Yale University Press, 1999.

Choe, K., F. Keil, and P. Bloom. "Developing Intuitions about Which Personal Properties Are Associated with the Brain." Unpublished manuscript, 2008.

Churchland, Paul M. *The Engine of Reason, the Seat of the Soul: A Philosophical Journey into the Brain.* Cambridge, MA: MIT Press, 1995.

Cobb, John B. Jr., and David Ray Griffin. *Process Theology: An Introductory Exposition.* Philadelphia: Westminster, 1976.

Connerton, Paul. *How Societies Remember.* New York: Cambridge University Press, 1989.

Conway-Morris, Simon. *The Crucible of Creation.* London: Oxford University Press, 1998.

Cowdell, Scott. *A Study of Recent Christology.* New York: Paulist, 1996.

Creech, James, Peggy Kamuf, and Jane Todd. "Deconstruction in America: An Interview with Jacques Derrida." *Critical Exchange* 17 (1985) 1–33.

Damasio, Antonio R. *Descartes' Error: Emotion, Reason, and the Human Brain.* New York: Putnams, 1994.

———. *The Feeling of What Happens.* New York: Harcourt Brace, 1999.

———. *Looking for Spinoza: Joy, Sorrow, and the Feeling Brain*. New York: Harcourt Brace, 2003.

Dambricourt, Anne. *La légende maudite du XXeme siecle: L'erreur darwinienne*. Strasbourg: La Nuee Bleue, 2000.

Dean, William. "American Religious Thought." *Journal of the American Academy of Religion* 20 (1992) 737–52.

———. "The Challenge of the New Historicism." *Journal of Religion* 66 (1986) 261–81.

De Duve, Christian. *Vital Dust*. New York: Basic, 1995.

Denton, Michael J. *Nature's Destiny*. New York: Free, 1998.

Derrida, Jacques. "Deconstruction and the Other." In *Dialogues with Contemporary Continental Thinkers*, edited by Richard Kearney, 107–25. Manchester, UK: University of Manchester Press, 1984.

———. *The Gift of Death*. Translated by David Wills. Chicago: University of Chicago Press, 1995.

———. *Limited, Inc. with Afterword*. Edited by Gerald Graff. Translated by Jeffrey Mehlman and Samuel Weber. Evanston, IL: Northwestern University Press, 1988.

———. *Specters of Marx*. Translated by Peggy Kamuf. New York: Routledge, 1994.

———. *Writing and Difference*. Translated by Alan Bass. Chicago: University of Chicago Press, 1978.

De Waal, Frans B. M. "Culture and Nature are Inseparable." *Chronicle of Higher Education*, June 4, 1999. "Do We Think That Machines Can Think." *TerraDaily: News about Planet Earth*, July 10, 2008.

———. "Do Humans Alone 'Feel Your Pain'?" *Chronicle of Higher Education*, October 26, 2001.

———. *Our Inner Ape*. New York: Riverhead, 2005.

———. "Pointing Primates: Sharing Knowledge . . . without Language." *Chronicle of Higher Education*, January 19, 2001.

Edelman, Gerald. *Bright Air, Brilliant Fire: On the Matter of the Mind*. New York: Harper Collins, 1992.

———. *The Remembered Present: A Biological Theory of Consciousness*. New York: Basic, 1989.

———. *Wider Than the Sky: The Phenomenal Gift of Consciousness*. New Haven, CT: Yale University Press, 2004.

Fuhrman, Gary. Review of *Descartes' Baby*, by Paul Bloom. Online: http://users.xplornet.com/~gnox/Bloom.htm, 2004.

Evans, James H. "African-American Christianity and the Postmodern Condition." *Journal of the American Academy of Religion* 18 (1990) 207–22.

Fiorenza, R. Francis Schussler. "Tradition: Between Identity and Reconstruction." Paper presented at the American Academy of Religion Annual Meeting, New Orleans, November 1996.

Fodor, Jerry. *Language of Thought*. Cambridge: Harvard University Press, 1980.

Foerst, Anne. "Cog, a Humanoid Robot, and the Question of the Image of God." *Zygon: Journal for Religion and Science* 33 (1998) 91–111.

Foster, Mary L. "The Growth of Symbolism in Culture." In *Symbol as Sense: New Approaches to the Analysis of Meaning*, edited by Mary L. Foster and Scott Brandes, 371–97. New York: Academic, 1980.

Foucault, Michel. *Power/Knowledge: Selected Interviews and Other Writings 1971–1977*. Edited by Colin Gordon. New York: Pantheon, 1980.

Fuller, Robert. "Spirituality in the Flesh: The Role of Discrete Emotions in Religious Life." *Journal of the American Academy of Religion* 75 (2007) 25–51.

———. "Wonder and the Religious Sensibility: A Study in Religion and Emotion." *Journal of Religion* 86 (2006) 364–84.

Gadamer, Hans-Georg. *Truth and Method*. New York: Seabury, 1975.

Gallagher, Shaun. *How the Body Shapes the Mind*. Oxford: Oxford University Press, 2005.

Gelernter, David. "Artificial Intelligence Is Lost In the Woods." *Technology Review*. Published by MIT, July/August, 2007.

Geraci, Robert M. "Apocalyptic AI: Religion and the Promise of Artificial Intelligence." *Journal of the American Academy of Religion* 76 (2008) 138–66.

Gibson, James J. *The Senses Considered As Perceptual Systems*. Boston: Houghton Mifflin, 1966.

Glass, Jay D. *The Animal within Us*. Corona del Mar, CA: Donnington, 1998.

Godlove, Terry F., Jr. *Religion, Interpretation, and Diversity of Belief: The Framework Model from Kant to Durkheim to Davidson*. Macon, GA: Mercer University Press, 1997.

Godzieba, Anthony J. "Ontotheology to Excess: Imagining God without Being." *Theological Studies* 56 (1995) 3–20.

Goodenough, Ursula, and Terrence W. Deacon. "From Biology to Consciousness to Morality." *Zygon: Journal of Religion and Science* 38 (2003) 801–19.

Goodman, Nelson. *Ways of Worldmaking*. Indianapolis: Hackett, 1978.

Gregersen, Neils Henrik. "Levels of Complexity." *Global Spiral* [formerly *Metanexus Digest*] 2 (January 21, 2002).

———. "Three Varieties of Panentheism." In *In Whom We Live and Move and Have Our Being*, edited by Philip Clayton and Arthur Peacocke, 19–35. Grand Rapids: Eerdmans, 2004.

Griffin, David Ray, editor. *Sacred Interconnections: Postmodern Spirituality, Political Economy, and Art*. Albany: State University of New York Press, 1996.

Guterman, Lila. "Do You Smell What I Hear? Neuroscientists Discover Crosstalk Among the Senses." *Chronicle of Higher Education*, December 14, 2001.

Harries, Karsten. *Infinity and Perspective*. Chicago: University of Chicago Press, 2003.

Harvey, Van A. *A Handbook of Theological Terms*. New York: Macmillan, 1964. S. v., "Inspiration of the Bible."

Hauerwas, Stanley. *Against the Nations: War and Survival in a Liberal Society*. Minneapolis: Winston, 1985.

———. *Christian Existence Today: Essays on Church, World, and Living in Between*. Durham, NC: Labyrinth, 1988.

———. *A Community of Character: Toward a Constructive Christian Social Ethic*. Notre Dame, IN: University of Notre Dame Press, 1981.

Head, H. *Studies in Neurology*. Vol. 2. London: Hodder & Stoughton, 1920.

"Hear, Hear: Genders Listen Differently." *Los Angeles Times,* November 29, 2000.

Heidegger, Martin. *Identity and Difference.* Translated by Joan Stambaugh. New York: Harper & Row, 1969.

Hick, John. *God Has Many Names.* Philadelphia: Westminster, 1980.

Hodgson, Peter C. *God in History: Shapes of Freedom.* Nashville: Abingdon, 1989.

Hopper, Jeffery. *Understanding Modern Theology II: Reinterpreting the Christian Faith for Changing Worlds.* Philadelphia: Fortress, 1987.

Hume, David. *Dialogues Concerning Natural Religion.* Edited and with commentary by Nelson Pike. Indianapolis: Bobbs-Merrill, 1970.

Hunt, Harry T. *On the Nature of Consciousness: Cognitive, Phenomenological, and Transpersonal Perspectives.* New Haven, CT: Yale University Press, 1995.

Jahme, Carole. *Beauty and the Beasts: Woman, Apes, and Evolution.* New York: Soho, 2001.

James, William. *The Principles of Psychology.* 2 vols. New York: Dover, 1890.

———. *The Varieties of Religious Experience.* New York: Dover, 1902.

———. "The Will to Believe." *New World,* June 1896.

———. *The Will to Believe and Other Essays in Popular Philosophy with Human Immortality.* New York: Dover, 1956.

Jameson, Frederic. "Postmodernism or the Cultural Logic of Late Capitalism." *New Left Review* 146 (1984) 53–92.

Jantzen, Grace M. *Becoming Divine: Towards a Feminist Philosophy of Religion.* Bloomington: Indiana University Press, 1999.

———. *God's World, God's Body.* Philadelphia: Westminster, 1984.

Jardine, Murray. "Sight, Sound, and Epistemology: the Experiential Sources of Ethical Concepts." *Journal of the American Academy of Religion* 64 (1996) 1–25.

Jencks, Charles. *Postmodernism: The New Classicism in Art and Architecture.* New York: Rizzoli, 1987.

Johnson, Mark. *The Body in the Mind: The Bodily Basis of Meaning, Imagination, and Reason.* Chicago: University of Chicago Press, 1987.

———. *The Meaning of the Body: The Aesthetics of Human Understanding.* Chicago: University of Chicago Press, 2007.

Johnson, Mark, and George Lakoff. *Philosophy in the Flesh: The Embodied Mind and Its Challenge to Western Thought.* New York: Basic, 1999.

Kant, Immanuel. *Critique of Pure Reason.* Translated by N. Kemp Smith. London: Macmillan, 1929.

Kasper, Walter. *The God of Jesus Christ.* Translated by Joan Stambaugh. New York: Crossroads, 1984.

Kaufman, Gordon. *In Face of Mystery: A Constructive Theology.* Cambrige, MA: Harvard University Press, 1993.

———. *In the Beginning . . . Creativity.* Minneapolis: Fortress, 2004.

———. *Systematic Theology: A Historicist Perspective.* New York: Scribners, 1968.

Kauffman, Stuart A. *The Origins of Order.* London: Oxford University Press, 1993.

———. *Reinventing the Sacred: A New View of Science, Reason, and Religion.* New York: Basic, 2008.

Keil, F. C. "The Origins of an Autonomous Biology." In *Minnesota Symposia on Child Psychology.* Vol. 25, *Modularity and Constraints in Language and Cognition,* 103–37. Hillsdale, NJ: Erlbaum, 1992.

Keleman, Deborah. "Are Children 'Intuitive Theists'?: Reasoning about Purpose and Design in Nature." *Psychological Science* 15 (2004) 295–301.

Kim, Jaegwon. *Supervenience and Mind: Selected Philosophical Essays.* Cambridge: Cambridge University Press, 1993.

Kirby, Alex. "Parrot's Oratory Stuns Scientists." BBC News, January 26, 2004.

Klemm, David E. "Toward a Rhetoric of Postmodern Theology: Through Barth and Heidegger." *Journal of the American Academy of Religion* 15 (1987) 457–66.

Kort, Wesley A. "Religion and Literature in Postmodernist Contexts." *Journal of the American Academy of Relgion* 18 (1990) 575–88.

Kurzweil, Ray. *The Age of Spiritual Machines: When Computers Exceed Human Intelligence.* New York: Viking, 1999.

Lakeland, Paul. *Postmodernity: Christian Identity in a Fragmented Age.* Minneapolis: Fortress, 1997.

Lakoff, George. *Women, Fire, and Dangerous Things: What Categories Reveal about the Mind.* Chicago: University of Chicago Press, 1987.

Lakoff, George, et al. *Where Mathematics Comes From: How the Embodied Mind Brings Mathematics into Being.* New York: Basic, 2000.

Lawson, Hilary. *Reflexivity: The Post-Modern Predicament.* La Salle, IL: Open Court, 1985.

Leahy, D. G. "To Create the Absolute Edge." With an introduction by Thomas J. J. Altizer. *Journal of the American Academy of Religion* 17 (1989) 773–89.

———. *Novitas Mundi: Perception of the History of Being.* New York: New York University Press, 1980.

Lindbeck, George. *The Nature of Doctrine: Religion and Theology in a Postliberal Age.* Philadelphia: Westminister, 1984.

Lowe, Walter. "A Deconstructionist Manifesto: Mark C. Taylor's *Erring.*" *Journal of Religion* 66 (1986) 324–31.

———. *Theology and Difference: The World of Reason.* Bloomington: Indiana University Press, 1993.

Lyotard, Jean-Francois. *The Differend: Phrases in Dispute.* Translated by George Van Den Abeele. Minneapolis: University of Minnesota Press, 1988.

———. *The Postmodern Condition: A Report on Knowledge.* Translated by Geoff Bennington and Brian Massumi with a Foreword by Frederic Jameson. Minneapolis: University of Minnesota Press, 1984.

Lyotard, Jean-Francois, and Jean-Loup Theband. *Just Gaming.* Translated by Wlad Godzich. Minneapolis: University of Minnesota Press, 1985.

MacIntyre, Alasdair. *Whose Justice? Which Rationality?* Notre Dame, IN: University of Notre Dame Press, 1988.

Mandler, Jean Matter. *The Foundations of Mind.* London: Oxford University Press, 2004.

Marion, Jean-Luc. *God without Being: Hors-Texte.* Translated by Thomas A. Carlson. Chicago: University of Chicago Press, 1991.

———. *In Excess: Studies of Saturated Phenomena.* Fordham University Press, 2002.

McFague, Sallie. *The Body of God.* Minneapolis: Fortress, 1993.

———. *Models of God: Theology for an Ecological, Nuclear Age.* Philadelphia: Fortress, 1987.

McHale, Brian. *Postmodernist Fiction.* New York: Methuen, 1987.

Mead, George Herbert. *Mind, Self, and Society*. Chicago: University of Chicago Press, 1934.

Meek, Esther L. "*Longing to Know* and the Complexities of Knowing God." *Tradition and Discovery* 31 (2005) 29–43.

———. *Longing to Know: The Philosophy of Knowledge for Ordinary People*. Grand Rapids: Brazos, 2003.

Merleau-Ponty, Maurice. *Phenomenology of Perception*. Translated by Colin Smith. London: Routledge and Kegan Paul, 1962.

———. *The Visible and the Invisible*. Translated by Alphonso Lingis. Evanston, IL: Northwestern University Press, 1968.

Metzinger, Thomas. *Being No One: The Self-Model Theory of Subjectivity*. Cambridge, MA: MIT Press, 2003.

Midgley, Mary. "The Soul's Successors: Philosophy and the 'Body.'" In *Religion and the Body*, edited by Sarah Coakley, 53–68. Cambridge: Cambridge University Press.

Milbank, John. Respondent. "Catherine Pickstock's *After Writing: On the Liturgical Consummation of Philosophy*." Session of the American Academy of Religion, Boston, November 1999.

Milbank, John, et al., editors. *Radical Orthodoxy: A New Theology*. London: Routledge, 1999.

MIT humanoid-robotics-group. "Overview." Online: http://www.ai.mit.edu/projects/humanoid-robotics-group, 2004.

"Monkeys Don't Monkey with Math." *Duke Magazine* 92 (2006) 19.

Moore, Stephen D. "The 'Post-'Age Stamp: Does It Stick—Biblical Studies and the Postmodernism Debate." *Journal of the American Academy of Religion* 17 (1989) 544–49.

Moravec, Hans. "Letter from Moravec to Penrose." In *Thinking Robots, an Aware Internet, and Cyberpunk Librarians: The 1992 LITA President's Program*, edited by R. Bruce Miller and Milton T. Wolf, 51–58. Chicago: Library and Information Technology Association, 1992.

Morell, Virginia. "Inside Animal Minds: Birds, Apes, Dolphins, and a Dog with a World-class Vocabulary." *National Geographic* 213 (2008) 36–61.

Murphy, Nancey. *Anglo-American Postmodernity: Philosophical Perspectives on Science, Religion, and Ethics*. Boulder, CO: Westview, 1997.

———. *Beyond Liberalism and Fundamentalism: How Modern and Postmodern Philosophy Set the Theological Agenda*. Valley Forge, PA: Trinity, 1996.

Nagatomo Shigenori. *Attunement through the Body*. Albany: State University of New York Press, 1992.

Neergaard, Lauran. "Scientists Rethink Origins of the Human Mind after Ape Studies." *Lincoln (NE) Journal Star*, May 11, 1998.

Neisser, Ulric. "Direct Perception and Recognition as Distinct Perceptual Systems." Paper presented to the Cognitive Science Society, Ann Arbor, MI, 1989.

Neville, Robert C. "The Depths of God." *Journal of the American Academy of Religion* 56 (1988) 1–22.

Neuhaus, Richard John. *The Catholic Moment: The Paradox of the Church in the Postmodern World*. San Francisco: Harper & Row, 1987.

Nikkel, David. "Negotiating the Nature of Mystical Experience, Guided by James and Tillich." *Bulletin of the North American Paul Tillich Society* 33 (2007) 29–39.

Nussbaum, Martha C. "Danger to Human Dignity: The Revival of Disgust and Shame in the Law." *Chronicle of Higher Education*, August 6, 2004, B6–9.

Orem, William. "The Magical Mind: How Do Adults Become Supernatural Thinkers." *Science and Theology News* 6 (2006) 18–19.

Peacocke, Arthur R. "Articulating God's Presence in and to the World Unveiled by the Sciences." In *In Whom We Live and Move and Have Our Being*, edited by Philip Clayton and Arthur Peacocke, 137–54. Grand Rapids: Eerdmans, 2004.

———. *Theology for a Scientific Age: Being and Becoming—Natural and Divine*. 2nd ed. Minneapolis: Fortress, 1993.

Peterson, Gregory R. "*Minding God* Symposium: A Response." Presented to the American Academy of Religion Annual Meeting, Atlanta, November 2003.

———. *Minding God: Theology and the Cognitive Sciences*. Minneapolis: Fortress, 2003.

Pinker, Steven. *How the Mind Works*. New York: Norton, 1997.

Plantinga, Alvin. "Reason and Belief in God." In *Faith and Rationality*, edited by Alvin Plantinga and Nicholas Wolterstorff, 16–93. Notre Dame, IN: University of Notre Dame Press, 1984.

Polanyi, Michael. *Knowing and Being: Essays by Michael Polanyi*. Edited by Majorie Grene. Chicago: University of Chicago Press, 1969.

———. *Personal Knowledge: Towards a Post-Critical Philosophy*. Chicago: University of Chicago Press, 1958.

———. *Personal Knowledge: Towards a Post-Critical Philosophy*. With Preface. New York: Harper Torchbooks, 1964.

———. *The Tacit Dimension*. Garden City, NY: Doubleday, 1966.

Polanyi, Michael, and Harry Prosch. *Meaning*. Chicago: University of Chicago Press, 1975.

Polkinghorne, John. *Faith, Science, and Understanding*. New Haven, CT: Yale University Press, 2000.

———. *The Faith of a Physicist: Reflections of a Bottom-up Thinker*. Princeton, NJ: Princeton University Press, 1994.

———. *Science and Creation*. London: SPCK, 1989.

Poteat, William H. *A Philosophical Daybook: Post-Critical Investigations*. Columbia: University of Missouri Press, 1990.

———. *Polanyian Meditations: In Search of a Post-Critical Logic*. Durham, NC: Duke University Press, 1985.

———. *Recovering the Ground: Critical Exercises in Recollection*. Albany: State University of New York Press, 1994.

Prinz, Jesse J. *Gut Reactions*. London: Oxford University Press, 2005.

Putnam, Hilary. *Reason, Truth and History*. Cambridge: Cambridge University Press, 1981.

"Q & A with Religion Professor, Mark C. Taylor." *Columbia News*, January 3, 2008.

Raschke, Carl A. "Fire and Roses: Toward Authentic Post-Modern Religious Thinking." *Journal of the American Academy of Religion* 18 (1990) 671–89.

Regier, Terry, Paul Kay, and Richard S. Cook. *Proceedings of the National Academy of Sciences*. Online: http://www.pnas.org.doi/10.1073/pnas.0503281102, 2005.

Reynolds, Terrence. "Walking Apart, Together: Lindbeck and McFague on Theological Method." *Journal of Religion* 77 (1987) 44–67.

Ricoeur, Paul and David Pellaner. *Time and Narrative*. 3 vols. Translated by Kathleen McLaughlin. Chicago: University of Chicago Press, 1984–1988.

Rieger, Gerulf, Meredith L. Chivers, and J. Michael Bailey. "Sexual Arousal Patterns of Bisexual Men." *Psychological Science* 16 (2005) 579–84.

Root-Bernstein, Robert S. and Michele. *Sparks of Genius: The Thirteen Thinking Tools of the World's Most Creative People*. New York: Houghton Mifflin, 1999.

Rorty, Richard. *Philosophy and the Mirror of Nature*. Princeton, NJ: Princeton University Press, 1979.

Rosch, Eleanor and Barbara B. Lloyd, editors. *Cognition and Categorization*. New York: Halsted, 1978.

Rutledge, David W. "Knowing as Unlocking the World: A Review Essay on E. L. Meek's *Longing to Know*." *Tradition and Discovery* 31 (2005) 21–28.

Rutler, George William. *Beyond Modernity: Reflections of a Post-Modern Catholic*. San Francisco: Ignatius, 1987.

Sapolsky, Robert M. *A Primate's Memoir: A Neuroscientist's Unconventional Life among the Baboons*. Waterville, ME: Thorndike, 2001.

Scarsellati, Brian. "Theory of Mind for a Humanoid Robot." Online: http://www.ai.mit.edu/projects/humanoid-robotics-group, 2004.

Scharlemamn, Robert P. Introduction in *Theology at the End of the Century: A Dialogue on the Postmodern*. Edited by Robert P. Schlarlemann. Charlottesville: University of Virginia Press, 1990.

Schreiner, Susan E. "Appearances and Reality in Luther, Montaigne, and Shakespeare." *Journal of Religion* 83 (2003) 345–80.

Searle, John R. "Minds, Brains and Programs." *Behavioral and Brain Sciences* 3 (1980) 417–57.

Slingerland, Edward. "The Study of Religion in the Age of Cognitive Science." *Journal of the American Academy of Religion* 76 (2008) 375–411.

Smolin, Lee. *The Life of the Cosmos*. New York: Oxford University Press, 1997.

Spelke, Elizabeth. "Origins of Physical Knowledge." In *Thought without Language*, edited by Lawrence Weiskrantz, 168–84. Oxford, UK: Clarendon, 1988.

Statile, Glenn. "Libet's Loophole: The Fight for Free Will." *Global Spiral* [formerly *Metanexus Digest*] 6, October 31, 2006.

Staune, Jean. "Darwinism, Design, and Purpose: A European Perspective." Paper presented at the Metanexus Conference, *Science and Religion: Global Perspectives*, Philadelphia, June 2005.

Stewart, Ian. *Life's Other Secret: The New Mathematics of the Living World*. New York: John Wiley, 1998.

Stout, Jeffrey. *Ethics after Babel: The Languages of Morals and Their Discontents*. Boston: Beacon, 1988.

Sullivan, Andrew. "Why Do Men Act the Way They Do?" *New York Times Magazine*, April 2, 2000. In *Reader's Digest*, September 2000.

Sweetser, Eve. *From Etymology to Pragmatics: The Mind-as-Body Metaphor in Semantic Structure and Semantic Change*. New York: Cambridge University Press, 1991.

Tanner, Kathryn. "Tradition and Theological Judgment in Light of Postmodern Cultural Criticism." Paper presented at the American Academy of Religion Annual Meeting, New Orleans. November 1996.

Taylor, Charles. *Sources of the Self: The Making of the Modern Identity*. Cambridge: Harvard University Press, 1989.

Taylor, Mark C. *After God*. Chicago: University of Chicago Press, 2007.

———. *Alterity*. Chicago: University of Chicago Press, 1987.

———. *Disfiguring: Art, Architecture, Religion*. Chicago: University of Chicago Press, 1992.

———. *Erring: A Postmodern A/theology*. Chicago: University of Chicago Press, 1984.

———. *Nots*. Chicago: University of Chicago Press, 1993.

———. "The Politics of Theo-ry." *Journal of the American Academy of Religion* 59 (1991) 1–37.

———. "Refiguring Religion." *Journal of American Academy of Religion* 77 (2009) 105–19.

———. *Tears*. Albany: State University of New York Press, 1989.

Tillich, Paul. *The Courage to Be*. New Haven, CT: Yale University Press, 1952.

———. *Systematic Theology*. 3 vols. Chicago: University of Chicago Press, 1951–1963.

———. *Theology of Culture*. Edited by Robert C. Kimball. New York: Oxford University Press, 1959.

Tracy, David. "Literary Theory and Return of the Forms for Naming and Thinking God. *Journal of Religion* 74 (1994) 302–19.

———. *Plurarity and Ambiguity: Hermeneutics, Religion, Hope*. San Francisco: Harper & Row, 1987.

Varela, Francisco J., Evan Thompson, and Eleanor Rosch. *The Embodied Mind: Cognitive Science and Human Experience*. Cambridge: MIT Press, 1991.

Wall, James A. "Meaning, Mystery, and Modernity." Lecture at the Futures Forum, United Methodist Publishing House, Nashville, TN, 1986. (On cassette, Newscope Lecture Series, June 1987.)

Ward, Keith. "The World as the Body of God: A Panentheistic Metaphor." In *In Whom We Live Have Our Being*, edited by Philip Clayton and Arthur Peacocke, 62–72. Grand Rapids: Eerdmans, 2004.

Wegner, Daniel. *The Illusion of Conscious Will*. Cambridge, MA: MIT Press, 2002.

Werpehowski, William A. "Ad Hoc Apologetics." *Journal of Religion* 66 (1986) 282–301.

Wheeler, David L. "A Neurologist Steps Back from the Brain to Look at Consciousness." *Chronicle of Higher Education*, November 26, 1999.

Whitehead, Alfred North. *Adventures of Ideas*. New York: Macmillan, 1933.

———. *Process and Reality: An Essay in Cosmology*. New York: Macmillan, 1929. Corrected ed. Edited by David Ray Griffin and Donald W. Sherburne. New York: Macmillan, 1978.

———. *Science and the Modern World*. New York: Macmillan, 1925.

"Will Our Future Brains Be Smaller." *TerraDaily: News about Planet Earth*, July 10, 2008.

Winquist, Charles. *Epiphanies of Darkness: Deconstruction in Theology*. Philadelphia: Fortress, 1986.

———. "The Silence of the Real: Theology at the End of the Twentieth Century." In *Theology at the End of the Century: A Dialogue on the Postmodern*, edited by Robert P. Scharlemann, 14–40. Charlottesville: University of Virginia Press, 1990.

Wittgenstein, Ludwig. *Philosophical Investigations.* 3rd ed. Translated by G. E. M. Anscombe. New York: Macmillan, 1958.

Yoder, John Howard. *The Priestly Kingdom: Social Ethics as Gospel.* Notre Dame, IN: University of Notre Dame Press, 1984.

Zhenhua Yu. "Tacit Knowledge: A Wittgensteinian Approach." *Tradition and Discovery* 33 (2007) 9–25.

———. "Tacit Knowledge: Knowing and the Problem of Articulation." *Tradition and Discovery* 30 (2003) 11–23.

Index

www.ingramcontent.com/pod-product-compliance
Lightning Source LLC
Chambersburg PA
CBHW061735270326
41928CB00011B/2250